ONE RUSSIA, TWO CHINAS

ALSO BY GEORGE FETHERLING

TRAVEL
Running Away to Sea: Round the World on a Tramp Freighter
Three Pagodas Pass: A Roundabout Journey to Burma

FICTION
The File on Arthur Moss
Jericho

MEMOIR
Travels by Night: A Memoir of the Sixties

POETRY
The Dreams of Ancient Peoples
Selected Poems
Madagascar: Poems & Translations
Singer, An Elegy

ONE RUSSIA
TWO CHINAS

GEORGE FETHERLING

an imprint of Beach Holme Publishing
PROSPECT BOOKS
VANCOUVER, BC

This book is published by Beach Holme Publishing, Suite 1010, 409 Granville Street, Vancouver, B.C. V6C 1T2. *www.beachholme.bc.ca*. This is a Prospect Book.

The publisher gratefully acknowledges the financial support of the Canada Council for the Arts and of the British Columbia Arts Council. The publisher also acknowledges the financial assistance received from the Government of Canada through the Book Publishing Industry Development Program (BPIDP) for its publishing activities.

The Canada Council | Le Conseil des Arts
for the Arts | du Canada

BRITISH
COLUMBIA
ARTS COUNCIL
Supported by the Province of British Columbia

Editor: Michael Carroll
Design and Production: Jen Hamilton
Cover Art: (Upper) *The Church of the Intercession of the Mother of God* Copyright © by Victor Potoskouev; (Lower) *The Island Pagoda* by John Thomson Copyright © by National Museum of Photography, Film and Television/Science & Society Picture Library

Author Photograph: Merrill Fearon

Printed and bound in Canada by AGMV Marquis Imprimeur

Library and Archives Canada Cataloguing in Publication Data

Fetherling, George, 1949-
      One Russia, two Chinas/by George Fetherling.

"A Prospect book."
ISBN 0-88878-433-3

      1. Fetherling, George, 1949- —Journeys. 2. Soviet Union—Description and travel. 3. China—Description and travel. 4. Taiwan—Description and travel. I. Title.

G465.F47 2004   910.4   C2003-910072-3

CONTENTS

FOREWORD

For such a modest book this one has taken a long time to finish, but that's because the story itself was incomplete. In the spring of 1990 I went on assignment through the Union of Soviet Socialist Republics and the People's Republic of China, heading towards Southeast Asia. At the time all those places, but especially the Soviet Union, seemed to be vibrating in the expectation that important events were underway or about to begin.

The end of the Cold War and the dismantling of the Eastern Bloc (and of the Berlin Wall that symbolized it) came with what struck many people as an unstoppable counter-revolution in the Soviet Union. The situation there was the mirror image of that in China, where the pro-democracy movement had been suppressed so cruelly. Yet the two occurrences clearly were manifestations of the same urge, a demand for democracy in many regions of the world that had had no recent experience of it.

The following year I went for the first time to Taiwan, which was still a one-party state in the long shadow of Chiang Kai-shek and his family. I returned there in 1995 when Taiwan had transformed itself into a vigorous and indeed raucous and rambunctious democracy. My purpose on these two trips to the island was similar to my purpose in going to Russia and China: to get a look at the effects of seismic change while it was still going on. I was not posing as a literary travel writer, making semi-fictional characters from pieces of individuals encountered along the way. Neither was I being a reporter, writing only of forces and background without reference to history and culture. These pages, set down shortly after returning from notes made on the spot, are from an older tradition. Most of the material appeared long ago, often in substantially different form, in two obscure books of mine, *Year of the Horse: A Journey Through Russia and China* and *The Other China: Journeys Around Taiwan*, both long out of print. Reading the texts now, I itch to rewrite them, obscuring my naïveté and bringing my spur-of-the-moment comments into line with what we all know actually happened next. But I resist and try to confine my perfect hindsight to an afterword. For all its infelicities, this collection of notes remains what it was then: simply an indication of how matters looked at the time to someone who was there because he wished to be.

RUSSIA 1990

1

On the Loose in Moscow

I once departed Canada for France aboard a ship with a Russian crew and came up on deck at dawn the next day to find them doing callisthenics in the rain. That had been my only experience of Soviets in groups. The recollection came back to me at once at Mirabel, that vast empty white elephant of an airport from which Aeroflot flew to Moscow several times a week. A crowd of a couple hundred people with the distinctive blood-coloured CCCP passports was going home—people with wide Slavic faces, many of them, some of the women with scarves on their heads and a large number of bulky bags or cartons tied with rope, some of the men wearing sweatshirts under their copious blue business suits. At neither end of the departure process—at the check-in counter or at the gate—was it necessary to ask them to form a queue, for they did so automatically day in and day out, though they didn't make a religious obligation of neatness the way the British do. Everybody jumped ahead of everybody else while somehow preserving the queue idea, despite the way that the lineup once threatened to become as wide as it was long. There was much weeping and waving goodbye to relatives. One man in his sixties wore not miniature decorations but full-size tin replicas of his military ribbons but was not otherwise formally dressed (I would see many such people in the Soviet Union). Quite aside from questions of age and fashion, the people of that

3

generation look fundamentally different from their sons and daughters and grandchildren. The younger people are simply more European.

The aircraft was bare-bones and the flight long—an all-nighter. Although, in obedience to Mikhail Gorbachev's drive against alcoholism, a light beer was the only strong drink served, the passengers became restive, shouting across the aisle, socializing, fiddling with all their bloody packages, a number of which, I observed, contained VCRs. If they had held live pigs instead, the level of tranquility would have been about the same. People were alert with anticipation. When they did settle down to sleep, a few slept with their heads on their crossed arms and their arms on the folding trays in front of them.

Sherenetyevo-2 Aeroport, the one where foreigners usually landed, resembled Mirabel in being big and empty and surrounded by farms and patches of boreal woods. In the Soviet Union many things resembled Mirabel. The wait lasted almost two hours, but when my turn came I breezed through passport control and customs. I struck up a conversation with the clerk while buying currency at the bureau de change, and she told me that the taxi fare to central Moscow should be no more than 15 rubles. Outside I was approached by six drivers in turn, each of whom refused to take me anywhere except for U.S. dollars or Marlboro cigarettes or some combination of the two. Finally I told one of them what they all knew already—that one's foreign currency is scrutinized and counted when one comes in and all hard currency exchanges (but not, it's true, purchases) are recorded on a customs form and must tally on one's departure with the amount remaining. The airport was full of warnings about the danger of selling dollars except at official kiosks; in the customs hall there were posters with photographs of the black marketeers of the week. It seemed clear that there was great pressure by the government to keep people from using dollars except in those places, run by the government and patronized by foreigners, where dollars were used exclusively. But no driver would take me on any other basis, and so I lugged my bags back inside and reported my consternation to Intourist. A young woman there shook her head sadly.

"Where do they think they are?" she said. "In U.S.S.R. or in U.S. of A.?" I responded sympathetically, but kept to myself the realization that I had just stepped into the present and learned my first lesson.

The driver who was shamed or browbeaten into accepting me for rubles was grumpy and sullen as we darted along the Leningradsky Highway, the main road linking the capital and the second city. He swerved in and out of traffic. On both sides were long buildings of various styles and ages, all impressive though many seemed a little shabby, albeit with the shabbiness that came with long use, not neglect. In the grassy median dividing the highway stood a modern sculpture, dedicated in 1966, that resembled a child's jacks but on a giant scale; it was a memorial to the citizens who had defended the city against the Nazis in the Great Patriotic War and was meant to suggest the hedgehogs, or tank traps, that had laced the eastern approaches. This stretch of highway was a showpiece, clearly. We roared past parks and stadiums and the Northern River Terminal which, with its open arches and high clock tower, suggested what the Ferry Building in San Francisco would have been like if an Italian had designed it. We rumbled past the Petrovsky Palace of Peter the Great, where Napoleon did his hasty logistical planning for the retreat from Moscow. This section was a distant suburb then, and clusters of small single-family homes show that it remained so until the 1920s, perhaps even as late at 1937 when the Moskva was connected to the Volga by canal, and Moscow, after 500 years as an inland city, finally became a seaport. At the House of the Newlyweds I spotted a bride getting out of a car with red and blue streamers tied to the rear bumper. The highway had long since dissolved into Leningradsky Prospekt, one of the 11 wide spokes that cross three ring roads before coming together at the Kremlin and Red Square. The driver was still glum when we arrived at the hotel. He wore jeans. Rubles in one pocket, dollars in the other. He made a big display of dredging up change from the one and not the other.

The next morning I watched dawn break over central Moscow from a hotel window on the 15th floor. It was like being in a photographer's darkroom, seeing the image come to life in the bath of developer. As the sky grew lighter—but without ever losing the suggestion of pewter—buildings were revealed row after row, following the contours of the river or else standing at attention along either side of the main boulevards. There were large patches of green everywhere, for a surprisingly high percentage of the city's area is given over to parks. Ugly high-rises jutted up from the trees in the foreground and in the distance, some with the construction cranes still in place, others dating, I would guess, from the 1960s or early 1970s, when the much-reported-on housing crisis was first addressed seriously (but of course never solved).

At a distance, it was not always easy in the Soviet Union to distinguish residential buildings from office blocks, owing in part to the absence of signage. One distinctive structure, which I soon learned was one of the seats of the government of the Russian Federation, resembles New City Hall in Toronto except that the two halves of the clamshell are back to back rather than face to face and so take on an X shape when viewed from above. There are also the seven High Gothic skyscrapers, serving various functions, built by Stalin, who compared them to the seven hills of Rome. One is the Ukraine Hotel; another is the Ministry of Foreign Affairs and International Trade, which sits across from a little pie-shaped park where I would see big protest demonstrations when Li Peng of China came to town. A third is the Moskva Hotel, which has mismatched wings. It is said that the architects submitted two plans to Stalin, expecting him to state his preference; when he did not, they built one of each and hoped for the best. As for some of the older structures, I noticed what I later saw confirmed in China as well: how one of the consequences of a revolution is that buildings are put to new uses that never quite eradicate all traces of their original purpose. Moscow's ordinary domestic architecture tends towards long blocks, four or five storeys high and with steep metal-ribbed roofs, such as you expect to see in the workaday parts of Paris and in the centre of the other old European capitals.

This was a special day, the 120th anniversary of Lenin's birth, and I decided to get my sightseeing out of the way and pay my respects to his mummified remains. After a breakfast of coleslaw and what I would call latkes, I bounded out into the crisp morning air for my ritual argument with a cab driver.

"Rubles!" he said. "Rubles I got here. And here and here." He touched all the pockets of his coat and trousers and a zippered bag on the dashboard. We eliminated dollars and cigarettes, leaving him to suggest that I might like to pay in caviar. A coals-to-Newcastle proposition, I would have imagined, though he perhaps meant the white variety often reserved for hard-currency tourists. I decided to walk to the Kremlin.

For a city of 8.5 million, and one so associated with industry, there was little air pollution in Moscow compared with other cities its size. This was no doubt because there were few automobiles, though private ones were becoming more common all the time and cars were one of the important local manufactures, even if not so important as radio electronics. I walked along the circular roadway and down one of the spokes, the Kalinin Prospekt, a Western-style shopping street for which long rows of historic Russian houses were pulled down. Outdoor advertising was still mercifully scarce, though I thought that might not be true much longer if the pace of Westernization continued at the present rate, and so I was startled to see an enormous theatre poster plastered on a hoarding along the pavement. Dozens of market stalls, most of them free-enterprise businesses, which the Soviets, in a reversal of nomenclature, called cooperatives, were being set up as I passed along, some with sticky buns and Pepsi (far more common than *Koka-Kola*), others selling manufactured goods from toy soldiers to women's blouses. The merchants did not seem to hustle, the way those in, for instance, an English market would do, but the customers were animated.

The closer I got to the Kremlin, the more soldiers were in evidence, and sailors as well. Officers with briefcases and young conscripts in groups with their girlfriends. It was in the crowds of military personnel, I noticed, that one was most likely to see all the various ethnic groups represented, including the distinctive Mongolians. Flags, too, became increasingly common. I sensed that I had crossed over into the official Moscow when I hit a duo-tone portrait of Lenin, several storeys high, suspended from one of the buildings of the Lenin Library. Just a bit farther on was 50th Anniversary of the October Revolution Square, delineated on one side by a Greek Revival building that once housed indoor equestrian events but was now the Central Exhibition Hall. Then there was a brick gatehouse connected to a bridge over the Alexandrovsky Gardens, which must once have been part of the Kremlin's defensive outerworks. I saw a few civil servants, bureaucrats, and military types flash their security passes to get across. The rest of us were pre-emptively sent down into the sunken garden where, before long, a queue began to assume shape. The Lenin Mausoleum wouldn't open for almost two hours yet, but I sensed that this was my opportunity to get in on the ground floor.

I had decided against getting a ticket at the hotel that would have allowed me to jump to the front, for I hoped to find people who spoke English. As luck would have it, the man in front of me possessed English he wished to exercise. He was in his late forties, I would guess, a Moldavian who took frequent trips to Moscow but had never before made the pilgrimage to see the father of the Revolution and the Soviet state. His nine-year-old daughter was with him, dressed in a kind of ski suit, with her long blonde hair tied back with pieces of bobbin lace. She kept staring at me for the exotic foreigner that I was but reverted to excessive shyness when I smiled in response or tried to speak with her. My companion also had a son, of 22, who had recently made him a grandfather. This was an important holiday for the family, though the man went on with genuine sadness about how Moscow was looking so decrepit these days, not full of life and freshly painted as it was when he began coming here 15 years ago. I couldn't determine to what extent it was his own—our own—advancing years he saw reflected in the surroundings.

The line now stretched for blocks and was suddenly made longer by the arrival of scores of Second World War veterans, some in uniform and others not, some with canes and crutches, most with at least a few medals or decorations, who placed roses on the monument to the unknown soldiers, a place where, on other days, brides and bridegrooms traditionally have their photographs taken. A children's marching band stood to attention, and the old soldiers were then given priority in the slow march around the corner and up the hill towards Red Square and another part of the Kremlin wall. "They no doubt feel bad at being made to go ahead of us," my friend said. But I saw only that they were caught up in their private memories. It is mildly shocking, yet somehow reassuring, to find one's clichés about a country so often revealed true—never wholly true, mind you, but true nonetheless in their sheer accessibility. First all those peasants at the airport in Montreal, struggling with parcels as lumpy as themselves, and then the fact that the Second World War, in which 20 million Soviets were killed, was still a palpable reality in everyone's life—and I hadn't even got as far as Leningrad where the fighting had been worse.

As we filed into Red Square, the people grew quiet. Hands came out of pockets. One woman quickly combed her hair and straightened her clothes. The clock on the Spasskaya Tower struck 11:00 a.m., and outside the mausoleum there was a changing-of-the-guard ceremony. The soldiers goose-stepped; I had already seen many soldiers, but these were the first ones whose boots were polished. Two others, on either side of the entrance when we arrived, were armed with old bolt-action rifles with bayonets fixed. Others made last-minute inspections of people's handbags, looking for cameras, which were forbidden inside, while another soldier moved up and down our part of the line photographing obvious foreigners (he snapped me twice, once, I suppose, because I was taller than most of the others, and again because I wear a beard). The interior was dark and cool and made of polished granite. We shuffled down some steps, turned a corner, and there he was, illuminated in his glass coffin, wearing a blue silk tie with white dots. He was a small man, and his goatee and the fringe of hair around the sides of his head were sandy red, which surprised me. By no stretch of the language could the corpse be called lifelike, though the fact that it had been preserved as well as this since 1924 does speak kindly of scientific method. Insensitive foreigners are renowned for remarking that the face and hands look like those of waxwork. On the contrary, it seems to me, the effect suggests wood carving.

One exits the sacred place to walk under a stretch of the Kremlin wall where state heroes, including John Reed, the Harvard alumnus who wrote *Ten Days That Shook the World*, are buried. Revolutionaries, artists, cosmonauts including Yuri Gagarin, have plaques set in the wall and small memorial stones in the turf below. A few foreign names catch the eye, such as that of Big Bill Haywood (1868–1928), the Wobbly from Chicago. Other figures of even higher rank are memorialized by a row of stone busts. Konstantin Chernenko is one of the most recent additions. Stalin is there, too, though he used to rest next to Lenin; Khrushchev had him demoted in 1961.

When I got back to my room, I turned on my little shortwave radio to hear Radio Moscow's report of the day's events. Gorbachev was quoted as saying, somewhat pointedly so in the faintness of his praise, "We shall rely on everything lasting in Lenin's intellectual heritage." But the people I was with, young as well as old, seemed to me to be genuinely moved, perhaps even awed, not much ready for revisionism insofar as the cult of Lenin's personality is concerned—a cult that is of course not justified in Lenin's own teachings but not difficult to explain in a culture where icons are such an important form of art. In the ensuing weeks I would meet people who cynically contradicted this first impression of mine.

Later in the day I fell into conversation about what I had seen with a woman who told me that she was first taken to see Lenin by her mother when she was a small girl and so took her own daughter there when the child was about the same age and expected her grandchildren to go one day as well. The notion of such deliberate continuity—as distinct from the unending sameness over which one has no control—seemed quite at odds with the mood of the moment, when everything in the society appeared to be either improving quickly or just as quickly getting worse but, in any event, changing. Two days later, a 49-year-old Lithuanian stood where I stood and threw two fire bombs in the direction of Lenin's body. No damage was done. He was arrested.

Events were moving so rapidly, in fact, that our memory of the present chronology is understandably jumbled. So perhaps I should pause here to give a more exact context to these remarks and observations.

At the time of which I write, Gorbachev was settling into the new presidential powers he had given himself and recently had gone so far in the direction of Western politics as to create the post of presidential press secretary. Politically and economically, chaos was barely being restrained. Ethnic tensions in Azerbaijan might have cooled, but the Lithuanians had declared themselves independent, forcing Gorbachev to cut off most shipments of natural gas and virtually all their supply of oil. His legal grounds for doing so were unclear, as there was simply no legislation on the matter one way or the other, but the action was better than sending in tanks; everyone was on tenterhooks waiting to see whether he could force the Lithuanians into a referendum on the succession question followed by a slow transition over five years. The Lithuanians had just responded with an embargo of their own involving those products, such as small electric motors and television tubes, on which their factories had been given a near monopoly long ago.

Back in Moscow, Gorbachev's adversaries were snapping at him, not only the communist old guard who distrusted reform, a group we heard less about in the West, but also the more highly profiled radicals who felt that the reforms were not proceeding nearly so quickly as they might. The most conspicuous of these was of course Boris Yeltsin, the brusque one-time construction foreman and former mayor of Moscow who periodically would accuse Gorbachev of becoming a dictator and who clearly wanted to set himself up as president of the core state, the Russian Federation that accounted for half of the Soviet Union's population and four-fifths of its territory. At this time, a few months before he succeeded in that goal, his image in the West was still coloured by the visit he had paid to the United States and elsewhere in 1989, when he drank and talked prodigiously, and coloured, too, by an incident in Moscow shortly afterwards when he claimed he was abducted by thugs and thrown in the river. In Britain, therefore, he was being seen by some in much the same light as George Brown was regarded in the 1960s, while in Canada his big square head and rough-hewn manners often recalled Eugene Whelan, Pierre Trudeau's perpetual agriculture minister. In fact, a closer approximation would have been a cross between William Lyon Mackenzie and René Lévesque.

When I arrived, Moscow was abuzz with the imminent swearing-in of a new mayor, Gavrill Popov, a free-market economist who had vowed to lease properties and businesses to organizations and individuals and otherwise move decisively towards a more workable economy, knowing that what Moscow does must inevitably be done in other cities and regions. When I got to know several leading journalists at Novosti, the state news agency, I asked whether these leases would be for long terms and whether they might one day be converted to freehold private property. "At the start, just leases," I was told. "But wait a few months." This was an answer I was to hear to several questions. For example, at that time there was still, officially, only one political party. But at the urging of Yegor Ligachev, the leading conservative in the Politburo, a number of radicals had been expelled before they could resign, and they were poised to set up their own party. They were already arguing about what the name on the letterhead should be. Similarly a green party was positioned to begin fielding candidates in the autumn, and there was a royalist party aborning, hoping to restore order by restoring the monarchy, as had happened in Spain. "In two months, you'll see, there will be a dozen parties." The number, like the timeframe, was arbitrary, but the thrust was accurate enough. There would no doubt be parties galore—reform and counter-reform, radical and reactionary, ones on specific issues, perhaps even religious ones; in time, they would probably be rationalized along economic and ethnic lines.

Most everyone I talked to was weary of the present and impatient for change, almost any kind of change, and yet at the same time fearful of what the immediate future would be like. Americans tended to interpret this unrest as a frantic desire to embrace Americanism, but that of course is ridiculous. People pursue some measure of democracy not out of the

Americans' cloying sentimentality about voting for its own sake but as a means of seeing a mixed economy in which their subsidized housing, unlimited education, and free social programmes might be enhanced by a convertible currency and a little decent food. The currency question was exceptionally thorny. To make the ruble convertible into dollars, Deutschmarks, sterling, and so forth would be instantly to erode the people's pensions and savings. (And because there was so little they could buy in the shops, Soviets were champion savers, having put away 340 billion rubles in the state bank even though the interest was only 1.5 percent—this was in addition to an estimated 200 billion rubles in "under the bed" savings.) Yet inflation was quickly eating up this pile anyway. In 1989 the government deficit was estimated by an outside specialist at 120 billion rubles, up from only 20 billion in 1982; to service the debt, Moscow simply printed more currency at the rate of 50 million rubles a day, 18 billion rubles a year. The most imaginative idea voiced to date was to back the ruble with gold, of which the Soviet Union was the second-largest producer, thus bringing all the world's savings and investment rushing in. Absurd of course, but wonderful. But the reason Gorbachev, the liberal reformer, could exist, and by existing save us by winding down the Cold War, was that he was a moderate who needed immoderates such as Yeltsin or the goldbugs to play himself off against. The phrase "five years" came to his lips as easily, and as frequently, as "two months" came to the lips of my newfound acquaintances in the press. I can only guess whether this carried an echo, in listeners' ears, of all those long-ago five-year plans.

Friends at Novosti promised to help arrange some interviews and meetings, including one at the literary magazine *Oktyabr*, which I hoped I could turn into access to some of the writers and painters I desired to meet. I had also asked to observe the meeting between Gorbachev and Li Peng when the Chinese leader arrived in Moscow to pay his respects and discuss border problems, but the indications were that this would be difficult to arrange. Earlier the response had been favourable when I sought permission to interview Yeltsin and a few other politicos, such as the minister of culture, Vasily Zakharov. But in the present situation the possibilities had receded. Before I could get in to see him, for example, Zakharov had been replaced by Nikolai Gobenko, putting me back at zero, though there was a much bigger factor working against me. "They're trying to keep foreign journalists away from politicians if they can," said Slava Bogdanov of Novosti's North American department with an admirable and characteristic frankness. He had been the press attaché in Ottawa but had returned home in 1988. He spoke perfectly idiomatic English and was the resident expert on English Canada. When I met him, he had just returned from three weeks in Vancouver and was soon to lead a delegation to a symposium in Ottawa.

Novosti is a difficult news agency to categorize. It was large, employing several thousand journalists to TASS's several hundred, and in further distinction to TASS, which provided the official news from the party and the government, it was "public," which the West usually interprets as meaning merely "semi-official." It published informal books and slick pamphlets about every aspect of the Soviet Union in a variety of languages and responded to requests for customized stories from the overseas media. More important, it ran its own network of correspondents both domestically and worldwide, and acted as a clearing house, though not as a telegraphic news agency like TASS or Canadian Press. It was also the publisher of the important *Moscow News*, which was considered not just radical but sometimes quite fearless. Recently it had ventured into television as well. For example, it bought a regular 90 minutes of airtime from the state network for the broadcast of such programmes as the first-ever look inside KGB headquarters in Dzerzinsky Square. Its highly distinctive building in Zoubovski Boulevard, opening on a courtyard with terraced balconies, was also a communications centre from which Soviet figures and foreign heads of state addressed press conferences. "During the Moscow Olympics," Bogdanov explained, sitting in a large meeting room with a bar, "this was full of TV monitors, and many distinguished sports journalists followed the various competitions from here, never venturing outside." He pantomimed the chugging of alcoholic beverages and laughed wryly.

His colleague, Alexey Lipovetsky, was also part of the North American desk, which with 30 personnel was quite the smallest of Novosti's branches. At 41 he was somewhat rumpled, with a drooping black moustache and a sly, cynical wit. Trained at the Moscow Institute for Foreign Languages to be a simultaneous translator, he was the agency's specialist on Quebec and spoke English with a Québécois accent. He was the most experienced and productive kind of journalist, the sort you find a few of in the top ranks of the profession in every country: unstoppably curious, at ease with all types of people, and with a love of imparting all the accurate information he has at his fingertips but with a discriminating filter that automatically weeds out the patently false or illogical. We spent a good bit of time together, talking about, among other things, the press. More than a need for shop talk motivated my enquiries. It was clear that the press had become an engine of change as well as an instrument to measure it. One day we were walking through Gorky Park, very near where Alexey grew up. It was spring, but it seemed like an early autumn day; there were few people about, and the Ferris wheel and other amusements were silent.

"The press is at the leading edge of the idea of a free market," he said. "Consider the case of *Pravda*." The official party newspaper was by no means the juggernaut it formerly had been (and perhaps remains in the heads of most Westerners who have occasion to consider the subject at all). Officials, and journalists who followed developments in the Central Committee, still consumed it and tried to decipher its levels of suggestion and implication, but millions of ordinary readers had dropped away. "As soon as a person realizes that there is something better, he changes his habits," Alexey said. Any publication that professed to throw light into the dark corners of societal administration, or even to chronicle the fresh evidence of change all around, was the beneficiary. The most remarkable success story, though remarkable is scarcely an adequate word, was an eight-page tabloid weekly whose name, translatable as *Arguments and Facts*, was a fair description of its method as well as its content. Four years after it was founded, its circulation stood at 34 million, the largest periodical in the world. In addition, there were some underground papers, so called even though they had ceased to be *samizdat* ventures, produced clandestinely and distributed furtively hand to hand.

"I was curious about how many there are, and so one day recently I asked the librarian at our agency how many of these we subscribe to," Alexey said. "It seems that we buy 210 of them. By no means all of these are from Moscow, of course, but no doubt there are many others we do not receive." One of the better-known examples riveted attention on itself by publishing an irreverent investigation of Mrs. Raisa Gorbachev's personal spending habits. (One day I looked out the window and saw an articulated lorry carrying rolls of newsprint and was reminded that this was another of the commodities included in the embargo against the Lithuanians.)

Some publications not previously considered radical began to take on a patina of radicalism. *Nedelya*, the weekly supplement of the decidedly middle-of-the-road *Izvestia*, is the obvious example. Only a thoroughgoing cynic, however, would suggest that they had done so solely in an attempt to lure readers by catering to fashion. Yet there was no doubt at least as to which were the true radical journals. They are the weekly newspaper *Moscow News* and the weekly magazine *Ogonyok*. I was counting on the freemasonry of journalists to gain me admittance to both places.

The *News* was founded in 1930 and owned jointly by Novosti and an organization called the Union of Soviet Societies for Friendship and Cultural Relations with Foreign Countries. Accordingly there were editions in English, French, German, Spanish, Hungarian, Estonian, and Arabic, with an aggregate circulation of 300,000, as compared with 500,000 copies of the Russian-language original. The offices were situated on one of the most advantageous pieces of real estate in Moscow. On a bright moderate day, too warm for a coat, too cool for just a pullover, I decided to walk there, a distance of several kilometres, rather than add to my knowledge of Moscow's extraordinarily ornate metro stations.

Gorky Street begins within easy sight of the Kremlin and runs north-west. Near the foot is the National Hotel, built at the turn of the century and once the U.S. embassy, before the Revolution forced its move to the present building in Tchaikovsky Street (and of course before the attempted new one, which the Americans discovered was riddled with hidden listening devices and so was razed even before they had finished constructing it). Farther up was the headquarters of TASS, the telegraph agency and news service. Its corner building is recognizable instantly by the huge globe over the entrance; the globe is supposed to revolve, but it had stopped working 20 some years ago and was never repaired. But mostly this wide and orderly boulevard, with some architecture going back to Napoleonic times, is lined with the city's, and the country's, finest shops; mews and side streets contain hidden parks and luxury flats. Many buildings are marked with commemorative tablets, each with a portrait relief, showing some historical figure who once lived there, and it seems clear that there will be a cause for more such plaques in future generations, for this is the haunt of the famous and the well rewarded. One richly decorated white building, I was told, is full mainly of ballet stars. My informant told me the flats have particularly high ceilings; I replied that this is probably best in the circumstances.

More than any other district, Gorky Street shows the extraordinary old European city that underlies our preconceived notions about Moscow, showing it to be the poor sister of London or Paris but a full sibling when it comes to complexity, age, size, style, and even grandeur. Which made it all the more significant that the *Moscow News* should occupy one corner of Gorky Street and Pushkin Square, the most Westernized place in this Westernized boulevard. Across the way, for example, is the world's largest and by no means most unpleasant McDonald's, owned by George Cohon of Toronto and employing 600 Muscovites. On opening day they faced a crowd of 30,000 customers and, as one of my new acquaintances put it, "ascended quickly to the record book of Guinness." Whenever I passed by during my stay, hundreds of people were queuing to get in—queuing eagerly, it seemed to me, without the resignation that always appears to mark the faces of those passing their time in the constant lineups for staple goods. But kitty-corner, outside the *News*, there was a large crowd hungry for something more nourishing. When the paper first came out each Tuesday, its 16 pages were pinned up in display cases running along the side of the building, and citizens jostled one another for the chance to read the news. That side of Pushkin Square is a traditional spot for such anticipation, and a perplexing variety of newspapers is vended there.

Many Soviet papers organized their physical plants on the German plan, with one composing room and one stand of presses working round the clock on a cooperative basis to produce newspapers of different sorts and allegiances, each of which maintained only its editorial shop as a separate operation apart from the rest. The *Moscow News* was different, though. It had its own exclusive plant, which was located some distance from the editorial rooms in Pushkin Square. The arrangement was made all the more awkward because the *News*, like virtually all the Soviet press, had not yet progressed to computerized production.

Two months before my visit, the offices were gutted by a fire, and I found the staff holed up in temporary quarters in an adjoining building whose lobby still smelled strongly of smoke. "There was no suggestion of arson," explained Sergei Volovets, one of the editors and the paper's former London correspondent, when I located him at the end of a slot-like room, perhaps two metres wide and six metres deep. "It was an accident. But the fire was several storeys up, and the fire brigade poured so much water on the blaze that the floors below were ruined, too." Hundreds of readers from many countries contributed to a relief fund. "We hope to get permission from city council to start rebuilding soon," he said. "The climate here makes it difficult to begin work of this sort except in the summer, and we must be finished before the cold comes, because the building we are in now has no heat." City Hall had bandied about the phrase "two months."

The *News* was the sort of newspaper that you wanted to hug or applaud. It was quick to attack the Chinese for the outrage at Tiananmen Square and was critical of Li Peng during his visit. It had been hard on both Gorbachev and Ligachev on point after point, sometimes even recklessly so, to judge by the English-language edition I read, but there was a consistent logical voice from behind the formidable amount of information it provided, information, it would seem, that was often available nowhere else. One of its memorable scoops dealt with two former prosecutors who became members of the Supreme Soviet only to discover organized corruption in the highest echelons of that chamber; the pair narrowly avoided being charged by the attorney general after the *News* began printing their revelations. Similarly it was the *News* that finally proved that the wartime massacre of Polish officers at Katyn, an event the Soviet Union had always attributed to the Nazis, was in fact the work of Stalin's henchmen, just as the Poles had suspected for 50 years. "And our stand on Lithuania differs from the official line in a number of respects," Volovets said with a smile of understatement. The paper was too extreme for the Cubans and at one point was banned even in Hungary.

What struck me most in the issues I read was a certain trenchancy, even down to the back pages devoted to culture, where one day I found this item by a contributor named Alexander Vershinin:

It is a cultural event when new books appear on a library shelf. When books disappear from the shelves—this, too, can be an important cultural event. But the main thing is to know what will be put there instead.

I got a call from the library where I used to lecture about the theatre: "Tomorrow Brezhnev's works will go into the shredder. If you want them, you'd better hurry."

I went and stared at the shelves. Hundreds of heavy volumes—the majority being red. The paper was high-grade, the covers were excellent, and the minimum printed copy runs were 100,000. But what was most remarkable were the titles. For about an hour I rummaged through them, getting pretty dusty in the process.

Brezhnev, *On Internationalism and Friendship of the People*—150,000 copies. Brezhnev, *The Virgin Lands*—3,250,000 copies. Brezhnev, *Rebirth*—3,250,000 copies. Brezhnev, *Following Lenin's Course* in nine volumes—each 300,000 copies. Brezhnev, *Matters of Topical Interest in the* CPSU *Ideological Work*, in two volumes, 1978—100,000. Brezhnev, *Matters of Topical Interest in the* CPSU *Ideological Work*, 1979, in two volumes, second edition, enlarged, 1979 (the only change is the Fourth Star of the Hero in the portrait)—300,000.

On Lenin and Leninism—100,000 copies. *Guarding Peace and Socialism*—100,000. *It Is for the Young to Build Communism. The Party and the Government's Concern About the People's Well-Being*, book two. *The Party and the Government's Concern About the People's Well-Being*, book three, part two. Ponomaryov, *Selected Works*. Romanov, *Selected Works*. Ustinov, *Selected Works*. Andropov, *Selected Works*. Grishin, *Selected Works*. Kunayev, *Selected Works*. Shcherbitsky, *To Master the Leninist Style of Work*. Chernenko, *The People and the Party Are United*.

For the people, about the people, with the people, but, alas, the ungrateful ignoramuses didn't appreciate it. The books are six, 10, 15, 20 years old and none of them have ever been opened. The jackets are brand-new. The cards are clean with no names of any readers in them. And this, although ours is the country with the biggest number of readers.

I collected books weighing more than 100 kilograms. Not to change for Dumas, no. I shall put them in my house, admire them, give them to friends as presents on May 1, November 7. I wanted to take a taxi but it was impossible. I caught an off-duty truck. We threw all this into it and hauled it to my apartment. Kids were playing in the yard—they rushed to help me. They dragged and panted: "Oh, uncle, where did you buy so much?" No, kids, I didn't purchase this. This is a present to the people. This is priceless. These turn thousands of square kilometres of fine forests into useless paper. This is our damned past. This is us.

I couldn't find Rashidov. Apparently, he came along a bit late. So much garbage! The paper is white, the covers are red and my hands are black. Only with great difficulty did I manage to get them clean.

"One of our biggest problems," Sergei Volovets told me, "is that we can't get enough paper to print on. There is a crisis of newsprint. To fill our needs we would have to buy paper from Finland for hard currency and..." He made a gesture to show the difficulty of that alternative. The Soviet Union had no newspaper recycling plants, but the Austrians and Finns sold to third parties the newsprint they recycled from Soviet sources. Space for news in the paper was further restricted by Soviet journalism's discovery of advertising—mostly for foreign airlines, to judge by the *Moscow News*. "But our advertising revenues will only be $150,000 this year, and the biggest part of that goes back to the government in taxes."

Two Western journalists, one American and the other British, had recently published a long article in *The New York Review of Books* entitled "How Free Is the Soviet Press?" based on a couple of weeks' travel and talking to people. Quite high up in the piece they identified Yegor Yakovlev, the editor-in-chief of the *Moscow News*, as "an associate of Gorbachev." It is precisely because of its opposition to Gorbachev, for supposedly being insufficiently committed to speedy reform, that the *News* was so popular and so important.

To find out about the pace and the twists in Gorbachev's plans, one was more likely to turn not to *Pravda* or *Izvestia* but to a magazine called *Ogonyok*, whose masthead used to proclaim that it was a journal of the Central Committee, a statement that had been dropped. *Ogonyok* was edited by Vitali Korotich, who kept making and then cancelling appointments with me as he tried to determine just what the status of my visit was. The day of the last scheduled meeting, word came down that he had been called away to the Central Committee on urgent business; I made a mental note of the phrase so that I could use it myself on those occasions when "a slight indisposition" is simply not a good enough excuse.

Korotich is a well-known poet and nonfiction writer from the Ukraine, but most assuredly not part of the stereotypical Ukrainian right wing. His literary life has permitted him a lot of travel to the West, including several trips to Canada, and he once spent six months at the United Nations, resulting in a book about the United States whose title could be translated as *The Ugly Face*; he has also written about France and about the life of Siberian oilfield workers. Early on he saw in the still-young Gorbachev a latent streak of liberalism, and formed an alliance. It was said, no doubt with a little exaggeration, that they spoke on the telephone daily.

When Korotich got involved in it, *Ogonyok* was a small general interest and cultural monthly with a circulation of 50,000 or 75,000. Now it had 3.3 million readers, lured to it by endless exposés about bureaucrats and the "mafia" and also by its hints about Gorbachev's current thinking and the delicate state of *perestroika*. It was in *Ogonyok*, for example, that the first sign of the anti-radical backlash in the army appeared.

So how free *was* the Soviet press? The Communist Party and the government still appointed the top editors, still imposed circulation ceilings, and still installed censors who sat in editorial offices—though admittedly the censors had little to do in the present mood of freedom. When I was in Moscow, the controversial Press Bill, the first in Soviet history, was meandering its way towards law in a few months' time. Its main provision was to permit individuals or collections of individuals to found and publish newspapers or periodicals of their own, without sanction by, or hindrance from, the party or the state.

2

Arts and Letters

If the press was in a state of flux, changing and growing according to no discernible plan beyond whatever tomorrow might bring, so too were the arts—but for some additional reasons. When liberalism is in the ascendant, art and culture always tend to flourish, as the energy pent up in more restrictive times is given an appreciative outlet, with results that are variously youthful, contagious, and self-intoxicating. The sexual revolution that was sputtering to a regressive and ignoble conclusion in the West, as AIDS and other factors ended the long holiday of public sensuality, was just beginning in the Soviet Union. Sex and nudity were now almost de rigueur in Soviet feature films and especially on the stage, "even in pieces from Chekhov and scenes from Shakespeare," I was told. But this also had to do with the depoliticization of art and the concurrent rise of the free market in culture and everything else. Public art, sanctioned art, subsidized art—it still had to be justified by what I more than once heard called *conjuncture*, or theoretical grounding in the social here-and-now for reasons of national pride. But partly this was force of habit. Soviet readers, for example, *liked* novels about politics, old ones and new ones, indigenous or foreign. Yet the demands that art be used to laud and justify the achievements of socialism— the basis for social realism in art—was already way in the past, and much of the job of simply promoting politics and community had been taken

21

over by the newly free press. The bureaucracy was therefore cutting back on some kinds of arts spending. Gorbachev took a bold pro-arts initiative, for example, when he appointed a prominent stage and cinema actor as culture minister. One of the minister's first important interviews revealed that many theatre companies would have to find free-market ways of contributing to their own keep. He also noted, with what mixture of emotions I found impossible to know, that the trend of so many professional artists letting themselves be subsumed into politics and public service was, well, a sort of double-edged sword. (Not long after my trip, the new culture minister led a performing artists' protest against the state of Soviet culture—in effect, against his own policies.)

So I set out to try to learn something of the current state of the arts, not just their political economy but also, so to say, their texture. I began at the point of easiest access, the offices of *Oktyabr*. They were located in Pravda Street, so named because much of the opposite side of the quaint tree-lined boulevard was occupied by that newspaper and its giant printing plant and various affiliated buildings, like the "palace of culture" (concert hall and all-purpose performing arts centre) and "sanatorium" (health club) for the use of its employees, such as most of the largest industries, unions, and professions enjoyed—another manifestation of the older, more rigidly planned approach to culture.

Oktyabr was in an old mansion with a large shady garden in front. Inside it looked like literary magazines everywhere: secondhand furniture; proofs, files, and manuscripts in permanent disarray; a few dedicated people, though more than one would find on a similar journal in the West. I drank glasses of tea with Nina Loshkareva, the deputy editor-in-chief, and Inessa Nazarova, the executive secretary. Another employee, a young copy editor, married to an editor at an encyclopedia publisher, kindly volunteered to take me the following day on a tour of Old Moscow, which carries many of the same associations as Bloomsbury, with a little bit of Soho thrown in. It was once the student quarter, but Moscow University long ago relocated to the Lenin Hills outside the city.

In this part of Moscow, abutting the famous Arbat, with its colourful shops, small cafés, and ensnared tourists, there are unexpected pieces of the architectural past, including a great many with literary, artistic, or musical associations, around every corner. One stately classical mansion in Vorovsky

Street is said to be the model for the home of the Rostov family in *War and Peace*; it had become a kind of retreat of the Association of Soviet Writers. Nearby is the House of Writers, a club and meeting hall, where I was invited a number of times. It was formerly a Masonic lodge, and the rich panelling in the dining room is carved with such motifs as the double-headed eagle of the tsars, while the cellar is a bar. I sensed that this was to Soviet writers what the Groucho Club is to English ones—there is a delicate ego system at work there.

The area is rich in museums dedicated to such figures as Pushkin. When one of the foreign embassies, which are also centred here, wanted to build on a small park, the protesters erected a sign indicating that the tree in the centre of it had strong associations with Pushkin, thereby mocking them-selves while preserving the spot. We also stopped at the place where Pushkin was married. My guide called it the Church-of-Jesus-Christ-Going-Up-in-the-Air, which I took to be the Church of the Ascension. It was being restored, but there was some debate as to whether it should be a museum or a living church; there was recent precedent for either, as Gorbachev had returned some old monasteries to the Russian Orthodox Church and caused some of them to be restored as well. Which brings home the fact that there are political currents even in the museum field. Only in the past few months had the state made a museum of the house occupied from 1843 to 1846 by Alexander Hersen, the revolutionary editor who spent most of his exile in England. He has risen from relative obscurity partly because it turns out that he was the first person to employ the word *glasnost* in the contemporary sense.

However refreshing such communion with the past—and to me it was one of the major pleasures of Moscow, to an extent that quite took me by surprise—my task was to report on the present. And so, over the course of several more days, I set out to make my rounds.

Book publishing was another point of entry. Western writers and readers all know the stories of how the classic Russian writers are revered, and even read, by the true proletariat as well as the allegorical working class, and how contemporary Soviet writers, or those who carry the seal of approval, saw their works gobbled up in editions of many hundreds of thousands of copies; how writers are debated, argued about, and accorded signs of importance such as in North America are only ever given to figures in big business, entertainment, sport, and crime. There is some truth in this supposition, but of course the situation is rather more complicated—as bad as it is good. In any event, the kind of Soviet publishing North Americans were most familiar with, the English-language editions of Soviet and Western writers associated with Progress Books in Toronto or International Publishers in New York—the loving editions of Walt Whitman, John Steinbeck, Langston Hughes, and so on, with their flimsy paper, mundane design, and quaint 1950s hot-lead typography—turned out to be another area, surprise, that was undergoing rapid change. Such was what I learned from a visit to Alexei Faingar, one of the editorial department chiefs at Progress Publishers, the state's foreign-literature works and, with 1,500 employees, the country's biggest publishing house. Each year it brought out 600 titles in 50 languages, and another 100 in Russian, in the fields of literature, history, politics, law, and the sciences.

Faingar was a beautifully tailored man in his fifties, polylingual, relaxed, and sophisticated, with the look of a shrewd negotiator and a keen judge of a fluid marketplace. He looked like any European publisher you would expect to find at the Frankfurt Book Fair. We met in the boardroom.

"How are the books selected? Ah, that is a complicated process, but I would say that we rely one-half on our editors here and one-half on outside specialists living in Moscow. The latter may work in some academic institution, as in, to take an example, the Institute for the United States and Canada. As for ourselves here, I offer as an illustration my own department, which is concerned with essays, works of quality journalism, and so on. We try to use every possible source of such literature, even private sources. We read foreign periodicals, especially the book-review sections; we have a special department for ordering what might be of interest, and we have [hard] currency for the purpose. As a result, we can plan a year's activities." When he spoke, in early spring 1990, he was engaged in planning his 1992 releases. On subsequent days I spent some time in the foreign-language bookshop in the same building. Recent releases in English literature included a selected writings of Evelyn Waugh, a lesser novel of Robert Penn Warren's, and an anthology of journalism with the status of literature that included a long extract from Daniel Defoe's *Tour thro' the Whole Island of Great Britain*. I perceived no common thread with respect to ideology—perhaps those days had already gone—nor with respect to the usefulness of the texts as teaching aids. Taste was the only basis for selection obvious to me.

The typical press run for a work of mass literature was 50,000 copies, a figure that corresponded roughly to Canadian numbers if you allowed for the fact that Canada had less than 10 percent of the Soviet Union's population. For the blockbusters, as many as half a million copies might be printed, while for specialized or scientific works, the total might be as few as 5,000 copies. Soviet publishers didn't ordinarily maintain extensive backlists of popular titles, but printed a book hoping to sell it out so they could move on to the next. People shopped for books as they shopped for food, gobbling up whatever was available on that particular day. So at least some small part of what outsiders took to be the average Soviet's voracious appetite for culture and learning was the buy-now-and-hoard-for-tomorrow-it-will-be-gone mentality. (I keep remembering the sight of a stylishly attired woman on a trolley-bus, opening her expensive Western handbag in search of a five-kopeck ticket to reveal a half dozen of some vegetable— it looked like a cousin of the rutabaga—caked in mud, just as they had come from the farmer's field. Whenever Soviets saw valuable goods being vended, they joined the queue and bought some, for these goods would soon be worth more than rubles.)

Not all that long ago it was commonly supposed in the West that Soviet publishers of foreign writers were motivated by a desire to show the West in an unfavourable light and would undertake athletic feats of editing to satisfy this ulterior motive. I remember Peter C. Newman showing me the Russian-language edition of *The Canadian Establishment*; it was a mere fraction of the length of the original, presumably because it retained only the material about Bay Street operators calculated to suggest that they are the norm of Canadian society. More recently, I know, the Soviets had published, without any interference or manipulation, Canadian writers whose unflattering views of the Soviet Union were well known. One house, for example, made a selected poems of Al Purdy available. Which is not to suggest that the Soviets rushed to find a special affinity with Canada, whatever geo-cultural logic there might be in such twinning. "Our geography section has published such writers as Farley Mowat on your northern regions," said Faingar on cue, "and I read and enjoyed his book on the Second World War [*And No Birds Sang*], but in the end we didn't publish it. I confess that

Canadian literature is our weak point. We learn not enough of it." He left the impression that Canadians themselves must take more of the initiative. This led us to discuss the whole question of payments received by authors, a topic in which I have a permanent interest, though one, sadly, that is rather more theoretical than not.

In the past, Soviet publishers would withhold royalties on Russian translations of Western books but permit an author to come in person and collect some or all of the money in his or her account, for spending inside the Soviet Union. In the 1960s many a fur hat and many a case of vodka were bought under pressure of deadline by poor drudges from the West with rubles burning a hole in their pockets. The clerks at the GUM Department Store in Red Square must have seen them coming for miles. But in May 1973, a dozen years before *glasnost*, the Soviets finally joined the Geneva Copyright Convention and now dutifully send foreign authors their royalties on books published after that date. Payments are made in the foreign currency of the writer's preference. Some time soon—a few months or a few years? I wasn't able to pin anyone down—they were expected to become signatories of the Berne Convention as well and then pay up on books predating 1973. Of course, publisher-author relations had always been touchy, with some writers, Americans particularly, refusing to cooperate with the Soviet Union. Tom Wolfe, for example, would not permit Progress to print a large portion of *The Right Stuff*, though he relented and allowed them to produce his novel *The Bonfire of the Vanities*.

In the West writers receive a percentage—usually 10 percent—of the retail price of the book, but in the Soviet Union they were paid according to the number of "signatures," which in the Soviet equation amounted to approximately 25 pages of typescript, as well as the "circulation," or size of the print run; actual sales, or the speed of sales, were irrelevant. This allowed the publisher to calculate the sum in advance (and pay 25 percent of it on signing the contract, 35 percent when typesetting was completed, and the final 40 percent on publication). But all this would change soon, for the whole process of getting the books to the readers was undergoing dramatic alteration, like so much else in the country. Formerly all newly printed books from all publishers went to the Book Union, a monopoly trade organization that supplied all the shops and took one-quarter of the retail price. And those prices, like all other financial details, were set out by

Goskompechat, the state committee for publishing, printing, and book-selling. "But two days ago," Faingar informed me, "the directors of 300 houses met in this building to establish the Soviet Publishing Association," with the purpose of finding a way to arrive at prices based upon what the market will bear. "This may be the beginning of the end of the Book Union's monopoly on bookselling," he said. "Maybe in a year's time there won't even be a state committee for publishing."

Far more so, I believe, than in literature, Moscow at this time was particularly rich in the visual arts, and I was fortunate to be able to see a variety of new work and various related activity. I was most pleased, for example, by a visit to an art auction preview, though it was a rather anemic affair by Western standards, held in an ugly, mostly vacant light-industrial space down by the river that bore the same name relationship to the London and New York sale rooms as the dreariest Moscow café bears to a four-star restaurant. But it was rewarding in a number of ways. Although without doubt much of Russia's movable past—books, pictures, antiques, and the like—was destroyed during successive revolutions and wars, it was probably not subjected to a deliberate policy of mass destruction except briefly when the Bolsheviks took power (quite a different situation from China's during the days of the Red Guards). Rather, it simply became irrelevant; Lenin's mission after all was to build a new world; *new* was the operative word. That the export of all art and antiquities of the remotest consequence was prohibited for so many decades contributed to the strength of the pool, as did the low level of disposable income. Now, in the secondhand bookshops, and not just those found among the upscale souvenir places in the Arbat, the European custom of selling old books under the same roof as pictures and prints seemed to be creating some bargains for collectors. Nothing of great importance in the art-historical sense, perhaps, but plenty of attic clutter from late tsarist times, which in shop windows or in the auction preview I mentioned hung side by side with minor contemporary work—not amateur but not really professional either—from which it was often indistinguishable in terms of manner.

This is an important point, it seems to me: the sheer force of accumulated tradition is a question young artists there must come to terms with. The response that painters and sculptors formulate is one of the many factors that determine whether they will be official artists or avant-garde ones.

The former term did not change its meaning much under *perestroika*; such artists are not like those in the Stalin era, working on huge murals of heroic workers marching behind tractors, but they did resemble the social realists of old in that they were members of the U.S.S.R. Artists' Guild or a similar body. *Avant-garde* takes a little more defining, and I was lucky in having a skilled explainer who could also get me inside studios representative of the two types of artists.

Maria Pustukhova, 26, was born in the closed city of Vladivostok in the Far East when her mother was the first woman in local television there; her father was a creative writer who then became a journalist with *Pravda*, which brought the family to Moscow when Maria was 12. Shopping trips to Prague helped her to cultivate the Western appearance admired by Soviet young people, at least of those in the big cities, but her look was altogether more stylish than the usual blue jeans and Reeboks. She was an art critic and art historian. "I live for the avant-garde," she told me as a plain statement of fact, without any of the faux-drama such phrases carry in English. She and I scampered along to a small street behind Starokonyushenny Lane, where the Canadian embassy is located, to the two-room basement apartment that Alexei Mironov used as his sculpture studio. The space, quite separate from the flat where he lived, in another part of the city, was crammed with works in stone, clay, wood, plaster, and various metals. Sometimes a painter friend used the space as well, and as we descended the dark steps we caught the faint smell of turps, which all studio-hounds love, whether they admit it or not.

Mironov, not yet 30, got a sound start. Both his parents were recognized artists, and he graduated from the Stroganov College of Industrial Design when he was 22. For monumental works he sometimes employed assistants, in the traditional manner. Maria told me going in, "He is very rich for an artist"—to the extent that he owned an automobile, or did until quite recently. By Soviet standards he was richer in experience: he had been to the West. He was represented in several public collections in the Soviet Union and in private ones there and elsewhere. In the past couple of years he had been able to accept invitations to visit Britain—first Glasgow, then London—where he had pieces in group exhibitions.

I noticed that like many of the young artists whose work I saw, Mironov used quite a lot of found materials (one exhibition of kinetic Rube

Goldberg-like structures included a room-size contraption that incorporated everything from hand saws to skis to an old pram). I was bound to
ask whether this element was part of his aesthetic or indicated that the flow
of normal supplies was tenuous. "Not problem getting what I need," he
replied. "I deal with, you know, Soviet robbers." He laughed, but I couldn't
tell whether he was joking, for he was a nervously gregarious fellow. Later
he played Russian folk songs on his guitar and poured brandies all round
and offered slices of what I first took to be a piece of wood, for it looked
like a carpenter's leavings, but turned out to be an Armenian meat, spiced
within an inch of its life—and of ours.

What impressed me about Mironov's work was not only its range but
its range of sincerity. Maybe *intensity* is a better word. His painted wooden
figures of contemporary everyman and everywoman, often with right
angles redesigning the human form and commenting perhaps on the angu-
larity of big-city existence, struck me as the most deeply felt, followed by
some very personal pieces in stone or wood, such as a torso of his wife
when she was pregnant with their son, who was now three. But the same
person could also commit an enormous plaster bust of Peter the Great, of
the sort appropriate to a schoolroom long ago—not as one of his many
lucrative commissions but totally self-assigned. The spectrum was so broad,
East to West, contemporary to traditional, that it was almost a kind of
doubt. Mironov couldn't be more different from Harry Vinogradov, a true
underground and decidedly unofficial artist who, for reasons that did not
quite survive the translation process, signed himself Bicapo.

At 32 he was of the same generation as Mironov. His great-grandfather
was a famous St. Petersburg mystic and faith healer, who was sent to Siberia
where in 1937 he was killed. Vinogradov/Bicapo carried on some of the
same fascination with the idea that madness was sometimes connected to
saintliness, a proposition that runs deep in Russian culture. "All people
have to do rituals," he said, "to help them to re-establish relations with
nature." His head was shaven, like a penitent's or a prisoner's rather than
like a skinhead's, and he affected unusual modes of dress. One day, he
recalled, he was wearing a scarf over his head with a hat jammed down over
top of that, and a police officer took him to task, saying, "You'll never be
another Marc Chagall unless you have a proper smoking suit." The cop
didn't know that at that moment Bicapo was naked under his coat.

He studied architecture, found work as a draughtsman, but gave it up "because it was an impossibility for one of my temperament—I prefer the status of a free artist." A number of Soviet painters found the term *free artist* useful. It suggested people who were not direct descendants of the old avant-garde of 1910–30, of the Kandinskys, Komardenkovs, and Konstamntinovs who paralleled the modernists in the West, but rather of the artists whose work, in one especially notorious incident, was ordered destroyed by Khrushchev in 1962—an entire group show ground up by bulldozers.

The point was not necessarily that Bicapo worked in art forms that the state did not recognize. Nor that performance art was exactly a state priority, though the ministry of culture now bragged that, in contrast to "the period of stagnation from Stalin to Chernenko," all disciplines might be recognized and rock and roll might even be perceived as an official export. Yet people like Bicapo didn't receive aid from the cultural arm of the government. Some other apartment artists (so called because they were forced to show their work at open houses rather than in galleries) had become prosperous through overseas sales—part of the new vogue for Soviet art in the West, a by-product of Gorbamania. "Sometimes the neighbours would call the police when they saw a foreigner come up the steps," Maria said. Bicapo, for his part, was in a group called the Kindergarten Artists, because for a time he and a few friends supported themselves as night guards at a day-care centre and school.

Like two million other Muscovites, Bicapo and his mother shared their apartment with another family, or they used to. One fellow tenant died, two others moved away. So now he had his studio space next to his living quarters, on the top floor of an apartment building that was built as recently as the 1930s but looked to be covered in at least a century's worth of grime. The lobby smelled of urine and the lift was broken; the stairs were lighted only partway up.

The essence of his current work involved the intersection of fire, water, and music. To explain "Bicapo consciousness," he first lit candles around the room and struck a series of chimes he had made by suspending different lengths of steel pipe from the ceiling; the sound lingered and then merged with that of a cassette tape he put on, one track of which consisted of the same chimes, while the others were strange sounds I could not identify, half human perhaps and half inorganic, climaxing in what might be screams. All this while two small beer kegs suspended from the ceiling were dripping water into a pair of shallow receptacles that looked like prospectors' gold pans, only larger. Also hanging from above was a circular wire basket in which the artist had put six or eight fuel pellets and ignited them with a blowtorch. The heat rising from the basket caused a large aluminium printing plate, slung over a wire as a blanket might be slung over a clothesline, to vibrate. A microphone connected to an amplifier was placed down a two-metre section of plastic flexi-pipe, the sort used for household plumbing, which pipe was dangled from a light chain and tilted, so that one end, the one with the mike, was close to the water pans, which continued to fill up, *drip-drip-drip*. Bicapo then passed the blowtorch along the length of the pipe, varying the size of the flame. The sounds picked up by the microphone varied accordingly. Clearly this was how he made the sounds that I heard on the tape; other tracks—of hammering and sawing, for example—had been mixed in later.

"I first did this with 10 metres of metal tubing at a construction site," Bicapo explained. "I inserted one end of the tube into a fire while a woman sang opera." This was not so much mere street theatre; he was quite earnest about musical structure and the mixing of created and found sound, but his high seriousness was more apparent from his conversation than from his writings on the theory of his art. He allowed me to look at a draft manifesto that described Bicapo as "radiant, equilibristic, superconducting super-rapid interaction momentary understanding." But his English orthography slipped in a handbill that he let me take away with me, which declared: "The water is drip, the fire is burn. Losting primordial human natur is manifest when thousands of Bicapo and Dzoings are sound. I am mystacal artist through my madness I am penetrate heavens and listen musik of sky forest."

I wasn't able to determine what Dzoings were.

3

Red Arrow, Red Square

I struck gold on the midnight train to Leningrad.

Like all the other overnight trains, such as those to Helsinki, Vilnius, or other points north and west, this one, called the Red Arrow, had compartments with two berths each, side by side, and I found myself sharing with a woman in her seventies, dressed in a very middle-class manner but with a ratty old cardigan over her suit. On her left lapel she had affixed pins or medals, ones I had never seen in that country of military decorations—both cameos of someone (not Lenin), one black, the other red and black. I asked her what they were, and she told me that they showed her membership in the Soviet Academy of Science and its Italian equivalent. "I do not usually feel disposed to wear insignia but today was different," she said. She was a retired mathematician, and the occasion was a gathering of the clan in Moscow, from which she was now returning home. She spoke the English of someone who had learned it before the Great Patriotic War—might almost have learned it before the Revolution, the last time Russia was part of Europe.

How long had she resided in Leningrad?

"It has been my home uninterruptedly since 1947."

Then she had not been there during the war, during the Nazi siege lasting 900 days?

"But I was there, yes. I was a young student, and I took very ill. The German circle around the city was complete except for one small opening, and I was evacuated and taken back to Moscow. When I recovered, I continued my studies there."

We talked for many kilometres. She sat perfectly upright; her eyes shone, and when she broke into a smile, as she did at every opportunity, the change in her expression took up the slack that the years had given her face, the lower part in particular.

I asked her how she had come to receive the pin from the Italian academy.

"It was given to me two years ago, I believe it was, when I travelled there for that purpose. Things were not always as you find them now. There is *libéralisme* in the Chamber of Deputies and throughout the government; it is in the air. But this was not always so," she said, taking advantage of her understatement to smile again. "I was the first woman mathematician to become a member of the Soviet academy." I gathered that her discipline was almost as much a barrier as her gender, and that even after she was elected there were still more obstacles to overcome. "Perhaps six years ago the international symposium was held in Montreal, but I was not permitted to go." But with the Gorbachev ascendancy, the mood changed instantly; the trip to Italy was her first and so far only visit to the West.

Finally we grew tired of talking. She put out the lamp, saying merrily, "There is too much illumination in the carriage." We lay back on our respective bunks. Whenever we passed through a town during the night, I could see her head silhouetted in the flickering light. It looked as though it belonged on an ancient coin.

As it happened, I saw Leningrad in strict sunshine, which it is possible to do only 65 or at most 100 days of the year. This good luck no doubt contributed to my general impression that Leningrad was on balance one of the handsomest cities I had ever been in. I mean the old central city, which became the capital in 1712, a few years after it was founded, and retained the distinction for 200 years. But even the outer districts, with rusty factories in the Soviet manner, were not without a 1930s late modernist charm. They made you forget for a moment how northern a city Leningrad really is, with its Baltic air and immense skies. When you move beyond the city—and such is the density that you don't have to move very far, considering that there are five million residents—you run into forests of white birch.

When leaving Canada, I had stuffed a bag with expendable secondhand paperbacks for consumption in queues and waiting rooms (and learned when I arrived that they made welcome gifts as the appetite for English books was hearty everywhere I went). Quite by chance I came upon a passage in *Walden* in which Henry David Thoreau enumerates his reasons for choosing to settle at Walden Pond. "No Neva marshes to be filled; though you must everywhere build on piles of your own driving," he writes. "It is said that a flood-tide, with a westerly wind, and ice in the Neva, would sweep St. Petersburg from the face of the earth." But it's not like that at all, at least not in the warmer months. The Neva is a broad river that cuts a deep blue pattern through the heart of the city, augmented by small canals that suggest a miniature (and cleaner) Venice. On both banks of the river, for as long as one can see in both directions, are perfect baroque buildings from the 18th century and classical ones from the early part of the 19th. Many are painted in pastel shades—not, as in Portugal, say, to display themselves best in direct sunlight but to fight back against the absence of it. The Winter Palace, I was surprised to discover, is wintergreen (a mnemonic device in the making for anyone who has difficulty remembering what buildings were stormed in the Revolution). The low line of harmonious rooftops was interrupted here and there by a church spire or a gold dome. One such dome, in the distance, belongs to St. Isaac's Cathedral, whose columns still bear some scars from the war. It is located across the square from the Astoria Hotel, which Hitler vowed to make into a museum of the conquest of Leningrad. Some chicken, some neck. The pockmarks on St. Isaac's are retained as a reminder, like a sign on a building in Nevsky Prospekt, the principal commercial street, requesting pedestrians to walk on the other side of the avenue during periods of bombardment.

The damage done during the war went beyond what would be suggested by the word *extensive*; it was heartbreaking. But the Soviets were the world's champion restorers and rebuilders, and neither the antiquarian symmetry of the riverfront nor the open-handed bustle of Nevsky Prospekt, with its often magnificent pre-Revolutionary shops, showed Leningrad for the tragic and violent place it had so often been. Granted that by now there should be no way of recalling that three-quarters of the buildings were destroyed in the war against Napoleon. What is implausible—and it flies in the face of all sensory logic, too—is that it is not easy to connect the place with its revolutionary past—Leningrad, where the Decembrists rose up, where the men of the cruiser *Aurora*, which is now a floating museum, fired some of the first shots of the Revolution, where Lenin disembarked at the Finland Station, his exile ended. But it is so. I found it much easier to conceive of Moscow, where intellectual and artistic ferment go together with a gritty workaday existence, as the epicentre of past political earthquakes than Leningrad, which was merely the hub of government, the aristocracy, and the capitalist business culture that were being overthrown. Not that it was remote from the present political turmoil. On the contrary. Only weeks earlier a crowd of 100,000 had gathered outside the Winter Palace to protest the possibility that the two former prosecutors whose stories of corruption had been printed in the *Moscow News* might lose their immunity. I saw graffiti such as FUCKEN POLICE and the letter A in a circle, the international sign for anarchism. Yet despite all that, Leningrad was definitely the quieter place, with both a deeper level of culture and a sense of inferiority, perhaps equally profound, about having become the second city. The comparisons are inexact enough to be odious, but Leningrad is to Moscow as Montreal is to Toronto, San Francisco is to Los Angeles, and Melbourne is to Sydney.

As befits a city that in tsarist times gave pride of place to its magnificent classical Stock Exchange (by now a naval museum), it was also, or so I found, a greedier place than Moscow in terms of the poor Soviets' eternal quest for the magical American dollars—greedier and so ruder, because the mission was clear and the time to accomplish it so brief. My experience of Intourist employees I dealt with in Moscow, for example, was that they were uniformly helpful and efficient and usually friendly to boot; but the ones in Leningrad wore *renfrogné* expressions that were matched by their voices. One or two of the foreigners' hotels in Moscow had a few discreet slot machines in the lobby to extract yet a few more dollars or pounds per year, but in Leningrad they were more numerous and not at all hidden; in one instance, there was a sort of miniature casino, gaudily lit. Maybe that kind of thing is to be expected in any city whose museums and treasures make it a place where tourism is disproportionately important to the economy (20,000 people per day visit the Hermitage museum, 40,000 per day in the summer and during holidays). One incident for me crystallized Leningrad's position in this matter.

Wherever I went, I found, as so many Western visitors do, that people were forever approaching me to change dollars into rubles at the best black-market *valuta* (you would have had to be crazy to run the risk of accepting) or to try to sell me wristwatches or vodka. Leningrad exceeded all the boundaries. Spotting me as a foreigner (it is my fate always to look like a foreigner wherever I am, even when I stay home), young men would enquire in whispers whether I might wish Soviet flags or icons or caviar (three jars for $10—"special price"). The most original was a chap not far from the main entrance of the Admiralty. He was in civilian attire, but I took him to be a sailor by his distinctive haircut—and because Leningrad has been full of sailors since it was established originally to be the country's Baltic seaport. He was carrying a bag of some rough cloth, bigger than a large pillow slip. I thought I saw it move, leading me to suppose that it contained a chicken or perhaps a litter of kittens. But what he wanted was to sell his—or somebody's—dress uniform, complete with braided cap and epaulets. I declined, and we each scurried off in stoic embarrassment like two people whose stomachs had been rumbling in public. Naval discipline, I gathered, was not what it once was.

I stayed in Leningrad a couple of days, looking at paintings and buildings and talking to as many people as I could, including bathers sunning themselves on the sand beneath the walls of Peter and Paul Fortress, the old political prison. I marvelled at the brevity of their costume, given that I found it cold enough to warrant something midway between a mackintosh and an overcoat. They're a hardy mob, those Leningraders.

I wish I could report that my return journey to Moscow was as rewarding as the trip up had been, but it was merely memorable. My roommate this time was a merchant seaman who kept addressing me as *Englander*. I had all the more reason to not split hairs, but simply accept this as the generous compliment it was, given that he was as drunk as a—well, as a sailor. He couldn't move more than a few steps without banging his head into something, and he kept dropping the sheaf of roses that he told me were for his wife in Moscow. He also confessed, rather needlessly, that he had been out with his friends and had consumed quite a lot of vodka. He told me that he knew my country well, and rhymed off the landmarks: Tilbury Docks, Tower Bridge, Big Ben.... By the end of the list he was singing rather than reciting them.

I confessed my fatigue and asked whether I might put out the light. But when I did he would simply turn it on again. And my plan of going to the Soviet Union with the intention of ignoring my own shyness and talking with as many different citizens as possible was put to the test by the fact that, after an hour or so, I still couldn't get him to shut the bloody hell up. So I was relieved when he announced that he was leaving our compartment in search of more vodka. When he found some, though, he returned to shake me awake and insist that I share it with him. I sent him away and fell asleep again. He then sent as an emissary to reawaken me the woman whose vodka it was. I told her to get out. Some while later the sailor barged back into the room to retrieve his wife's roses, presumably for redistribution among women elsewhere in the carriage. That must have been 3:00 a.m. or so. When we pulled into the station at seven, he was asleep, slouched over like a big sack of onions, snoring a deafening snore. I left him there and went in search of a taxi driver I could bribe.

For all the reverence I saw in people's behaviour at the Lenin Mausoleum, I also heard, throughout my stay, a lot of condemnation of his shade or maybe of the Lenin cult. Much of it was expressed at the level of satire or humour, however seriously it was felt. One person told me that in his lifetime he had seen 50 coats or suits that once belonged to Lenin hanging in various museums—"and they're all different sizes." At another exhibit I heard a woman argue quite seriously and cogently that Leningrad should be given back its old name; this surprised me, but soon a powerful movement would spring up around the idea. But of Stalin who betrayed the Revolution and commenced not only the Era of Stagnation but the long reign of terror, I heard much less derision. I couldn't quite tell to what extent this was because his statue had been kicked over long ago and to what extent it was because the plinth was still warm. Maybe hatred of Stalin was simply taken for granted. Taking a poke at Lenin was certainly a different matter, a safe novelty, part of the new freedom, the changes in change itself, the liberal counter-revolution.

The joyous assumptions of Americans to the contrary, this new revolution was not necessarily a purblind rush to embrace America or the right.

No one was advocating turning the Soviet Union into another United States; surely Gorbachev, faced with a deepening national emergency, was only making socialism far more flexible, as Franklin Roosevelt, when in a similar corner, made capitalism more flexible. The point wasn't the Cold War except to the extent that the Cold War was too expensive for either side to continue fighting, most of all the Soviets, who had a standing army of four million but, according to the more liberal military planners at defence headquarters across the river from Gorky Park, needed a mere 1.7 million. It was simply about moving nearer the middle, with more democracy and a more mixed economy than in the past, trying to improve the lot of individuals (and preserving the power of those now bringing about the improvement). Yet the changes were abrupt. They could still turn out to be violent. Certainly they would cause some aspects of Soviet life to worsen before they improved. This much was brought home to me again and again as I spoke with people about their fears and aspirations.

It is obvious to the least observant visitor that the present system guaranteed full employment only by perpetuating a ridiculous level of overstaffing. Four people worked in a cloakroom that might be handled by one. To buy a plane ticket or rent a hotel room or get a loaf of bread in a bakery, you were passed from person to person, each of whom undertook some further perfunctory part of the process. A retail purchase that in a state-run shop in China might require the services of two or three persons could easily, in the Soviet Union, take those of four or five—one to show you where the item was, a second to fetch it down, another to take your money, yet another to take your receipt and do the wrapping. As the old socialist jest had it, "We pretend to work and they pretend to pay us." There was an important difference between this arrangement in the Soviet Union and the impression I got in China that the government was at least making the best use of its most obvious asset—the labour force. That it was difficult to feel the same way about Soviets was no doubt coloured by the way the country was routinely rumoured to be on the brink of collapse—an ethnocentric Western view, I feel, since we had no real understanding of how long it had been as bad as it was and no way to measure the Russians' extraordinary capacity for swallowing adversity and making the best of chaos.

This was the difficulty in trying to interpret events in the socialist world at the time: the Americans refused to believe anything good about the

Soviets, that the people were generally better educated, less violent, and leading perhaps altogether deeper lives than they themselves were, whereas the Soviets, or the young ones at least, refused to believe anything bad about the West—the drugs, the crime, the homelessness, the AIDS. A general lack of attention to reality obscured the simple truth that the quality of life in the one place was improving and in the other place deteriorating but that, in any event, they were becoming more alike.

I was told that it wouldn't be long before Soviet citizens would be free to possess credit cards—despite the absence, so far, of all the necessary mainframes and software. One can imagine what a mess eventually resulted, given that virtually every place of business in the country still used the abacus in preference to the cash register. They had cash registers, all right, but they didn't use them for any form of tabulation but merely as places to keep large-denomination notes, as one might use a microwave oven as a bookcase. In that environment the moves towards a market economy were bound to be painful. People may cheer when bureaucrats are put out of work, but what about when they themselves must go on and living standards plummet? As things then stood, 45 million Soviets lived on 70 rubles a month. In Moscow alone there were 1.7 million people below the official poverty line, and when I was there the new mayor announced plans for municipally funded soup kitchens. Before they could be opened, it was expected that the price of most consumer goods would rise 100 percent. No one disputed that such changes were necessary or that the existing social net had to be remade, but with new measures to protect pensioners and others on fixed incomes, if the country was to stabilize its currency. Stabilizing it was the first step towards internationalizing it. At that time the much-vaunted joint ventures between Soviets and Western businesspeople, about 1,300 of them when I was there, didn't work because the Westerners didn't want to be paid in worthless rubles and there were not enough dollars or Deutschmarks for that purpose. The joint ventures were necessary, however, to improve the supply and quality of consumer goods. To an extent I was prepared to accept but couldn't quite fathom until I saw the situation with my own eyes, the problem of the Soviet Union was the problem of food. No one actually starved to death, as of old, but Gorbachev must have been aware all too acutely of a rule that has cautioned leaders for thousands of years, that hungry people are dangerous people.

Then there were social ills we don't usually see, for a variety of reasons. There was indeed a slight drug problem in the Soviet Union, though hardly on the scale of any western European country. One of the reasons you heard so little about it was that it did not involve smuggling and international borders, for the drugs came from areas of the country close to Afghanistan (though intelligence specialists have long insisted that China illicitly supplies drugs to its old adversary, just as it is supposed to have flooded the Vietnamese market 35 years ago to help demoralize the American troops). Crime was rising in the big cities, as it is in big cities everywhere, I suppose. There were places in Moscow, just as in the West, where for fear of rape women were afraid to enter their own apartment buildings alone after dark. I saw beggars in the subway underpasses, but not many; so far there was virtually no homelessness as such, though the extent and quality of housing was a pressing problem and a major subject of anxiety—but having said so, there seems no point getting sucked up into any East–West comparisons when the systems are so fundamentally different.

By contrast, the whole range of women's issues is a useful illustration of the similarities and differences. "There is no feminist movement," a teacher in her forties explained to me. "We have equal pay for equal work, and women do about all the jobs that men do." There is, however, a "women's lobby," which is expected to challenge the spread of such complacency and to address imbalances, such as that only eight percent of political offices in the Soviet Union were held by women (as compared, for example, with the House of Commons in Ottawa, where at the time 13.5 percent of the MPs were women—hardly a figure to justify smugness). Perhaps the harshest fact of women's existence is that though both partners must work, the woman still performs all the domestic functions previously expected of her, and moreover that this presents even greater difficulty than in the West. The father does not usually take part in child care. It is also the woman who spends two or three hours shopping for food for the night's supper (only to find sometimes, after getting to the head of the line, that the food is spoiled). Women are not *social* equals. What was called male chauvinism in the West in the 1970s was the common currency in the Soviet Union, though there was no name for it and it was almost completely unremarked on by either gender so far as public discussion went; it was simply part of the culture. If lucky enough to be invited into a private home, the Western visitor was often shocked by how the husband denigrated his wife's domestic skills as a means of apologizing, needlessly of course, for the lack of what he imagined to be Western comfort. No wonder that 33 percent of marriages ended in divorce, which accounted for 70 percent of all activity in the courts; in more than 98 percent of divorce cases involving children, the mother was given custody. The parting couple paid a 300-ruble divorce tax (until recently 200 rubles—inflation again). Child-support payments were generous but of course that never really solves the problem. The nation might now be self-sufficient in blue jeans, much to the impoverishment of black marketeers and shrewd Western tourists. What it lacked so conspicuously were condoms which, when available at all, were of unreliable quality. I was told that for Western visitors to give their host or hostess condoms would not be misunderstood but, on the contrary, would seem considerate. Abortion might be free on demand, but it was virtually the only form of birth control worthy of the name. Fully 20 percent of first pregnancies ended in abortion.

Alcoholism was another factor in marriage breakdown as it was in poor work productivity. One of Gorbachev's first initiatives was the major campaign against alcohol abuse, even to the extent of banning the sale of hard liquor (but not its consumption) on trains and planes. Reaction against the "authoritarian" campaign was among the causes that enabled Yeltsin to get his political comeback underway. One sensed that economic loss, not health, was the primary concern, given that virtually no acknowledgement was made of the fact that 78 percent of adult males and 38 percent of adult females smoked cigarettes. The Soviet Union was, in fact, a nation of inveterate chain-smokers. "Sure, we have free housing, or virtually free," I was told. One person I talked to paid just 17 rubles a month for an apartment in downtown Moscow, a tiny portion of his middle-class salary. "But the quality is poor. With health care, it was similar. It was free of charge, and available to everyone, but the quality I believe you would call lousy." I heard stories, which I was not able to confirm, of a drug shortage so severe that patients in polyclinics had died from infection after routine operations such as appendectomies. People wanted change to come and soon, sooner than seemed possible, in fact. The good thing about the present, after all, is that there are no surprises.

Kropotkin Street, named to honour the great anarchist, was formerly known as Blessed Virgin Street. It contains a sinister building partly hidden by a high wall topped with barbed wire; this is one of the psychiatric institutions where dissidents were held against their will and, in a few cases, still were, if rumours were correct. A short distance along is a building that was long home to two elderly women who kept scores of cats. Five years earlier, however, the cats were removed and the house became Moscow's first cooperative, which is to say free-enterprise, restaurant, known simply as No. 36 Kropotkin. It wouldn't even accept dollars much less rubles but took only credit cards and was frequented by groups of foreigners or by single foreigners like me, eager to repay the genuine hospitality of some Soviet acquaintances. It was not the most expensive of the seven or eight such eating places in the city; I was advised in a hushed tone that at a Chinese restaurant called the Peking the shark's fin soup cost 100 rubles. But it was representative, I believe, and symbolic.

Eating in any Soviet restaurant, you were conscious first of all that the printed menu, considered as literature and theatre, served quite a different function than in the West. In our tradition the menu is a basic list. You expect the waiter to ooze over to the table and say something like, "Good evening, my name is Mark, and I'll be your server this evening. In addition to our menu selections, chef has prepared the following specials...." Soviet menus by comparison were little encyclopedias, page after page of every conceivable chicken dish, fish dish, vegetable dish. The job of the server was to explain, in response to your enquiries, that the dishes you wanted were not available—until you began to suspect that they had never been available. "So what, then, do you suggest this evening?" you were finally forced to ask.

"Bifsteak." Boiled beef.

"What would you recommend to go with that?"

"Cabbage."

"Is there anything else available?"

"Cabbage."

A cold fish course came first; the meat was the second course and was always boiled. Fresh fruit and vegetables were almost nonexistent. No. 36 was offering carrots that night, but they were cold. It was amusing to see the head waiter in evening clothes and the junior staff in stiff white tunics, trying to suggest the pre-Revolutionary style. They had the snooty looks down pat but kept serving and taking away from the wrong sides. The example might be a small one, but the point was bigger: one of the reasons why individual entrepreneurship was far more widespread and obviously more successful in China than in the Soviet Union, I heard it said, was that in China there was still an old generation that remembered how the salary system worked; 1917 was just that much longer ago than 1949 to make the same continuity impossible in the Soviet Union.

Outside in the street, however, the world before the Revolution is apparent enough, in the old apartment blocks, the former private houses, the hotels or public buildings that serve completely different functions now but are so clearly a part of their own time and place—and class. Even the arrangement of the streets and boulevards shows the wealth that once obtained there. It is like London in that respect, though in general the similarity to the United States seems more pressing and germane: another of those sprawling, powerful, ungovernable countries that can proceed only by lurching from extreme to extreme in a kind of slow-motion ricochet in which innocent people so often get hurt.

I managed to wangle a VIP pass to the May Day parade in Red Square, but was told to bring my passport and visa (the latter is a separate document, not something stamped in the former). Security promised to be tight because this was not an ordinary May Day, or Day of the International Solidarity of the Working People, to give it its full official name. For one thing, it was the 100th consecutive May Day parade to be held in Red Square. Some will be surprised to learn that this was a pre-Revolutionary holiday in new red clothes. It is in fact a pre-Christian celebration of the return of spring; even some of the Russian songs associated with it may date back the better part of a millennium. Some elements of the original ceremony survived into the era when aging patriarchs standing side by side atop the Lenin Mausoleum would give feeble geriatric waves to the endless line of troops and missile carriers passing below. That is the May Day we in the West know from years of television clips, though in fact the displays of unending might have always been more important as a feature of Victory Day on May 9.

In any case, this year was to be very different. No military parade at all and no rogues' gallery of Red Army generals to take the salute—that would have been too Stalinist in tone and, in the present atmosphere, too provocative. This time the various trade unions and such would do the marching, organized not by the government but by the Society of Moscow Voters, a pro-reform organization, and others, but with the approval of the Council of Ministers, which also gave permission for a demonstration—a manifestation, as the Soviets said—to be held around the corner, so to speak, in Revolution Square. I couldn't find anyone who knew for certain whether Gorbachev himself would turn up. In Leningrad and other cities the holiday would be marked in similarly radical ways; in Kiev local people did without government representation in the reviewing stand altogether.

By 9:30 or so the area around the Kremlin was filling up with humanity. I heard the size of the crowd estimated variously at 100,000 and 300,000— the latter seemed too high to me, but it made no difference really. I kept track of the number of times my papers were scrutinized at different checkpoints as I got closer to Lenin's tomb; the final tally was nine. The soldiers were equally careful with diplomats, I noticed. From the concrete steps where I perched, closer to the reviewing stand, downwind, than to the Historical Museum to my left, where the marchers would proceed from, I had a fine view of the goings-on. I could see columns mustering, banners being unfurled and tested, brightly coloured groups of walkers pacing like horses impatient for the race to begin. To the right, TV camera crews on an unstable-looking scaffold were training their equipment on the top of the mausoleum, where the new extra-military dignitaries would stand. Soldiers were everywhere. There were also many security men in black leather trench coats with walkie-talkies. Through the long lens of my camera I could see others directly ahead, across the great cobblestone square, positioned along the rooftops.

I moved my gaze downward and began scanning faces in the crowd through my viewfinder. During one pan, I stopped with a jolt of recognition. The face was unmistakable. Yes, it was Honest Ed Mirvish, the zillionaire proprietor of Toronto's oldest, largest, and altogether most garish discount store, a man who had parlayed the nine-cent light bulb and the job lot of slightly imperfect ladies' ready-to-wear into a famous dynastic fortune. He was wearing a beautifully tailored dark blue wool suit and handmade Italian shoes that shone like obsidian. He seemed to be giving some people his business card. For just a moment, before he was swallowed by the crowd, I saw him framed against the GUM Department Store and could imagine it as perhaps he might hope to see it, its 2.4 kilometres of counter space brimming with toilet rolls and polyester tank tops, its long facade plastered in neon and witty sayings and blow-ups of articles from the Toronto *Telegram* extolling the legend of Honest Ed (boy, what a card). I couldn't help but wonder whether he knew the significance of what he was about to see or whether it reminded him of the Eaton's Santa Claus parade when he was a kid.

At the stroke of 10:00 band music came over the public-address system, followed by short speeches from a series of sonorous disembodied voices. The first speech was booed but not consistently or with real persistence. By now I could see the thin line of figures on the reviewing stand. The pent-up marchers were released, and there was another flurry of brass and drums, but live this time, from somewhere within the multitude. The participants lunged forward, men in suits, women in dresses, lots of children, some holding red flowers straight out in front of them like votive offerings. Suddenly I realized what a sea of colour it was, how surprised I was to see all the bright fabrics together, for after even so short a time in the country my eyes had become accustomed to the more limited spectrum that was certainly one of the features of existence there, quite apart from any quality-of-life considerations.

The parade went on. Then it went on some more, and some more. My vantage point was privileged, but I realized that it was also constricted. I couldn't see Gorbachev from where I was; I couldn't even see whether he had turned up. There were gasps now at the wording on some of the placards and banners bobbing over the heads of the crowd. I asked someone to translate. One read THE COMMUNIST PARTY OF THE SOVIET UNION EXPLOITS US. Another ran: GET OUT OF OUR POCKETS NOW! I felt compelled to see how the fellows on the reviewing stand were reacting. I needed to move to the east, but whenever I tried I was stopped by the militia police or by the plainclothes security. For the same reasons it seemed hopeless to try to make a circuitous route, westward to the museum at the edge of the square and then along 25th October Street, through the back door, as it were; that would have put the whole crowd between me and the mausoleum and I wasn't certain I would find a sufficiently elevated spot there such as the one I already enjoyed where I was. The only thing to do was to join the parade and become one of the marchers myself. If anyone tried to prevent me from doing so, I would make a fuss and insist I was one of the cultural workers (for such is how my editor must think of me, I said to myself).

An organization of machinists was going past. I could identify them by the logotype of meshing gears on their signboards. I stepped down and slipped sideways between the guards and was swept up in the marchers before anyone could stop me. We hadn't gone many metres before I caught sight of Gorbachev. He was the 12th from the right, in his trademark top-coat and little grey hat. His wool scarf had an irregular pattern of red in it, no doubt to honour the occasion. He was looking impassive and occasionally he waved in somewhat the same way we associate with the Queen. I got to look at him only for half a minute before the momentum of the crowd pushed me and my fellow machinists along. I didn't see any obvious concern on his face, but my intuition, I believe, was correct. Shortly afterwards, thanks partly to an administrative mix-up, the demonstration in Revolution Square was permitted to tag on to the end of our parade, not far behind me, and when these other marchers reached the vicinity of the reviewing stand, they produced loud-hailers and began shouting personal insults at the president, who lost his patience and walked off.

The next day this incident was the talk of the town, though the media were cautious at first, referring only to evidence of displeasure in the parade and in the unofficial demonstration. Radio Moscow merely referred to some slogan of "an explicit and controversial nature" that would have been unthinkable at any time in the past. But gradually, as time went on and the various weeklies appeared, the story came out a few details at a time, to the point where *Moskovskaya Pravda*, as the local edition was called, one day ran a long front-page interview with the first secretary of the party. It was headed "On the Wave of Irresponsibility."

4

Diseases of the Soul

There are naturally two museums in central Moscow devoted to Maxim Gorky. One of them is the house where he spent his last few years and wrote his last books. It was there that he died—murdered by his doctors, some say. The story is that they were acting on orders from Stalin, who apparently feared that Gorky was becoming too much of a folk hero. Others believe that Stalin personally killed him, by giving him poisoned candy. How many Soviet biographies end this way—"murdered by Stalin"?—though the motive was not usually jealousy.

What makes the Gorky house truly interesting is not the memorabilia displayed there but the structure itself, which dates to about 1900. It was confiscated from the person who built it, a manufacturer and banker named Ryabushinsky. He was a great patron of the modern artists, whom he commissioned to design stained-glass windows and balustrades and every other sort of decorative component. The result suggests what might have come about if Roger Fry and his Omega Workshop had been given carte blanche to create a total environment. Something about the front entrance struck me immediately. There were large brass hinges on the thick double doors. I couldn't be certain, for the design was somewhat stylized, but it certainly seemed to me that the hinges were meant to represent a menorah. I remember this detail because it is impossible to conceive of anyone in Moscow since the turn of the century who would have been brave enough, or foolhardy enough, to flaunt his or her Jewishness in quite that way. Certainly no one would do so when I was there. The Soviet Union, unfortunately, seemed a very anti-Semitic place. The evidence suggests that Russia has always been so, of course, but the new mood of relative freedom had permitted the old animosities to be expressed publicly.

In the couple of months before I arrived in the country, anti-Semitism appeared to be breaking out everywhere, from Irkutsk in Siberia, where there were outcries about the number of Jews supposedly holding scientific appointments, to Baku in Azerbaijan, where Muslims not ethnic Russians were the persecutors of the 20,000 local Jews, to Odessa on the Black Sea, where the authorities had to issue reminders that inciting racial hatred was a crime. In general the new wave of anti-Semitism was bound up with the politics of Russian nationalism. One of the main instigators was Pamyat (the word means *memory*), an ultra-rightist group based in Moscow and Leningrad. It had called for keeping Jews out of teaching jobs, doctoral programmes, local governments, and even the CPSU. When I was there, rumours about a pogrom—that was the word being used—in Leningrad on May 5 were gaining currency. Fortunately they were just rumours, but they had been circulated with a certain desired effect. Officially there were only about 1.5 million Jews in the Soviet Union, because many of them went to pains to disguise or submerge their Jewishness during the Stalin years and later. The true figure was a least 50 percent greater and might have been twice as large; the heaviest concentration was in Moscow, about 200,000. A majority of Soviet Jews were intending to emigrate to Israel.

In 1990 for the first time Passover was proudly covered on Soviet television, and I saw posters announcing exhibits of Jewish art and Jewish history. Yet such activity carried a suggestion that the culture it represented was passing from the Soviet scene, though at this time Gorbachev was threatening to keep the Jews from leaving unless Israel undertook not to settle them on the occupied West Bank and Gaza Strip (a demand it eventually agreed to). In any event, the new religious freedom being granted the Christians had resulted only in more anti-Semitism. That China has no noticeable anti-Semitism has less to do with the fact that it has only a handful of Jews than with the fact that it has so little political freedom. (Buddhism there is mostly for show. In Tibet, for example, there were

106,000 priests and 2,400 monasteries as late as 1960, after the refugees had left. Today there are 2,000 priests and only 10 monasteries. The most important feature of religious freedom, perhaps, is that it needs political freedom in order to flourish.)

Another hotbed of anti-Semitism in the Soviet Union—though also of reaction against it—was the literary community, in particular the Writers' Union of the Russian Republic, where there had been actual fistfights over the issue. Only a very few writers, such as Stanislav Kunyaev, were anti-Semitic agitators, but they had a disruptive effect, and as I learned one evening over dinner in the union's dining room, the polarization extended deep into the profession. I was with two young people, both junior editors. They were well educated, not at all susceptible to the crude canards of *The Protocols of the Elders of Zion*, which the tsars and Hitler used to fan hatred of Jews and which various groups in the provinces were once again spreading about as "proof" of a worldwide Jewish conspiracy. Nonetheless, they were quite firm in what they did believe.

"Most of the leaders of the Revolution were Jews," one of the editors told me. Well, some were, of course, but the significance of that fact is that the Revolution was hatched by intellectuals as a revolution of ideas. "They planted the seeds for the Soviet system, and you see what condition the Soviet system is in." He was deadly serious about this syllogism and expected others to take it seriously as well: the food shortages were the Jews' fault! I was appalled. This was the view of the Pamyat leaders like Dmitry Vasiliev, though the person across the table from me was hardly a Pamyat type. The other young editor was of the contrary opinion and announced that he was prepared to hide Jews in his home when the situation came to that. Both positions were proclaimed with feverish emotion. Even the person taking the second position, however, kept using the phrase "the Jewish problem," a term that made my blood run cold. I believe that was my second scariest moment in the Soviet Union. The scariest was when a moderate liberal democrat told me, "There are only perhaps four million of us right now who believe as I do. Now people are speaking out, but the door could close on us at any time. Stalin killed how many? Ten million? Twenty million? Gorbachev could kill four million and it wouldn't make a particularly large grave." In fairness to him my informant was drunk at the time. The young people discussing "the Jewish problem" were deadly sober.

I was relieved to see that the *Literaturnaya Gazeta* came out forcefully in support whenever the government brandished the anti-hate laws against the most blatant offenders, but the whole subject left me worried and weak-kneed. As economic conditions worsened, as they were bound to do before they began to improve, the anti-Semitism would worsen as well, even though, like so much of the present turmoil, its basis was less in matters of money than in ones of race. When I was there, three of the Baltic republics and three Muslim ones were engaged in plotting to break away from the federal union, and later, with Yeltsin's election, the opposite possibility started to be talked about openly—the possibility of the centre breaking away from the edges.

By a vivid coincidence, the period covered by my trip saw news about census-taking in the United States, China, and the Soviet Union. The U.S. census turned into a shambles of inaccuracy, because there was no effective way, it seemed, of enumerating all the transients, bag ladies and other homeless people, winos, junkies, and illegal aliens. China announced that it would begin a thorough new census of the country, a daunting task involving six million enumerators to count an estimated 1.1 billion people, and one that immediately aroused suspicions that the operation would be a cover for new means of tightening the grip of authority. In the Soviet Union, by contrast, there were stories about why the census undertaken the previous year had yet to be released and perhaps never would be. The reason, it was supposed, was that results showed the number of Soviet Muslims up by 33 percent while the number of ethnic Russians had increased by only 5.6 percent. The whole question was enormously complicated and fraught with great emotion.

In the same room where I eavesdropped on the discussion of anti-Semitism, I later had dinner with Igor Shkliarevsky, who was acknowledged to be one of the country's four or five most important poets. He was popular as well as important, so popular, in fact, that the sales of his books provided him with an independent income, which had freed him from much of the cliquishness of Soviet literary life. In recent years he had acquired renown as an ecological activist. His interest in the environment had been with him all his life. One of his poems spoke of Canada, which he had never visited, as the "beloved country of my childhood." He of course meant a sort of metaphorical Canada of clean rivers and clear skies;

when I disabused him of the image, he was not surprised, for he was not a utopian. Quite the opposite. He had no use for green politics. "No politics," he said. "Everyone now likes to get into politics. There was a plenary session [on the environment] in Moscow city council recently. Nothing but speakers! Not one bird or tree is better for such talk. I'm sick and tired of it." His approach, rather, was the familiar one of individual responsibility, with people tending first to conditions "within their own region, their own state, and their own persona," combined with a massive educational effort to turn out graduates in "new trades such as ecological engineering and such others as will be needed in large numbers before long. Not that we lack ecologists already." He used the word *ecologists* with a note of disdain, to express the view that they were too concerned with theory. With the accident at Chernobyl, he seemed to be saying, the time for theory ended and the time for treatment of shock and trauma began.

Thanks partly to the exposés of the *Moscow News*, it was now known, or at least argued convincingly, that the amount of radiation let loose when the Chernobyl power station burned in April 1986 was more than 20 times greater than the authorities admitted back then—and that the same authorities not only knew beforehand that the reactor's design was unsafe but failed, after the fact, to evacuate all the people who were in danger. The accident took place on April 26. But five days later, in nearby Kiev, a city of 2.6 million people, the annual May Day celebration was allowed to proceed as usual, though radiation levels had risen to 100 times what was considered safe. According to the *News*, it was only the day after the big parade that a decision was made to evacuate the town of Chernobyl, 14 kilometres from the reactor—and little more than a month before the scheme was fully completed. Eventually 25,000 people were removed to the 175 resettlement villages built for that purpose, and it was not long before a 30-kilometre area around the plant was sealed off with concrete and wire, punctuated by armed checkpoints. At least 1,000 people who lived in what was now called the Dead Zone found adjustment to their new homes so difficult that they sneaked back, hoping to carry on life as it had been, in their telling phrase, "before the war." The authorities first re-expelled them. Later the people were permitted to pursue this form of slow suicide, given that most of them were elderly.

Only now were all the medical consequences of the tragedy becoming known: 1.4 million adults and 600,000 children had been contaminated by cesium-137, strontium-90, plutonium-239, and other radioactive isotopes. They required immediate treatment for leukosis and a long list of other diseases, spanning the range from anemia to respiratory and gastroenteric problems to immune disorders and psychological difficulties. Thyroid complaints were particularly common. Deformities in newborn infants and farm animals became frequent.

The political implications could hardly be divorced from the medical ones, yet they were of freestanding significance. Chernobyl seemed to give a new force to dissent in the Ukraine, the second largest of the republics, supplying a quarter of the Soviet Union's food and conducting a third of its industry, yet the one where Stalinism and the Stalinist aesthetic lingered longest. There were four large nationalist movements, one of them led by the poet Ivan Drach. They espoused an array of causes, some of them having to do with the Ukrainian language, others centring on the Ukrainian Catholic Church. But environmental concerns were not very far from most people's minds, no matter what the nominal agenda. Forty percent of the Soviet Union's nuclear reactors were in the Ukraine, and one separatist group claimed to know of a secret government plan to build another 27 there. True or not, the story added to an already well founded fear.

An estimated 70 percent of the land contaminated by the Chernobyl accident lies not in the Ukraine but in Byelorussia, the neighbouring republic that was home to 10.2 million people, a quarter of them 14 years old or younger. Even in Minsk, the capital, which received the smallest dose of any city in the region, there had recently been huge demonstrations, complete with black flags and the tolling of funeral bells. Many people in Byelorussia should have gone abroad for treatment but lacked the hard currency to do so, for it is an especially poor place, without the money for all the cleanup work that needed to be done. Some citizens were urging that Minsk stop contributing to the Soviet budget until the situation changed. Meanwhile, the republic appealed to the rest of the world for help in moving 10 million people from 27 cities and 2,600 villages. The response was shamefully lackadaisical.

Writers, such as Oles Honchar in the Ukraine, took a considerable role in this combination of nationalism and environmental activism, but none more so than Shkliarevsky perhaps. By the end of summer 1986, he had visited the danger area, up to the limit of the barriers, 30 kilometres from the reactor. "When I got back, I got rid of my clothes, shoes, everything. I had a throat infection. I still cough today." Later he added his purse to the battle. When he received one of the country's largest literary prizes, 10,000 rubles, he gave away the money to plant 30 hectares of trees, half in Byelorussia, half in the Ukraine. It was a lot of money—especially when you consider "that the fine for polluting rivers is only 500 rubles."

He feared that more than a way of life was being lost, that some part of the soul was dying, not only around Chernobyl but across the face of the country, and had been doing so for a long time. "I first went to Siberia, for instance, in 1959, as a Young Pioneer. I was sent to near Vladivostok. I then went back in 1963. Superficially conditions were improved, but I was unnerved my first day to find out that a particular type of big fish the people used to love eating was no longer caught. Soon the people forgot how to fish. In the Ukraine and Byelorussia, people for hundreds of years have been gathering mushrooms and strawberries in the forest, and tending their gardens, and doing some fishing in small lakes and rivers. Such activity is strictly forbidden now. Life in the small cities is dead, shops are empty. People are on rafts in an ocean of disaster. There has been some psychological shift in human consciousness, some loss of life-recognition. The sparks of consciousness disappear if you look beneath people's skulls."

5

Transsib

For the past couple of weeks I hadn't slept more than three or four hours at a stretch. Such rest as I did get took place mostly on a blanket on the floor, because I had sprained my back. The poor diet was beginning to wear me down as well, and the malaria prophylaxis I had begun to take in anticipation of Southeast Asia had started to affect my vision, or so I imagined. More than anything, I suppose, I was talked out, and I looked forward to what I fancied would be the comparative silence of the long train trip through Siberia. I arrived at the station at one in the morning and joined the eager crowd of fellow masochists already assembled there. One was a German wearing a backpack from which a police truncheon protruded. A light rain was falling. It made a high-pitched sound, like Japanese women giggling.

The Trans-Siberian, which the Soviets know as the Rossiya and the Germans call the Transsib, was built in stages between 1891 and 1916, as a matter of economic policy, to open up the barren fastnesses. Until that time people went overland by *troika*, wrapped up in bearskins in winter, stopping at log post-houses every 40 kilometres. The railway has always had a military and geographical purpose as well. On another level, as a national achievement, it was inspired by the Canadian Pacific, though the engineering problems were quite different. One of the project's prime movers was Count Nikolai Ignatieff, a tsarist minister and the great-grandfather of Michael Ignatieff, the Canadian man of letters. A complete route map, taking in the later additions, some as recent as the 1950s, is a complicated affair. Basically the idea is to dip southeasterly from Moscow, climb over the Ural Mountains, and maintain a more or less straight course across the enormous back of lower Siberia as far as Lake Baikal (where in the early days the railway carriages were transferred to barge-ferries). After that one line goes northeast to Khabarovsk, where connections can be made to a passenger ferry that plies to Yokohama across the Sea of Japan, while another line cuts sharply south to Mongolia. The terminus of both lines is Beijing, following a passage through Manchuria from one direction or the other. I had bought a ticket that skirted Mongolia, to avoid the necessity of fighting for a Mongolian visa at the Mongol embassy in Moscow, and would be deposited at the Chinese capital via Harbin. I was to travel hard class rather than soft. I wasn't being stoical or going native. I was told that nothing else was available.

There is an extensive literature about the Trans-Siberian, by people as different as the pianist Artur Rubinstein, who crossed in the 1920s, and Laurens van der Post, who made the trip in the 1960s. Two of the seminal British travel writers of the 1930s, Robert Byron and Peter Fleming, described their own journeys in memorable terms. As for contemporaries, Paul Theroux has written on the subject more than once, beginning with *The Great Railway Bazaar* and continuing in *Riding the Iron Rooster*. The latter episode is apparently the one he also deals with in his novel *My Secret History*, and I prefer the fictional version as being truer and less marked by his usual rancour and dislike of foreigners. There are views from the side of the track as well: Yevgeny Yevtushenko grew up in Siberia and writes about the train hurtling through his childhood. Altogether there is enough to make an attractive little anthology, sufficient for whiling away another couple of hours on a ride that seems, towards the end especially, as though it will never end, what with the nature of the accommodations and the nature of the landscape and the curious way they interact.

Before the Revolution the train had grand pianos and marble bathtubs. No more. But then it is not really designed for tourists, though tourists take it in increasing numbers—to the extent that Siberian prostitutes seeking dollars or marks are said to board the train at one isolated station, ply their trade for a while, then disembark at another godforsaken whistle stop farther down the line. I saw none of this particular brand of *perestroika*, perhaps because I was on the so-called express, which makes only short pauses at some of the largest towns and cities.

Like the BAM line in eastern Siberia, which runs parallel some distance to the north but is off-limits to foreigners because of its military connotations, the Trans-Siberian is the public highway of the country it passes through—one might almost say, as one would of a great river, of the country it drains. All forms of development, including highways, drop off quickly a short distance from the right-of-way. Thus while the view from a train window is not usually a reliable indication of the country one is passing through, what is seen in this particular case is a more complete picture than the rule of thumb suggests, as would also have been true of the Canadian Pacific across the Prairies and the mountains in 1910 or so, before large-scale investment and settlement had spread over much of the territory away from the tracks. Census figures make the point neatly. As already mentioned, the 1988 Soviet census has never been released and perhaps never will be, so I fell back on one from 10 years earlier. It showed 21.6 million people living in Siberia, an area covering a quarter of the Asian continent. That was less than nine percent of the Soviet population, and most of it hugs the railway line; a few millions are found in big cities, Novosibirsk and Irkutsk, but most of the people are in thousands of desperate little settlements hacked out of the taiga. Along the various tracks there average about 30 inhabitants per square kilometre; in the north, the figure drops to less than one person per square kilometre. Siberia, then, has nearly as many people as Canada, but it is as though there were no Halifax, no Montreal, no Toronto, no Vancouver, only northern Quebec, northern Ontario, the Lakehead and the north generally, with perhaps two or three Winnipegs thrown in.

Siberia bears some comparison with Canada in visual terms as well. Until we neared steppe-like terrain in the last few days of the trip, as the train began its climb towards Inner Mongolia and Manchuria, the vegetation was mostly birch and fir and the topography mostly flat. After the first day or two, I was reminded of the crude back-projection techniques of old Hollywood movies in which, if the scene lasted long enough and you paid close enough attention to the background, you could see the couple in the car drive past the exact same stretch of scenery time and again. Significantly the long curve between Moscow and Japan was the last part of the world not hooked up to the fibre-optic cable system that passes around the globe like a second equator.

Nearly everyone I told about my plans for the Transsib advised me to take my own food or as much of it as I could. So when I was in London some months earlier I called the manager of the food hamper department at Fortnum & Mason in Piccadilly and put to the test the famous claim that the shop can deliver anywhere in the world. Could they make me a custom hamper of cheeses, choice meats, marmalades, "gentlemen's relish," and so on, with a decent selection of ports and brandies, and have it waiting for me at Yaroslavl Station in Moscow at the appointed hour? The firm would be game to try on a no-fault basis, I was told, but the manager felt duty bound to inform me that he had never known one of the baskets to arrive intact anywhere inside the Soviet Union. So I had brought my own food from Canada. I had been dragging it around with me for weeks, resisting the temptation to break into the stock during the nutritional emergencies that were so much a feature of Soviet life. I now repacked it all according to a daily menu plan and reassured myself that there was more than enough. In fact, enough to share, which was precisely what I ended up doing.

The locomotive that stood waiting for us was a Soviet-made electric engine built in 1964. The carriages were of East German construction (I suppose this is probably the last time I shall write *East German* except in some historical connection); they had wooden trim and were painted the standard Soviet railway green, which was brighter than dark olive but not by much. I found myself in an upper berth, sharing a compartment with a middle-aged Frenchman who came from the same gene pool as Valéry Giscard d'Estaing, and his young wife from, I gather, the French West Indies, and a heavily tattooed Siberian male of about 50 who instantly hung cheeses and sausages from the ceiling for safekeeping. In view of Gorbachev's prohibition of alcohol on the trains, he, like many of the passengers, had brought his own supply of vodka. For the first few hours he slept curled up around the bottles, then awoke and began swigging from one of them and discoursing loudly on the Soviet political scene. I caught the drift, which was that he saw no choice between Gorbachev and Yeltsin in that they were both scoundrels. I'm expressing the point rather more gently than I believe he was doing. As the train pitched and yawed, his cheeses and sausages swayed in unison, like the strands of a beaded curtain in some sleazy bagnio. My reading lamp was broken and the windowpane was almost too caked with mud to admit light. I sensed I was in for a discouraging passage.

I was rescued by Tian Hsueh, a 27-year-old reporter from the *Commercial Times* in Taipei. We had struck up a conversation on the platform at Yaroslavl Station. His paper was sending him through Eastern Europe, the Soviet Union, and finally China, the land his father had fled in 1948 without ever going back. As he travelled through all the hot spots in this *annus mirabilis*, he was faxing back his stories to his paper: page after page of beautiful Chinese calligraphy. Now he spotted me languishing in steerage and invited me to share his cabin, which he had all to himself. A few extra rubles made the upgrading official, and he helped me drag my luggage from one moving car to the next. A week later the reverse process would have been easier, for by then we had demolished my heavy supplies of ham, crabmeat, biscuits, and gin. He was the perfect companion, full of insight and mischievous wit. We exchanged books, confidences, and professional gossip.

The country east of Moscow pretty quickly loses its urbanity, but not its history. Ancient churches, sometimes all the more imposing for the way they sit almost proudly, almost derelict, in rusty old heavy-industrial towns like Yaroslavl, can give only some hint of all the centuries of suffering that make up much of the heritage of that portion of the world: involuntary suffering and sometimes suffering deliberately sought for its spiritual benefit. Between the cities, the settlements are tiny. The wooden buildings stand in clusters—a dwelling and assorted outbuildings. Sometimes they are weather-beaten and bare, sometimes painted a near-Wedgwood blue; in still other cases, only the traditional shutters are painted. Once we crossed the Volga River near Yaroslavl, I began to sense that we were in the Russia of the Russian novels. The name Kirov alone was enough to suggest the feeling.

Kirov the city, about 950 kilometres into the journey (we reached it at 3:00 p.m. on the second day), was a trading centre whose history already went back 700 years when it became part of Russia in the 18th century and began its association with the wretched exile system. We in the West tend to think of exiles first when Siberia is mentioned and perhaps most of all political prisoners of the Stalin years. As early as 1932, five years before the infamous purges, there were 265,000 of his "special settlers" there, a figure that is more remarkable for being acknowledged than for being accurate. There is no way of knowing how many hundreds of thousands he sent to the gulags, just as there is no way of knowing how many millions he had killed in his career overall. Kirov, the person after whom the city is named, was another of those colleagues of Stalin who looked to become a rival. Why Kirov the city kept that name instead of reverting to its original name, Vyatka, is a mystery, considering that Perm, the next big city, a half day farther along, was allowed to drop the temporary name Molotov after Stalin's death. It's easier to change names than to restore them, I suppose.

Even in spring, life along this part of the line is hard. Vegetation alternates between birch and conifers and between both of these on the one hand and open scrub land on the other, in maddening variations and repetitions of variations. I saw one man working a wooden plough pulled by a tired shaggy horse. I couldn't learn to what extent, if any, *perestroika* had begun to penetrate here, but most of what seemed small tenancies were, I was informed, merely tiny co-ops that happened to be incredibly poor. Houses as well as gardens tend to be fenced, almost palisaded in some cases, not merely to delineate them and keep out small pests but perhaps also to discourage larger game. The hoardings may also supplement the lines of trees used as windbreaks. It was May, but in several places there was still snow in the shadows. I got the impression that though the snow may melt, the shadows never completely disappear. There is some pasture, but it looked poor. What I noticed most were the woodpiles and how big they were in proportion to the size of the dwellings. People must spend most of the transient summer preparing as best they can for the intransigent winters.

I was making inroads on my gin supply, and so it was that I went to bed drunk in Europe and woke up hungover in Asia. Not that I could have seen the signatory obelisk in any case, for we passed it sometime in the middle of the night, high up in the Urals. By using my pocket watch as an odometer, I calculated that we were making a top speed of over 100 kilometres per hour, but most of the time the pace was much slower and some of the time it was little short of retrograde. People were constantly getting on and getting off, so cars were being added and subtracted at some of the stations, though at other spots the train halted seemingly for no reason at all.

Sverdlovsk is a place with two claims on history: it is where Tsar Nicholas and his family were murdered, back when it was called Yekaterinburg, and is close to where Francis Gary Powers, the American pilot, was shot down in his U-2 spy plane, whose existence Dwight Eisenhower flatly denied. There we had the longest scheduled stop of the whole trip—15 minutes, to change locomotives. I have been calling the territory Siberia, but actually we were still in the Russian Federation; Siberia, strictly speaking, began only after another 250 kilometres or so, once we had reached Bogdanovich but before we got to Tyumen, a place we hit at 10:00 a.m., by which time I was fully awake and functioning, thanks to several glasses of strong coffee in the restaurant car that I otherwise avoided as much as possible.

The names of the towns through this stretch started to take on an intoxicating ring by the simple arrangement of the syllables. Ishim, Tobolsk, Nazyvaevskaya, and finally—the name falling with the thud of end punctuation—Omsk. Most of these places were founded as long ago as the 16th century as forts, either for fur traders or the Cossacks. Tobolsk was where many of the Decembrists were imprisoned after their abortive uprising in St. Petersburg in 1825 (the jail had recently been given to a seminary). Omsk, whose population is now more than a million, was an *ostrog* or political prison as well; it was here that Dostoyevsky served four years at hard labour. By contrast, Novosibirsk, the largest centre in Siberia, with 1.5 million people (and a subway to move them), came into existence because of the railway. This part of western Siberia is above all a land of mighty rivers—the Ob, the Tom, the Yenisei.

It was Krasnoyarsk, a large industrial city on the Yenisei, that we were heading for on the third day. By late morning, the landscape had changed; the vistas were bigger and there were rolling foothills in the distance. The human element, though as bleak as before, was changing as well. There were more abandoned buildings, though we also saw some log houses being put up, and from time to time there were small irregular pens or corrals, indicating that farming was giving way to ranching. Just when I began to get used to the wider angles, however, there would be a quick change, and the train would descend into woods once more. We passed, without stopping, many small stations, which we would not have known were stations at all but for the tattered red flags fluttering in front. Along the entire route there was a sense that the Trans-Siberian keeps shedding its skin like a snake. There are old water towers left over from the days of steam locomotives and sometimes even the steam locomotives themselves, either abandoned to the elements or relegated to shunting in the bigger marshalling yards (a distinct contrast to China, where steam is still common on the railways, thanks largely to China's abundance of coal, which is far less sulphurous than the sorts we're most familiar with in Canada). Across the whole country you see disused rolling stock by the sidings; some of it is apparently used for housing. One farmer had a root cellar made of old ties.

All of this helped to strengthen the impression that the natural world was infinitely more varied than the man-made. By the close of the day, the terrain first became hillier, then took on a distinctive British Columbian cast, with tall timber and big peaks. At other points the hills had sharp and unexpected twists and edges, like driftwood; the wind had put its signature on them as plainly as on, say, the Sussex Coast. By dusk we were coming up on a coal-mining town called Ilanskaya.

A policy of full disclosure compels me to admit that I was not a totally reliable witness to all these changes. In my attempt to combat the dehydration resulting from the period of inebriation, I had broken one of my cardinal rules of travel—always boil the drinking water for five minutes in any place, such as Siberia or Texas, where one cannot buy the *Globe and Mail*. At one stage all I could do was to place my spectacles on the night table in such a way that I would lie in my bunk and see the Soviet Union reflected in the lenses. The impression I had then was of a horizon with serrated edges, like the metal strip used to tear lengths of Saran Wrap from the roll. Sometime during the night we passed the halfway mark between Moscow and Beijing.

Naturally enough, the closer we got to China, the more Asian faces there were on the train, and the more children as well, though some had been with us from the outset. The conductor of the Shanghai Philharmonic was aboard, for instance, along with 15 of his musicians and all their instruments. These poor people had first gone by train from their home to Beijing, a trip of 19 hours, there to wait in the station for the train not just to Moscow but to Leningrad, even more distant by some 1,700 kilometres or so. In that city they had played a 10-day engagement and then started back without delay. How I can't imagine, but the conductor, a round jovial man in his late forties and one of the few Chinese symphony conductors who hadn't succumbed to the brain drain, was bearing up with weary good humour. "This is the train through hell," he said, "but suffering on such a scale is food for artistic endeavour." As for my fellow Westerners, they included a German middle-manager in a large computer firm, a sous-chef at the Windsor Arms Hotel in Toronto, a young Englishwoman who wore a zircon in her left earlobe and when I saw her was reading *Alice in Wonderland*, a couple of Kiwis with haversacks, and a cinema usher from California who kept saying *wow* and *man* and once asked Tian whether Taiwan was part of Japan. Intourist had thoughtfully sent along a guide; she had red hair (most unusual in the Soviet Union) and O-level German and a nodding acquaintance with English. That is to say, when she heard English being spoken at her, she nodded. This fostered the totally false impression that she understood at least a little bit of what was being said. She lived in Siberia, about three-quarters of the way along, and rather than teach German, as she was certified to do, she made her living travelling back and forth, like a wooden duck in a shooting gallery.

One of the major disadvantages of life on the Transsib is that there are no facilities for bathing. This design fault becomes only too apparent after three or four days. There are small lavatories at either end of each sleeping car, but they don't have warm water. In any case, Russian signs on the doors request passengers not to attempt bathing. I gathered that the tone was rather more abrupt than that of the famous signs once found in the men's loo of the British Museum Reading Room, put there to keep Karl Marx and his disreputable friends from continuing to treat the place like a hotel: THESE BASINS ARE FOR CASUAL ABLUTIONS ONLY. I tried breaking the rule, first filling a goatskin bag with hot water from the *batchok*, the boiler from which most people made tea and on which the resident guard-chambermaid in each carriage cooked her rude meals. But I had no sooner mixed the scalding water with cold when the martinet in question, having seen me siphon off the water, came pounding on the locked WC door, demanding an explanation and threatening punishment. After that I was careful to take only enough water to fill a metal cup I carried, as though I were indeed brewing tea. I found that by diluting it and not wasting a drop, I could wash my hair, sort of, or bathe—again, after a fashion—on alternating days; but the level of hygiene never really exceeded what one might expect in, say, a jailhouse in Karachi. Yet I was luckier than the people who were also dependent on the system for all their meals. The food started out quite adequate by Soviet standards. Terrible meats and not many vegetables but lots of subsidized bread (the fresh loaves were stored under the seats in the booths the diners sat in) and a few local delicacies, such as yoghurt taken aboard in the kind of glass milk bottles that even the English haven't seen for years. But the quality deteriorated quickly, I observed, and with it the quantity. The last meal before the Chinese border was a piece of volcanic cheese and two bits of salami, all of which people soon had to forfeit to the Chinese health authorities who searched the cars for animal and vegetable products that might be diseased. At times I felt quite guilty, eating strawberries and turkey and granola, though the guilt passed more quickly than the landscape.

Some of the places remain in my memory almost by accident. Tayshet, 4,522 kilometres east of Moscow, is distinguished only by being situated where the mainline meets the line running north to the mammoth hydro dam at Bratsk, which I recalled because of Yevtushenko's long poem "Bratsk Station." I remember grassy hillsides, too, and the smiling worn-out faces of local people for whom the arrival of the train, even though it did not stop, might, to the extent that it relieved tedium, be one of the high points of their day. There was also one spectacular cemetery, spread over the slope of a hillside but confined within a fence, as most everything man-made in those parts was; some of the markers were at precarious angles but they were freshly painted and had been carved in the same manner as the door- and window-frames of the local houses. The graves of exiles, I thought, political or otherwise. As I believe Farley Mowat has noted, Siberia seems to serve the same social function that the Yukon sometimes does in Canada: young people go there to break away and older people to start over.

The last considerable city on the Soviet side of the route is Irkutsk, where we rolled, slammed, and hissed to a stop at 9:30 a.m. on the fourth day. It is famous for having once been called the Paris of Siberia. That seems a reckless use of a hyperbole, though the place does have an interesting history. Some of the Decembrists were sent there, and later a gold rush of sorts took place.

The main attraction of this part of Siberia is Lake Baikal, which the rail line follows for nearly half its total circumference after first hugging one of the main rivers feeding it. Because it is the world's deepest lake (1,741 metres; Lake Ontario by comparison reaches a depth of only 237 metres), Baikal is said to contain 20 percent of the world's lake-water reserves, and it is the habitat of many creatures and plants not found elsewhere. Siberians are said to refer to it as the Siberian Sea. It does seem a tiny ecological world of its own, occupying the space between ranges of mountains, tipped by birch forests and, when we passed by in early May, still thick with ice pileups quite far from shore.

Even the most recent editions of some of the best-known English-language guidebooks raved on about the purity of the water and the generally paradisical nature of the whole environment there. The Soviets knew better. Pulp-and-paper mills have been dumping waste into the lake for many years, and cities like Irkutsk have contributed their sewage; the writer Valentin Rasputin became an important public figure as much as a literary one after his advocacy of Baikal's cause, in somewhat the same manner as Igor Shkliarevksy, more recently, with respect to Chernobyl. The government had done a great deal in response to the situation, not only banning log rafts but also in building a pipeline to take Irkutsk's waste far away. Moscow claimed that the water was now 50 percent cleaner than it was a few years ago, yet species continued to die, and even the authorities estimated that 20 billion rubles would have to be spent on a proper cleanup. One of the effects of the emerging economic order in Eastern Europe and South Asia is that Moscow, and the world, have begun to recognize that the damage done to the environment and health under a rigid planned economy is no less than under open-throttle capitalism. Poland, for example, is easily the most polluted nation on the whole European continent. Siberia is said to be the second-largest source of oxygen on Earth, after the now quickly disappearing rainforests of the Amazon basin. Acknowledging the fact might not have been Gorbachev's first priority, but he seemed much more aware of such matters than his predecessors or even most of his neighbours.

We hit Ulan Ude the next night. This was once a very important stop for caravans going to China—our first clue that we were in hope of getting to the People's Republic, still 1,000 kilometres away at the nearest point. It is also here that the line veers off to Beijing, the easy way, through Mongolia. By late the next morning, we were stopped at Karymskaya, near where we took the track to Manchuria instead. The countryside to the north and south, but especially to the south, resembled steppes, and there were mounted shepherds with Mongolian features tending their sheep and goats from the saddle. There was also trash strewn all along the roadbed by generations of train crews. In only 36 hours or so we would be in Beijing, though eight or more would be spent straddling the border.

In China and virtually all other major countries, the distance between the rails is 141.25 centimetres, but the Russians use a different gauge—150 centimetres. People commonly suppose that this indicates Russian backwardness. On the contrary, the Russians have adhered to the safer more expensive standard while the other countries, one by one, have sacrificed stability to savings, though there are other factors involved as well. By clinging to the older size, the Russians heightened security at the frontier and generally reduced the risk of invasion by rail. So it was that at Zabaikalsk, the last point in the Soviet Union, 6,293 kilometres from Moscow, we turned in our visas and filed into a huge old building with Corinthian pillars to exchange our leftover rubles for dollars. Meanwhile, the train was taken away so that the bogies on all the cars could be changed. Lingering in the smelly, overcrowded station, it was easy to chafe at the waste of time, but the wait was as nothing compared to the 10 hours one might expect on a train crossing from India to Pakistan or vice versa, for delays of that magnitude result mainly when the two nations despise each other, and it was clear despite the presence of some soldiers with rifles that tensions were very much relaxed here. Foreigners were even allowed to take photographs of the platform, an activity forbidden at many another less sensitive facility of the Soviet Railways.

Finally we reboarded and progressed 12 kilometres until Manzhouli, where Chinese immigration officials climbed aboard and there was a wait of several hours more, during which the Chinese dining car full of delicious food took the place of the long-empty Russian one. A patriotic Chinese locomotive—Chinese locomotives have names like East Wind, Red in the

East, or Progress—was added as well. At the station where we changed our freshly retrieved dollars for Chinese Foreign Exchange Certificates, the yuan used by foreigners, was a large notice board hung with news photographs; I was told that sometimes the display showed the likenesses of recently executed criminals. Nevertheless, I couldn't help but breathe easier now that I was in China, notwithstanding the present perception that it and not the Soviet Union was the more obstinate and authoritarian place. The officials were courteous as well as efficient. A customs inspector, age 23, came into our compartment and asked if he might sit down and join me in a conversation to practise his English. To my disappointment, he mentioned Dr. Norman Bethune, whose name I had hoped to travel in China without either hearing or speaking, just as I was resolved not to give people any bloody maple leaf pins for their lapels. Alas, there was even a toast to the old boy at a banquet in Chongqing thrown by the local newspaper editors.

Anyway, the train got up steam, and we set off to see a bit of Inner Mongolia and then Manchuria. I glanced out the window to find two Chinese soldiers looking in. One had his rifle slung upside down; the other was unarmed and the sleeves of his tunic were far too long for his arms; they smiled. Tian and I got into the gin once more to celebrate.

We awoke the next morning, our sixth on the train, just in time to catch a glimpse of Angangxi, whose notoriety is its proximity to Tsitsihar (now Qigihar), where there is a public space once devoted to the execution of bandits and other wrongdoers. The belief in those days was that people who died with parts of their bodies missing could not be admitted to heaven, and the prisoners, once decapitated, had their heads sewn back on—but backward, so that they wouldn't be mistaken for the righteous. At breakfast we were at Daqing, a city synonymous with oil wells; we saw numerous small ones pumping away in the middle of the fields, and a refinery and a pipeline in the distance. By lunch we were in Harbin, just beyond the banks of the Pine Flower River. This was once a White Russian stronghold, a fact that recalls one of the most colourful incidents in the history of the whole Trans-Siberian system. When the Bolsheviks pulled out of the First World War, the Czech Legion was left stranded, with the Bolsheviks now hostile to them, certain that they would join up with the White forces. With their way back to Europe blocked and nothing to lose, the Czechs hijacked the trains and shot their way across Siberia towards Vladivostok. By tea time we had crossed into Jilin Province and were at Changchun, its capital. It was once the centre of the puppet state established by the Japanese, with Puyi, the last emperor of China, as its titular head.

The deeper we penetrated into China, the more complex, and inexpressible, became Tian's feelings about his ancestral home, which he had visited only once before, a year earlier, right after the Tiananmen massacre. The event had affected him very deeply, more deeply than I could imagine or he could articulate. Around Changchun we passed, again without stopping or even tooting the throaty whistle, a series of small stations, each bearing a family name as the name of the community or district.

"My father tells me that when he was a boy, about 90 percent of the people in the county of the province where he lived had the same family name," Tian said. "In China there is only the self and the concept of family. There is no Chinese ideogram to express the idea of personal privacy, for instance. And because there is no personal privacy there is no corresponding sense of what is public responsibility. Until that breaks down it will be a stumbling block to democracy. They don't know that democracy is not something you do for yourself or your family. It's supposed to be for the public good. All that will take time."

He was looking out the window. He appeared wistful but determined. When I looked out the same window, I couldn't help but see how much less harsh life here seemed to be than in the Soviet Union.

Northeast China is one of the most thickly industrialized regions, yet like the rest of the country it is under intense cultivation, with hardly the smallest bit of arable land left untilled. Its people are supposed to be strong, silent, and self-reliant: it's a Chinese cliché. Everybody was working hard. They worked in factories, which were decorated with slogans such as WE MUST BE HAPPY TO WORK HERE SO THAT WE WILL BE HAPPY TO RETURN HOME or WE MUST KEEP THIS PLANT SAFE SO THAT WE CAN PRODUCE GOODS FOR THE SAFETY OF SOCIETY. Or they worked in the fields or paddies. But everyone was busy and everyone was in motion constantly, without the almost paralytic despair I sensed so often across the Soviet Union.

In Siberia I saw surprisingly few farm animals, and many of those I did were so emaciated I could count their ribs. I remember one poor cow that was covered in sores as well. China was full of healthy animals—ducks, goats, sheep, everything, all making noise at once; even lots of dogs, which I hadn't expected. At one point the tracks were clogged with cows, a scene reminiscent of India except that these were fat, happy cows and their presence, I believe, the result of a bovine jailbreak. Farm machinery was abundant, too. Much of it was recent, though the new stuff coexisted with the simplest type of plough. Such juxtaposition was typical. Later in my stay I saw people working on the long-term project of building a reservoir. First bulldozers had cleared the way, then hundreds of men worked with spades and wheel-barrows and wicker baskets to complete the job. A Westerner would say, "Why not use heavy equipment and complete the whole project in a short time with only a handful of personnel?" The Chinese would answer: "And what will the remaining people do the rest of the year?" Westerner: "Why, they'd make more bulldozers in a bulldozer factory, of course...." The idea seemed incomprehensible to the Chinese, who feared the present system, one of the greatest organizational feats in human history perhaps and certainly an extraordinary improvement over generations of bloody tyranny by a patchwork quilt of nationalists, bandits, and warlords, might begin to unravel. Hence the tightened grip on political power even while economic power was being freed up ever so slowly. This lay at the heart of the contrast with the Soviet Union. Gorbachev could change all at once, as Poland did, with chaotic results, or change slowly, with a combination of both political and economic reforms, hoping that speed would prove neither too fast nor too slow and the mixture not too volatile. At what point does decay make change inevitable? At what point is change decay and not progress?

The previous year an auto factory in this northeastern part of China manufactured 80,000 lorries, though the government had placed orders for only 60,000 or so. Without recourse to layoffs, or even variable production schedules, the plant continued to churn them out to keep everyone work-ing, filling up huge car parks with light trucks. Meanwhile, in southern and western China, production of staple commodities lagged far behind. The small enterprise businesses, which were the first hint of reform when they began springing up throughout China in numbers almost beyond counting, seemed to offer the best hope of acting as a pressure gauge for use in making the difficult adjustment; at the least they were an acknowledgement of the marketplace as a legitimate consideration within the total economic equation. That the Chinese are such irrepressible entrepreneurs, whether in the state's service or their own, is after all one of the reasons they are able to feed themselves, a quarter of the world's population. But since September 1988, the government's strict credit policy, introduced to fight inflation, had forced more than three million small businesses to close. God only knows what the effects of the political crackdown had been.

I looked out the window just as a young pig took it into its head to chase the train, as a puppy might chase a car. It ran after us for several carriage lengths, its big ears flopping in the wind. People were building houses and then building courtyard walls around them, often with shards of glass set along the top to discourage thieves but also to reinforce the idea of the family compound—and of family solidarity against outside forces. People were buying and others were selling. Women were carrying strange vegetables and men were carrying tools. Motorbikes became conspicuous among the bicycles. Most older people still wore shapeless blue Mao suits, but the young affected the Western look, especially in their footwear, which you could tell they were proud of by the way they walked. Everyone seemed to be rushing somewhere under the weight of a great unseen burden, physical or psychological. Kids in a schoolyard played basketball with a grown-up intensity, for they were doing more than passing time or taking exercise. We had journeyed into the middle of some spectacle that the participants for some reason didn't seem to recognize as such. Eventually, when the light failed completely, I went to bed, though reluctantly. I woke up the next morning in time to pack and re-sort and clean myself up and dispose of rubbish before we came to a stop at Beijing at 6:35 a.m. We had been on the train for one week and had come exactly 9,001 kilometres. Nine thousand and two would have been too many.

CHINA 1990

1

Comparative Embalming

In a few days' time it would be the first anniversary of the student hunger strike that led, a couple of weeks later, to the tragedy in Tiananmen Square. Accordingly Beijing was on edge. It would not be overstating the case to say that the joint was crawling with cops. And soldiers. And even, for some reason, sailors, their shiny helmets incongruous with their traditional blouses and scarves. "Those people on the street corners who look like secret police," a Western diplomat explained to me, "they're secret police." The day I arrived the government announced that it was freeing 211 of the dissidents who had been taken alive, including one major figure; 431 others were still being "investigated"; this was the second such release since the incident. It was thought to be designed to curb the threat that the U.S. Congress might try to take away China's most-favoured-nation status, but of course the principal reason was to avoid or lessen dissent on the June 4 anniversary. Feelings were running high on both sides, and it was easy to make matters worse. While I was there I saw a telecast of the Cable News Network from Atlanta reporting a speech in Beijing by CNN's founder, Ted Turner. He had the temerity to tell the audience that he felt sympathy for the soldiers who had done the shooting. He later backtracked by way of apology.

All this tension was brought home to me the moment I stepped off the train. Someone was calling my name, though I hadn't expected to be met. The person introduced himself as Wen Dong of the All-China Journalists' Association. I had got by in the Soviet Union without a handler and I thought that I could avoid one here as well. But I was quickly faced with an ultimatum. I could cancel all my existing tickets and accommodations (they were prepaid, alas) and buy completely new ones both for myself and Wen, who would accompany me everywhere. Or I could go to the foreign affairs ministry to plead for an exemption from the tough new restrictions on foreign journalists (which no one had yet been exempted from). The cost of the Chinese portion of my trip had just been trebled and the amount of slack reduced to—well, I didn't know to what level. "To be blunt about it," I was told bluntly when the time finally came for me to hint safely at the question, "we didn't want you here. Your visa request was first turned down and then you got your foreign minister to intercede. The situation is uncertain, and more foreign journalists aren't welcome in the present atmosphere. We've been widely criticized for this decision, but it's a matter of safety." It seems that I had inadvertently made myself the first North American since the massacre to ask for a visiting journalist's permit for the capital.

In any case, there I was in the company of Wen Dong, 35, a fellow of quick humour and a skilled expeditor. He had many contacts in the West. His wife, the daughter of the Chinese ambassador to Egypt, was a student in Toronto, and Wen himself was widely travelled; he had recently been to England, for example, as the guest of Sir David English of the *Daily Mail*. A good companion, it seemed to me, so I resolved to make the best of the situation and to see and learn what I could.

Several months earlier Taiwan had decided to permit its citizens free egress to visit the People's Republic for pleasure or business, even though, despite the increasingly important economic ties binding them together, the two countries remained officially at war. The idea was that the Taiwanese would see socialism at first hand and soon return home thankful for the Kuomintang (which while I was crossing Siberia made a move even farther to the right, installing a former general, Hua Pei-tsun, as premier). The practical effect of the liberalization in the midst of capitalist authoritarianism was that China was suddenly full of tourists from Taiwan. They were all the more conspicuous because there were so few from the West with whom to contrast them.

At the luxury-class joint-venture hotel to which I hurried, ravenous for a hot shower and some news in English, the ratio of staff to guest rooms would normally, I should think, be about two to one, as it would be in an equivalent hotel in Europe or North America. Such had been the drop in tourism following Tiananmen Square that I shouldn't be surprised if the figure was ten to one. I saw not even a handful of Westerners there and not many more in Beijing as a whole. But then people were keeping out of sight. It didn't seem to me that the danger of another uprising was very great. Such, at least, was what instinct and common sense told me; there might be a commemorative disturbance, perhaps, but the leading democrats were in prison, in exile, or dead. It was simply a case of rumour and anxiety feeding on themselves, but there was enough danger of another kind, I suppose. Wiser heads than mine were keeping low.

The journalists' association made it plain that they didn't wish me hanging around Beijing for long, yet I managed to enjoy it for several days at least. I believe it is a city that Canadians usually take to. The main streets are tree-lined and spacious, and the pace is slow compared with that of most other capitals its size, even Moscow. I feel that the climate favours it, too, though many would disagree. In summer it is hot and dry, with a wind blowing in from the Gobi Desert. As recently as the 1940s, water was hauled in by camel; there was little dust when I was there, though two weeks earlier the city had suffered its fourth dust storm of the year. In winter it's beastly cold, but there is seldom enough snow to impede bicycles. These were the main means of transport despite an adequate bus system and a modern subway (for the construction of which, in the 1960s, Mao ordered the razing of the 500-year-old city walls, one of the larger acts of wanton destruction to take place during the Cultural Revolution era). My secret theory is that people prefer bicycles as tiny acts of rebellion against the system and against their own Confucian deference to authority, in somewhat the same way that most Soviets simply laid their seatbelts loosely across their laps without buckling them, adhering to the spirit of the law while violating the letter of it. To ride the bus or subway is to cast your destiny with that of strangers, far beyond family. To ride a bike (one cost an average office worker perhaps two months' salary) is to stay in control. In any case, the scarcity of automobiles, like the abundance of horse-drawn wagons and pedicab drivers, added to the comparatively low levels of pollution and high level of history. The second of these, however, is sometimes an illusion.

If there were still an emperor to look down from the higher structures in the Forbidden City, he would see a number of construction cranes and massive electronic advertisements. The change in name from Peking to Beijing has a symbolic importance reflecting more than just the administrative shift to Pinyin, for, since 1949, in fact since the early 1960s, the city has been virtually replaced by another one built on the same spot. Some historical buildings remain, but then the Chinese way is to rebuild historical monuments exactly as they were before, so that continuity is more important than the true age of anything. The most famous section of the Great Wall open to visitors, at Badaling, about 70 kilometres northwest of the city, dates from both the second century B.C., when it was built as a communication line across the top of razorback mountains almost impregnable against either mounted or dismounted enemy, and equally from 1957, when it was rebuilt with the same materials. The second time, handrails were included; they're necessary; the thin line of tourists climbing up to the top, almost hand over hand to an elevation of 1,000 metres, resembles nothing so much as cheechakos going over the Chilkoot Pass in 1898. Or take the Temple of Heaven, built in 1420 and again in 1890 and then restored in the 1970s. In China history is everywhere and yet it's never quite tangible the way it often is in the West; Westerners in China find it hard to experience the sensation of the distant past being right at their elbow, even when at the site of great events, even in the Forbidden City, amazing though it is in its complexity and scope. History, in China, is more a question of landscape and of streetscape than of individual buildings and monuments. The Ming Tombs seem less "historical" than the mountains surrounding them, which appear to have been painted with a calligrapher's brush.

All of which is to say that Beijing seemed very crisp, very modern, very clean. The big Western hotels and other such joint ventures worked in a way that their Soviet equivalents did not. It was not a case of Beijing being a tourist trap exactly. I was slightly shocked to drive past Tiananmen Square and see the Great Hall of the People and the huge portrait of Mao atop the Gate of Heavenly Peace. Such places look like postcards of themselves. One looks with morbid curiosity at the same spot where the students erected the so-called Goddess of Democracy statue. (However much I sympathize with the cause, however much I see the site becoming a sort of shrine in the history of anti-authoritarianism, like the Decembrists' square or the Eureka Stockade only more vast in its significance, I remember thinking what bad taste it was to imitate the Americans' Statue of Liberty—the poor people were so cut off that they bought the premise of America being synonymous with freedom or of having an exclusive claim to the democratic tradition.)

This is a long-winded way of saying that Beijing does not especially seem like a city for foreigners. It is more or less up to date without the least pretence of being fashionable, and even after all these years it must be a hardship posting for diplomats and executives, at least emotionally. But neither does it seethe with its own importance, as Washington does or once did, or as I have no doubt Tokyo does. For all their power the eunuchs in the Forbidden City trod softly and their successors still adhere to this approach. What sticks out most forcefully about Beijing is that it is probably a delightful place for the elderly. I saw them everywhere. Old women whose feet were once bound—they still exist. Old men with white beards who play chess and listen to Beijing opera in the park surrounding the Temple of Heaven. They patronize the Bird Market, where parakeets are sold by the thousands along with parrots, goldfish, lizards, turtles, monkeys—all manner of small creatures, even worms. (Walking through, I could imagine how the activity there might be reported by the Western media: "Goldfish were active today amid renewed inflation fears while worms were sluggish and turtles moved slowly....") At a time when taxi drivers made 1,000 yuan in a month and an independent businessman as much as 10,000 during the same period, one wondered what would happen to the city's elderly, one of the city's great resources, the only one perhaps that hadn't been reconstructed in the recent past.

Only one public statue of Mao remains in the capital, though it is colossal. Like Lenin's, his memory has been undergoing downward revision. In Mao's case the process began with his death in 1976 and has not been without sharp upturns along the way. One facile illustration of the difference between Mao's stature and Lenin's is that the queues are much, much shorter at the former's mausoleum than at the latter's—only about 10 or 15 minutes' wait.

While I stood in line to pursue my newfound interest in comparative embalming (I was looking forward to gazing on the body of Ho Chi Minh in a couple of weeks' time), a professor of Japanese, who had been removed to manual labour in the countryside during the Cultural Revolution, gave me the current line on Mao. "His theme was constant struggle rather than gradual change. He was a very great man of course, but he was narrow in his outlook. Except for the Soviet Union he never set foot in any other country than China." Such language teachers are in a particularly vulnerable position. The Western view is that the democracy movement was born and peopled by students at Beijing University on the city's northwest side. In China much of the suspicion is focused more narrowly, on the adjacent campus of the much smaller Qinghua University, which houses the foreign language institute and is always littered with Americans and other bad influences.

Mao's ghost is at the centre of a paradox. His policies are held to blame for much that is wrong with the present but are also reverted to for safety when the present brings uncertainty. He opposed all forms of population control, for example, believing that China was a peasant that needed as large a family as possible to work the land. Now, when the resources are stretched even more dangerously beyond capacity, he is rebuked, but the remedy is sought in a typically Maoist scheme—punishing women who have a second child, usually by taking away their jobs, even though both parents' incomes are necessary to feed the permissible family of three. Since Tiananmen Square, Maoism, as a thing in itself distinct from both socialism and Mao the man, has been creeping back. One day a person called my attention to some music coming out over a public-address system. "These are political songs of the early 1960s, songs about struggle. They were played all the time just before the Cultural Revolution. It was recently decreed that they be revived."

I had absolutely no reason whatever to believe that the authorities were keeping an eye on me except through the gentle agency of the All-China Journalists' Association, but I shouldn't have been surprised to learn that they were. (I had no equivalent suspicion while in the Soviet Union.) Given even the possibility that I might have been followed, I therefore took a foolish risk in making a rendezvous with Tian, my companion from the train, for I might have brought him to official notice as well. I told him as much when we met for dinner. I offered the opinion that he was putting too much faith in his appearance and his fluent Mandarin to carry him along unnoticed, especially in that he carried a visitor's permit describing himself as a "merchant" but had papers showing clearly that he was nothing of the sort, but an undercover journalist intending to report on the June 4 anniversary. We discussed all this at a Muslim restaurant called Coming Smoothly from the East, a steamy unpainted room above some small shops. When we left, we hired a pedicab. As we got underway, the elderly hunchbacked driver asked Tian whether I was a Pakistani—he knew there was some sort of Pakistani delegation in town and I was so white that he thought I might be part of it. I was glad that we clopped along through narrow alleys near Long North Street because it showed there was absolutely no one behind us as far as the eye could see. We wound our way through the maze to emerge in traffic once again, engendering one or two near-accidents in the process.

At one point we turned a corner and came face-to-face with an enormous billboard with emphatic red type two metres high on a white background. It dwarfed the nearby buildings and looked so exclamatory that I thought it must certainly contain some reference to foreign devils. Tian laughed. "It says DRIVE YOUR BICYCLE ON THE RIGHT-HAND SIDE." Some do and some don't. "It promises unspecified punishments for those who disobey. This is typical in that the threat is general and also large—far out of proportion to the violation." Thus alerted, I spotted a number of English signs in China that bore him out. This one for example—THERE IS A FINE FOR BOTH OFFENCES! PLEASE DO NOT SPIT AND LITTERING!—with the penalty before the misdemeanours. Tian professed to find significance in this, as it fitted his theory about the Chinese family as a concept and as a stumbling block to further social progress by way of some form of democratic movement. In former times the Chinese man, once married, would begin to ready himself for his death, the second great event in the existence of the family. Whether a northerner or a southerner, he would prepare his own coffin, giving it pride of place in the courtyard of the home and finishing it with expensive lacquers, one coat per year; visitors might tell the age of a very old man by the thickness and brilliance of the finish, as one might count the rings of a tree. Tian's point was that some of the underlying assumptions remain. "The Chinese people are difficult to motivate because of the family," he told me—the long history of peasant rebellions, large and small, notwithstanding. Beijing was vying, unsuccessfully, to be the site of the Olympics for the year 2000. When I was there, preparations were underway for the Asia Games to be held in four months' time, which would serve as a small-scale dress rehearsal. It was to accommodate the expected crowds that authorities had recently rewritten some of the local traffic regulations, changing the direction of certain one-way streets and the like. Some people professed that this was merely part of a more subtle plan to preclude any crowds of protesters from assembling in the centre of the city.

As Tian and I rode along, we passed Tiananmen Square. Normally at that time, after offices, factories, and schools were let out, it would be full of strollers and lollers, and on Sundays it would be especially crowded, with children flying huge dragon kites. Locals had been banned on Sundays now, and Chinese from other cities were scarcer than before, just as the number of foreigners was way down. The Sunday I was in attendance only one kite was evident. It was small and simple and was being flown by an old man from the countryside. He had apparently been hired for that purpose. Without expression he stood tending the end of the long cord, watched by dozens of troops with automatic weapons.

2

Chongqing!

Air travel within China was not highly developed. To the extent that
this meant that it was also not terribly efficient, the result could be
frustrating. Arranging to fly us out of Beijing, Wen Dong confirmed that
our plane was to leave at 6:00 p.m., as the printed schedule stated. We
arrived at the airport at 4:30 to learn the departure had been put back to
3:20. Fortunately the flight was delayed and wouldn't be taking off until
7:00. We went to the proper gate, where the NOW BOARDING sign was
flashing even though the aircraft had not yet arrived. When it did appear,
we nearly missed it because the gate was changed at the last minute and no
one told us. Such difficulties are more than made up for by the fact that
rail, land, and river travel are cheap and convenient. By flying to
Chongqing, a place I had always wanted to visit, we were going to put this
to the test.

Chinese airports tend to be small and simple. Beijing's is what you
would expect in the West for a provincial city with only five percent of
Beijing's population. Chongqing's, stuck up in the mountains of Sichuan,
2,500 kilometres to the southwest, is even more basic.

We were met at our destination by a woman of about 25 who was to
be our driver. She first corrected her posture behind the wheel and tested
the pedals. Then she neatly folded the hem of her skirt back to the knees,

exposing the top of her stockings, and put on a pair of white gloves of thin cotton, the kind archivists wear when handling rare maps. Whereupon she took off like a drag racer, sometimes veering into the parallel lane and honking the horn at every opportunity, however remote the danger. We threaded our way down through the mountains, which were planted in corn or winter wheat above, overlooking rice paddies in the valley below. Given the repressed or at least rigidly private nature of sexuality in contemporary China, I was somewhat surprised when we passed a topless woman standing all alone in the middle of the road, staring into space. "There are many mental patients in this area," I was informed. "Their families cannot always afford to send them for treatment in some other city and so they are given work on the farms here." As we pulled up to the hotel, three prostitutes were standing out front, spitting on the steps. They were only part-time prostitutes. During the day, they worked hard as illegal money-changers.

Growing up in the 1950s and 1960s, just on the cusp of the Cultural Revolution, I read many books on China in which Chongqing, under its former name Chungking, played an important role. The foreign correspondents of the Second World War, such as Edgar Snow and Theodore H. White, wrote of it when it was both the capital of China and what one writer called "the most heavily bombed city in history" (this was before the Blitz, before Dresden, and of course before Hiroshima). The humanists, such as Robert Payne and Lin Yutang, wrote of it in much the same terms: as a remote, backward place that had suddenly been thrust into the spotlight of world history and subjected to the horror of modern warfare.

Chongqing is cut into the side of a mountain that sits at the place where the Jialing River, strong, wide, and imposing, gives up its identity and joins the Yangtze. Thus in its situation it bears some superficial resemblance to Pittsburgh; but it is a primal Pittsburgh on a grand and profane scale. At the point where the rivers meet there is a long series of steep stone steps carved out of the mountainside. For centuries, hundreds, maybe thousands of water coolies trudged up and then down, in a constant single motion, bringing the city's drinking water directly from the Jialing, where dead bodies and who knows what else floated by. In about 1920 the English adventurer One-Arm Sutton conceived of a plan to build a modern waterworks in Chongqing. He had come to China to help the warlords after a career of mining gold in Siberia. But he wasn't able to put down a revolt by the coolies, who were fearful that they would lose their livelihood such as it was, and not until the 1950s, after the communists took over, was the old system replaced. Chongqing is full of stories like that. I found the place wonderful, even in some ways I hadn't quite expected.

It was one of the last of the treaty ports, opened to European and American power only as late as 1890, but there are no foreign concessions there as rude reminders of the days of swagger and extraterritoriality. There never were many Western traders there, only Western scoundrels like Sutton or his contemporary Two-Gun Cohen, the Canadian. In 1990 there weren't many Westerners of any kind in Chongqing. Air travel being as already described, the city was still reached most commonly by boat. China established a state-run adventure-tour company to lure American rafters to the white-water areas nearer the source of the Yangtze, but Chongqing, in the middle stretches of that enormously long river, is as free from foreigners as Shanghai, an equal distance in the other direction, is full of them. I was the only big-nose in town. As such, I had a selfish sense of having the place to myself.

The fact is hilarious to contemplate, but Chongqing was "twinned" with Toronto, with which it has almost as much in common as it does with its three other unofficial siblings, Toulouse, Seattle, and Hiroshima. It is even difficult to say how big Chongqing is. Chinese policy seems to be to speak of it only in the context of the vast region whose administrative centre it is, an area of nine districts, 12 counties, 2,300 square kilometres, and 14 million people. The *Times Atlas* gives the city's population as six million. In fact, the core appears to be a place of a million or two—it's hard to say because the density is so obviously high and the twisting narrow hilly streets, which are far too steep for bicycles, make it difficult to get an overview. More to the point, there is nothing in the least postmodern about it. Chongqing has old-fashioned skyscrapers and streets that are absolutely alive. Stand still for five minutes and you will be passed by women in high-collared and high-slit silk dresses (as though their grand-mothers had described how Myrna Loy looked playing Fu Manchu's daughter) and old men carrying coal in baskets suspended from bamboo poles, or soldiers wearing tennis shoes with their uniforms, and people buying and selling rice and wristwatches and furniture and medicines and God knows what all. Everybody is on the move, and on the make, all of the time. The streets are constantly full of honking cars and lorries, but it is the honking that is extinct everywhere else, which you hear otherwise only on the soundtracks of movies made in the 1940s.

I think that date is significant. It was during the War of Resistance Against Japan that Chongqing entered modern history. Chiang Kai-shek was driven out of Nanjing (Nanking), his original capital, and moved his army and the whole corrupt bureaucracy to Wuhan (Hankou). The Japanese air force and army drove him out of there as well; 300,000 were killed. So he withdrew even deeper in-country. Accordingly it was in Chongqing that the Allies maintained the Far Eastern Division headquarters, and it was at Chongqing that Mao and Chiang forged, or had forced on them, their rather short-lived alliance against the Japanese. Edgar Snow described the city in *Red Star over China* as a "place of moist heat, dust and wide confusion...." The first day I was there the heat and dust were kept in abeyance by a constant torrential rain, but the wide confusion was still in effect, proving that it exists independent of warfare, which was what Snow was describing.

As much as half of Chongqing was damaged or destroyed by the Japanese; tens of thousands more people were killed. The citizens dug shelters into the sides of the mountain; the shelters are still there and are used as workshops, warehouses, retail stores, in one case as a dance hall. Perhaps even more so than in most other Chinese centres, the people turn all usable space to good account, aided by a degree of new economic freedom not found in many of the other provincial cities. I saw a lot of family-run restaurants with as few as four tables, and other matchbox enterprises. With the rain persisting, I saw one man stick up a light tarpaulin over a little patch of pavement, put an old crate beneath it, and go into business as a barber. On another street was an alfresco pool table, protected by a sheet of heavy PVC, its four corners tied to trees and poles. Precisely because of the people's resilience, it was easy to visualize how Chongqing must have been during the war, when Japanese bombers had only to follow the Yangtze to the peanut-shape peninsula formed by the confluence of the two rivers. Despite American aid, and in part because of China's own extraordinary systemic corruption at the time, the Kuomintang was sorely pressed for supplies and matériel, and the city was only lightly defended against air raids.

The wartime residence of Mao, Zhou Enlai, and other leading communists, called Red Crag Village, was pulled down after the war for a museum to commemorate that which had been razed: the Red Crag Revolutionary Memorial Hall. Chongqing also has a chamber of horrors that tells the story of SACO, the Sino-American Cooperation Agreement, under which Americans trained China's secret police in torture techniques and so on. But that is as much official acknowledgement as Chiang is given. The houses he built for himself and his pro-communist sister-in-law up on the face of Yellow Mountain were handed over to a local hospital as auxiliary space and now were slowly being reclaimed by rainforest, unmarked and unremarked on. I was determined to visit if I could.

We should have had a Jeep rather than a car to travel the mountain road. For much of the way we inched behind a truck full of armed police. Our driver kept honking at them, which struck me as an imprudent thing to do. The windshield wipers couldn't begin to deal with the problem of so much rain. Rivers of water were running down the leaves of trees, leaves the size of elephant ears, and falling onto the ones below, so that the whole forest on either side of the road was like some elaborate water clock in the emperor's collection in the Forbidden City.

Near the summit, at an elevation of maybe 600 metres, was a long tropical-style building: the hospital. It seemed deserted except for a few nurses walking along the verandah, unconcerned with the way the rain was blowing in. Chiang's house was farther up still, at the end of a long series of twisting steps cut into the steep side of the mountain. We trudged up, slipping in the mud and soaked to the skin.

The house is sometimes described as a villa by Chinese, but they are using the term in the English sense not the European, to mean a small country house rather than a large luxurious one. Yet in this case the location alone, overlooking the city and the river valley far below, might almost justify the grander usage, though the structure is only a tiny two-storey dwelling, plain but sturdily built, with its own water tower. It is a house that would have been easy to defend, except against air attack—which was precisely the danger Chiang faced. Accordingly he used to come here only after dark and always left before daybreak. The sight of his motorcade departing the city became the signal for an exodus in rickshaws, on pack animals, and on foot.

An old man was living there now. He pretty much kept to the first floor, giving over the ground floor to his chickens and ducks. He slept on a cot in what was once the Generalissimo's bathroom, because part of the roof above the bedroom had rotted away, admitting water freely. His possessions included a couple of pots and pans and a few rice bowls. Whatever he could not grow he lugged up all the way from the city. Perhaps 100 metres away, along a slippery, overgrown path, is the slightly smaller house built for the U.S. military adviser in the region. It is used for the spillover from the hospital down below. There are only two rooms on the ground floor, one for sleeping and one that served as the war room for strategic conferences and such. In the latter we found six old women playing dominoes. They seemed surprised by our turning up, our hair wet like seaweed and our boots squeaking. One sensed they had no visitors even in dry weather. We tried to chat them up and soon they were quite jolly about our presence. I got the impression, I wasn't sure how exactly, perhaps only from their expression, that they were tubercular.

When we got back down into the city, traffic was in an even greater snarl than usual. While we were stalled with everyone honking at us and us honking back, I had one of those experiences, so common in China if you were alert to receive them, in which past and present became confused for a second. A man came out of his house, which was perched precariously on a cliff overlooking the Yangtze docks, and held up what looked at first like a bandolier of rifle cartridges but was actually an enormously long string of firecrackers. With great ceremony he held a lighted match to the bottom end, with results that drowned out the noise of the impatient cars and lorries. It was exactly noon. Someone in his house had died. Each day for three days—perhaps four, if there were relatives who had to travel a great distance to the funeral—he would perform this ceremony at 6:00 a.m., noon, 6:00 p.m., and midnight. Then the body would be taken away for disposal.

When I returned to the hotel to put on some dry clothes, the television was showing highlights of the Calgary Stampede in Chinese.

Two of the areas in which I was least ill-equipped to make comparisons between conditions in China and those in the Soviet Union were the press and the fine arts, both quite useful indicators of social health in addition to their other importance. I knew that since the era of reform started 10 years earlier the *People's Daily* had lost millions of readers, just as *Pravda* had done. I had not been aware of just how the situation had been corrected following the massacre. It seemed that as part of the plan to strengthen the party, a certain quota of persons at every factory, office, and neighbourhood committee were required to purchase subscriptions, with the cost subsidized by the state. Beijing actually paying people to read its own newspaper might strike the West as curious, but the policy apparently had the desired effect. No one foresaw any likelihood that China would allow the type of semi-independent newspapers represented in the Soviet Union by the *Moscow News* or *Arguments and Facts*, though the *China Daily*, the English-language paper the party began producing in 1981, came close to free expression by including material from foreign agencies and publications with government information not commonly available except in this translated form. People said of it what people said of Radio Moscow's English service in contrast to Russian-language radio and television: that because it was for foreigners it could afford to be more candid or at least much less secretive, putting the best possible face on a situation but not denying the situation's existence. But that was as far as the Chinese and Soviet press could be compared at the time. The *China Daily*—and in this, I was assured, it was just like the Chinese-language media—placed an unnatural and not always credible emphasis on good news about production and the economy. One might be tempted to dismiss this practice as universal socialist procedure if not actually attribute it to government manipulation, but I felt the trait might also reflect a basic difference in Chinese culture. Westerners go to China wanting to see ancient temples only to find the Chinese eager to show them hydroelectric projects and ugly sky needles that look like Toronto's CN Tower (the Soviet Union was full of them as well). Frustration naturally results. And when the Chinese, in an effort to give the foreign public what it wants, erect brand-new temples in the old style (the original having most likely been destroyed in the Cultural Revolution), the tourists are disappointed and the Chinese hurt and perplexed by such a reaction.

In its way, the press of Chongqing provided an unexpected example of this phenomenon—an unexpectedly pleasant one for me. Zhao Xiaoci, a short, slight middle-aged man with thin spectacles and a quick energetic manner, took up my presence with enthusiasm. He was chief editor of *Chongqing Daily*, the morning paper, which together with its sister publication, *Chongqing Evening*, and a combined weekly edition for farmers, had a total circulation of about 600,000 copies. He gave me the tour.

When I was there, the newspaper, which I was led to believe rose above the standard-issue propaganda only in its local coverage, was in the process of moving to a new plant near the Chaoqian Docks on the banks of the Jialing on the north side of town, though it was still being edited, set, and printed at a rambling complex in Jiefang Lu, on the southern (Yangtze) side of the peninsula. The structures were erected in 1953, the same year that Deng Xiaoping, who was then the party secretary for southwest China, did the calligraphy that was still being used in the newspaper's nameplate at the head of page one. They could have been erected in 1923 or 1913. The publisher's office and the conference room were bright, airy, and modern, but the other spaces in the editorial building harked back to another era, one that ended so long ago in Western newspapers that it was beyond the reach of even my own elastic recollection. Corridors and cubbyholes were dark and stale-smelling, with brown and yellow paint peeling in leaf-size pieces from the wall. One room was full of reporters with their feet up on the desks, some talking into phones, others pointedly doing nothing. An old girlie calendar hung from one wall. There was, I swear to God, a ceiling fan revolving ever so slowly. The sickly sweet smell of clogged urinals hung in the atmosphere. Many a spavined old hack at the Toronto Press Club would have been quite overcome with nostalgia.

The back shop and the press room were fascinating, too. The paper used an unholy alliance of technologies, both offset and letterpress. No evidence here of the Chinese typewriter invented by Lin Yutang, that remarkable writer about due for revival; copy was written with pen on graph paper, one character per square. The manuscript pages were then given to young female compositors, 21 of them spaced over two shifts, who worked not just with the California case familiar to my fellow fogies but sat surrounded by a multitude of cases, with thousands of characters, which they plucked out in proper order and put onto their composing sticks. Excepting the extent of the choice the compositors were faced with, the procedures would have been instantly familiar to William Lyon Mackenzie or Joseph

Howe if those gentlemen were resurrected to witness the scene. Compositors could set 1,500 characters per hour; the very best might reach a speed of 1,800. There was something wonderfully Dickensian in how they went about the labour, proud of their skill and content with their place in the greater scheme of things.

That realization brought me to another one that affected me very much in Chongqing particularly, but everywhere else I went in China as well. The problem with writing about travel in China, I thought—and it applies to all countries that use corrugated iron for roofing material (a distinction I prefer to the term *Third World*)—is that one is constantly coming upon strange sights and ways long lost in the West, which it is too easy to categorize as obsolescent or imitative or backward or otherwise inferior but which one secretly enjoys as proof of one's own now sadly irretrievable past. It is of course a hideous double standard, and generally counterproductive to any understanding of the contemporary scene. But I consoled myself that it was perhaps not completely worthless with respect to the history of China's relations with (or reactions to) the West. To walk into the Bank of China's Chongqing branch was to see two generations of cultural imperialism. Beneath the grime, the half-light, and the chaos, all somewhat suggestive of an Indian railway station, was a magnificent old banking hall from the days when banks were designed to convey security and stability rather than convenience. It was reclaimed for Chinese culture, but a new kind of internationalism was making inroads. The woman who waited on me at the foreign-exchange wicket sat on a high stool like a Scots clerk in a counting house, and she used an abacus. Above her was a plastic sign reading: USE "GREAT WALL MASTERCARD" FROM THE BANK OF CHINA.

My next call was on Fan Pu, vice-president of the Sichuan Fine Art Institute, the only such place of learning in all of southwestern China and one of only four in the country. He was 56 but seemed far younger and was himself a painter, or used to be; what with all the administration he looked after, he found he had little time for his own work, even on the two one-month holidays, summer and winter. This put him at a disadvantage in terms of his personal economics as well as his spirit, as he had to live on his monthly salary, the equivalent of $30 to $50, and not supplement it with the occasional sale of works for a couple thousand yuan each, as the other staff, and many of the students, did.

He was from a village in Shanxi in north-central China and fell into art education by way of the military. He was a very young war artist attached to the Eighth Route Army, assigned to paint slogans and such. Later he was involved in an art education programme for the troops generally, which proved to be a springboard to art training after Liberation. A few years later, in 1956, Mao would make one of his better-known pronouncements on the subject: "Let a hundred flowers blossom and let a hundred schools exist." But, in fact, the process was already well underway. The Southwest People's College of Art had begun in 1950, and in 1953, as part of national "adjustments" in the education system, merged with the Chengdu School of Art to make the Southwest Training College of Art, with the emphasis on turning out teachers. In 1959 the school got its present name to reflect a broader approach. In 1990 there were 800 students—700 of them under-graduates moving towards their state-assigned craft or design jobs once they got their degrees, the rest postgrads hoping to teach one day. There were 200 staff, from full professors to teaching assistants. Most teachers were Sichuan School graduates. The campus is a pleasant enclave of build-ings on 11 hectares on the north side of the Yangtze, a surprisingly quiet spot in the middle of such a noisy urban area. The centrepiece is a six-storey sextagonal building with several floors of exhibition space, complete with spittoons in the corners.

Only about one in 20 applicants is accepted as a student, for people wishing to enrol must show at least some ability in most of the major areas of the curriculum, which includes painting (both Chinese and Western), drawing, colour theory, and the philosophy of art. Great emphasis is put on the last one. They must also pass the standard exam set by the National Committee for Education in such fields as mathematics, philosophy, poli-tics, and language, though they need achieve a mark of only 200, not 400 as required of students in other fields, at other institutions. I had hoped to meet the students, but my visit fell on Monday afternoon when they were all away for their weekly dose of political indoctrination, a rite that was reintroduced following Tiananmen Square after many years' absence. Fan was apologetic, but no doubt his superiors scheduled my appointment with this coincidence in mind. In any case, it was impossible not to admire his own adroitness when the subject of politics came up.

Mao had great concern for art education, great plans, Fan insisted, "but these were not implemented till after the Cultural Revolution was finished." Nicely put, I thought. I wondered how the place had survived the wave after wave of carnage, destruction, and mayhem. "The past 10 years, however, have been the best and most valuable time we've ever had." The reference was to the Third Plenary of the Central Committee in 1979, which freed artists and art schools from strict adherence to social realism and useful propaganda to pursue whatever might, within reasonable limits, result in "quality."

"Painters enjoy greater freedom now if they're not against the teachings of the Communist Party or of socialism," Fan told me. "On the other hand, no one in my school is against those things, but of course such matters are harder to judge here than at, say, a drama school." He was too subtle to mention it, and I was too polite to bring it up, but each knew that the other knew that the issue was not political content of the art but rather the degree of political correctness inherent in various types of art, quite apart from imagery.

The watershed event in the modern story of free artistic expression in China, an event as important as the Soviet show of "modern" work closed down by Khrushchev, was an exhibition at the National Gallery in Beijing little more than a year earlier, right before Tiananmen Square, when the liberalization movement reached its peak. The show was devoted to the work of students from throughout China and featured stuff that would have provoked only ennui in the West. There were a lot of pop images, for example, and large imitation abstract-expressionist canvases onto which the artists had shot paint from a great distance. Found art found expression in such objects as condoms filled with water. The authorities were outraged. The show, which was to have run for a month, closed early. Yet that did not presage a retreat to the bad old days but only an acceptance that Western ideas must be assimilated slowly, that new eras should not be entered into until the previous ones had been dissected, digested, and understood. "We try to absorb more Western culture" was how Fan put it, "but we don't want to make a copy. We need to consider the condition of China and the customs and to try to absorb quality, whether East or West."

As a result, I got the sense of telescoping time as I wandered through the rooms of the gallery, as though the main purpose of the instruction in art history and technique were to find ways of applying the one to the other. I saw traditional Chinese scroll paintings with the unmistakable influence of the Mexican muralists of the 1920s and even some that tried to acknowledge cubism, and one large lacquer-ware mosaic of a field of flowers that incorporated the vocabulary of pointillism. Sometimes the institute picked up the least likely of Western ideas. Students in the fashion course, for example, were crazy about 1960s tie-dying, which was sometimes used in figurative work; some silk tie-dye pandas by Fan's wife were on display. But then that seems somehow appropriate. Chinese artists were fighting the battle and making the discoveries that Western art worked its way through in the early 1960s. Which in no way made the issues any less important or the lessons any less real, for the time difference was a vital part of the context needed to decipher such events, which were themselves a useful illustration of changes the larger society was going through.

One of the former students of whom the institute was proudest was Luo Zhonghi, whose 1979 painting *Fathers*, a sort of super-realist portrait done in earth colours but with a nod towards neo-expressionism, is considered a masterpiece. It depicts an old farmer holding up a soup bowl or rice bowl, as though offering sustenance to the viewers or begging from them. It was praised by some critics in France when it appeared there in a group show; it now hangs permanently in the National Gallery in Beijing. Its wide acceptance in China would seem to rest on the way it uses a variety of "international" techniques to acceptable documentary ends. Although, despite its descriptive content, it is not what a Western audience would immediately think of as overtly socialist art, it is greatly esteemed in China at least partly because it is not considered too Western despite its form.

The closest work to this ideal middle ground that I saw on display in the students' gallery was a reclining female nude in the manner that a Canadian viewer might associate with Ken Danby or Jeremy Smith. It was the work of a female graduate student. The faint, very faint, element of eroticism added to the effectiveness of the compromise between mission and explanation. I asked Fan whether there were any life classes, thinking that they might have been banished from the syllabus when the recent crackdown came. He said, "Oh, yes, and mixed classes at that. But it is hard to find female models. They fear that young men won't want to be their friends if they know that other people have seen them undressed, and this is often the case. We must therefore use girls from the distant countryside, and they are not the best models. They're not trained." Male models did not face the same stigma. But then I should have guessed that life-drawing classes continued to be important. Students at the institute still drew from the antique as well, using copies, made by teachers 30 years earlier, of the ancient sculptures from nearby caves. I was reminded of the old copies of Greek and Roman sculpture once used for the same purpose in Moscow but now relegated to display in the Pushkin Museum of Fine Arts in lieu of any genuine classical statuary for the people to look at.

In short, Fan explained, "abstraction moves slowly here," as though abstraction were the one barrier Western art had had to break through, as though, now having done so, all was stable and static. "But the students are aggressive." Later he would mention their penchant for long hair, speaking like a Canadian high school principal of 35 years ago. "There is a new atmosphere in the school." I got the impression that this new atmosphere might be described as a kind of enlightened pragmatism.

To judge from what I saw, the level of craft in the students' work was quite high and the interdisciplinary breadth remarkable. A person might ultimately specialize in the plastic arts but was expected to have a reasonable grasp of ceramics or, in a pinch, be able to execute a portrait. This approach is apparently the outcome of several factors. The socialist tradition for one. Students, and their teachers, did a lot of urban design work and public art. Sichuan graduates worked on Mao's mausoleum, for example, and the sculpture department was responsible for the allegorical sculptures, representing the four seasons, that decorate the approaches to the nearby Yangtze Bridge. Another factor is the deliberate attempt to meld the visual imperative of Chinese art with that of the Western modernist tradition. (To this end, incidentally, the institute often set up exchanges of staff and students with those in Canada, apparently feeling that Canada provided Western culture in its least virulent form.) You can see the results of this policy in all but the most traditional work. It is particularly strong in commercial design, which the students undertook for Chinese factories in need of help with their packaging. As the more market-driven economy has grown, such skill has been in greater demand. That may not have much to do with art, but it is the institute's safe-conduct pass into the future.

3

Downriver

S hortly after dawn on the day of departure from Chongqing I stood at
the head of the long flight of steps looking down the hill to the Jialing
and, beyond it, the Yangtze. There was motion everywhere. Fifty or 60 sizable ships were loading or unloading or crisscrossing their fellow vessels'
wakes in the one river or the other—passenger steamers, river freighters,
ore carriers, ferry boats. A few more were careened up on the mud flats
where workers were going at them on bamboo scaffolding. In addition, a
disorganized flotilla of smaller craft, some with family laundry flapping
from the rigging, loitered about, like birds following behind hoping to pick
up a little food when the garbage was thrown overboard—or rather, hoping
to pick up any spare bits of commerce that the big vessels couldn't be both-
ered with. Hundreds of people were moving back and forth between ships and
the shore. Many were passengers, others were stevedores and roustabouts.
They walked along rickety gangplanks that oscillated alarmingly under
the weight. Some carried enormous cloth bundles tied with rope, bundles
that dwarfed the people under them and gave the suggestion of ants trying to make off with someone's picnic food. Still others trotted along with
wicker baskets on their heads or two of them bouncing suspended from
bamboo poles that dug deeply into their shoulders. A number of people
appeared to be carrying all their worldly possessions with them—mattresses,

cooking utensils, small animals. Children cried, dogs barked, and whistles hooted hoarsely. The New Orleans levee in 1855 cannot have looked or felt much different.

It was time to respond to one of my original motivations in coming to China and begin passage downriver through the Three Gorges, an area only about 200 kilometres in length but possessing some of the most famous scenery in Asia. To get the tickets I had to queue up in an old river-front terminal where people were sleeping on the hard wooden benches while elderly women fanned themselves and Public Security officers strolled up and down with utterly unconvincing nonchalance, alert to the ways of beggars and pickpockets.

In socialist China there were no first-class cabins. There were entire first-class boats, you see, big sleek motor yachts for the exclusive use of tourists and important officials, where people could sit in swivel chairs in air-conditioned comfort and watch through the glass while the scenery came to them. Wen Dong and I were going to take one of the hundreds of ordinary Chinese boats that went up and down the river. Except that they were steel-hulled and weren't driven by paddlewheels, they looked like the old riverboats we associated with the Mississippi or the Yukon—and for a reason. They had the same shallow spoon-shape hull, drawing only a metre or so of water, in order to glide over incipient sandbars when the river was low. Atop that were three decks, with a sort of parlour forward, on the uppermost one, and the pilot house on what would once have been called the texas deck.

The highest order of accommodation was second class, in which two people—Wen and I in this instance—shared a small outward-facing cabin containing a basin, a vacuum bottle of tea water, and two life jackets. The toilets were common to all second-class passengers and consisted of stinking holes in the floor. In third class, one deck below, there were four small chromium-plated bunks to a cabin instead of two single beds, whereas fourth class, on the waterline, was made up of 24-bunk dormitories. There was also fifth class, below decks, in which people simply sprawled on the steel decking, moaning and tossing like prisoners, without much in the way of light or air but sometimes with a pig or two for additional company (for it was a strict rule—and a sound one, I felt—that all farm creatures had to travel fifth class). The uniqueness I had experienced as a Westerner in

Chongqing was continued aboard ship, as I was again the only foreigner in sight unless you counted a few Taiwanese. The next most exotic person was a wealthy Tibetan. I assume he was wealthy, for all of his teeth, uppers and lowers, were of gold. And by comparison he didn't excite much curiosity at all. At 7:00 a.m. we steamed out into the Yangtze channel and began moving eastward. We were underway. Over the PA system, very loudly, came a recording of "Auld Lang Syne" played on Chinese instruments.

The rains were early and determined, and the river was a little higher than usual. It was also, I had pointed out to me, more red than yellow, an indication of the amount of farmland it was taking away with it over its course of 3,600 kilometres. The Yangtze is by far China's largest river and one of the three biggest on the planet, but all other statistics about it incline towards meaningless numbers with many digits. Almost at once, however, I had a sense of its power as a thief, constantly stealing earth where it was most needed and depositing it where it was wanted least, on channels and berths, which then had to be dredged, or in new bars and shoals, which posed a hazard to navigation. The government estimated that 1990 could see the worst flooding on the Yangtze, especially in the middle ranges, since 1954, when the snows in Tibet were particularly deep and 30,000 people were killed and whole villages destroyed. Even in a good year 3,000 Chinese are killed in floods.

For the first while beyond Chongqing the view was industrial. The plants looked heavy and old-fashioned, but without the sense of industrial autumn you get seeing similar scenes in America or Britain. There was no leading edge to Chinese manufacturing; it simply existed and did its job and kept its share of the workforce busy in the process. Between the industrialized areas were sizable stretches of open country, and as the built-up places got farther apart, the countryside in between became both more rugged-looking and more intensively cultivated.

Here, gazing up at the sides of hills and cliffs to find small square vegetable patches, I saw my first examples of the almost completely vertical gardening at which the Chinese excelled. In the Soviet Union I had been surprised to realize to what extent food shortages underlay the urgency of reform. Now I saw the miracle by which the Chinese managed to feed themselves and that gave government a level of stability that could be compared to the Soviets'. I could only guess at all the reasons for the difference, but some were purely practical. In the Soviet Union the Stalinist legacy of enormous collective farms for crops like winter wheat and potatoes—crops that more or less took care of themselves between planting and harvest—gave permanence to a serious misapplication of human resources. The Chinese scheme of small communes, often no more than a few families, growing labour-intensive crops like rice, was much more efficient. Although the statement is not terribly scientific, it must also be said that the Russians probably just aren't as good farmers as the Chinese; the Doukhobors seem to have taken their special genius with them when they emigrated. Given controlled conditions and identical adjoining plots in a neutral third country, the Russian would starve and the Chinese would feed an extended family of 23 people. What was it Bertolt Brecht wrote in *The Threepenny Opera? "Erst Kommt das Fressen, dann Kommt die Moral."* First food, then morals. A lot of other words could be substituted for *Moral* without altering the meaning.

We passed a number of villages that would have reminded Mark Twain of his boyhood in Hannibal: towns with only a few streets, all of them running parallel to the muddy river, where people seemed willing to interrupt their work and watch, with what combination of emotions I could hardly imagine, whenever a riverboat like ours chugged by without stopping—rather as I had observed people doing in the case of the Trans-Siberian train.

Before noon we came to the first sizable city, called Fuling, which looked like one of the villages that long ago had been multiplied in size by the addition of industry. The river there was full of rocks and whaleback shoals, which had to be major protrusions indeed when the water was low. It was also particularly dirty along this stretch, with bottles and every other form of rubbish floating by, including polystyrene packaging and other permanent waste. Such conditions seemed to have no noticeable effect on the people whose lives were spent along the river. At almost every bend for the next two days we saw lone fishermen perched on smooth rocks near the bank, casting huge conical nets attached to long poles, and small individual fishing boats with women sitting on deck, mending nets. Sometimes there were hawks circling overhead. The river had been up to one and a quarter kilometres wide, but at about 2:00 p.m. it suddenly narrowed for a brief stretch and grew rougher, as though to remind us that we were on the right course if we intended to pass through the gorges the next day. It was near here that China planned to build the Three Gorges Dam, a structure 200 metres high that would create a reservoir an estimated 400 kilometres long, flooding a vast inhabited area, including entire cities, and dispossessing millions of people. The project was proposed in the 1950s; the most recent stage was yet another feasibility study, this one partly funded by the Canadian government.

The hills were very high—as much as 500 metres in some places, I would guess. They were covered in vegetation of different textures, from the leafy to the woolly, and painted many shades of green. The summits were often decorated with a fringe of mountain foliage, while close to the river the style was more subtropical, with elongated fronds overhanging the water. At a distance the steep face of the hills sometimes looked like green velour. High up there were periodic flashes of silver, as the sun caught waterfalls that made their way down the rocks in a series of graduated leaps before spilling quietly into the river.

The buildings we passed along the way were usually situated on narrow shelves notched into the hillside for that purpose, but the architecture was surprisingly varied. In the countryside farmers built and owned their own houses, unlike people in the towns and cities, where all real property was held in common by the state and assigned for use according to complicated formulae that met with few people's satisfaction. These farmhouses were usually a single storey consisting of two or three rooms; no two were of precisely the same plan, though all seemed to be built sturdily and with great vernacular skill. In some cases local brick was used. Certain people had elected, or been permitted, to settle off by themselves, surrounded by their own kitchen and market gardens, while other houses had grown up in clusters, no doubt through the dictates of family need. I saw several instances of what first appeared, from upriver, to be a lone house near a stream but turned out, as we passed, to be only the most visible part of a village strung out along the shores of the tributary for what looked like some considerable distance. Each such place would be governed, some might say ruled, by the rural equivalent of the neighbourhood committees that were the dominant feature of life in the big cities.

Perched up in the hills were two or three impressive temples and also many larger residences with their own boat slips or even their own private docks below, reached by stone steps or a smooth, steep span or roadway or some combination of the two. As with so many buildings in China, it was impossible to tell what they once must have been or how old they were or even what purpose they were put to now. It seemed to me, though, that some had walls that went beyond the needs of the traditional Chinese courtyard to suggest fortification. And it was brought home to me that although virtually the entire Yangtze valley had once been de facto a protectorate of the British, who had kept it so with a fleet of gunboats named for various species of English birds, this countryside, and indeed much of China, had been in the hands of warlords as recently as 60 years ago. Perhaps such thoughts came more easily to mind aboard a riverboat like ours. A tablet affixed to one of the bulkheads informed me that the boat was launched in 1981, but to judge by the design, the rust, the battered wooden doors, and the general signs of rough handling, it might just as easily have been built in 1921.

Our boat was never alone on the river for long. Downward-bound vessels naturally had the right of way, and we forever seemed to be passing, or being passed by, other identical ones, always with an exchange of whistle blasts. Also, there were work boats galore, from two-person fishing craft of four metres or less to more substantial wooden-hulled affairs that were probably operated by communes and used to deliver crops to market. At one place where the channel hugged the north bank we passed close enough to a boat slip to see that it was rice that the long line of men were carrying aboard in slow, methodical single file. Usually we could only guess at what cargo was being carried, except of course in the case of unpackaged commodities. Salt and tung oil were two common cargoes, but coal was the most obvious. All along the river, as far as we went, there were coal mines close to the shore. Some were so small that they seemed to be worked by only a handful of men; in one instance, the coal was being dug out of the hillside and shovelled directly into the belly of a waiting scow. In other cases, miners underground sent it up by lift, tram, or conveyor, building up huge stockpiles on the surface, which other men would transfer to wheelbarrows and push along a wobbly tipple before dumping the coal into the vessel perhaps 25 metres below. It must have taken forever to fill the three holds of a respectable-size ship of the sort that carried most such trade between Shanghai and all manner of little places up the river.

Towards late afternoon we put into Fengdu on the northern bank. The procedure of tying up at such cities was to come abreast of a large barge with a high superstructure that was permanently moored to the dock; each barge bore a number corresponding to that of the particular boat it serviced. The barge thus acted as a kind of bridge between life on the river and life in town. As soon as the deckhands had secured the boat to it with hawsers, the barge came to life. Even before the gangplank was put in place, men and women on the barge were selling to the passengers sodas and packets of dried beef and pieces of some rubbery white vegetable, passing the goods and making change over a gap of slurping water. The stops lasted only a few minutes, just long enough to discharge some people and take on others, but folks were eager to step onto land again and they penetrated as far into town as they could before the all-aboard bell called them back. The townspeople knew they had to conduct their trade swiftly. The street nearest the dock was always a miniature market for those who could afford to buy food for the next leg of the journey.

There was a restaurant of sorts below deck, in the fifth-class section, but the food was slop (I never thought I'd ever say that about what was basically Cantonese cooking—we had now gone beyond the jurisdiction of Sichuan cuisine, though Sichuan accents, which were almost equally spicy, were still common enough). The diners huddled together at small tables and sat on square handmade stools about 30 centimetres off the ground. There were more people than stools and fisticuffs broke out between two patrons, both of whom had the look of street toughs. Police rode all the boats as a matter of routine, and a Public Security officer broke up the dispute before the violence became general.

The channel was well marked and well monitored. There were frequent stations along the way where conditions were checked and information disseminated; these facilities were housed in red-and-white buildings with flagpoles out front and with depth markers painted on the rocks leading up the hillside. Despite that, rocks, sandbars, logs and other obstacles, and even occasional wrecks, made night travel impossible. It would certainly have been foolhardy to attempt a nocturnal passage of the gorges, where the water levels could vary as much as 25 or 30 metres according to the season. So at seven o'clock we tied up for the night at Wanxian, an old city on the north bank with a wide stone staircase leading up from the dock into the commercial section, where a market was conducted after dark more for the benefit of the citizens than for the passengers. In other words, it was not primarily a market for crafts and packaged food but for furniture and clothing, and housewares as well, though any Chinese market, in however provincial a town, had enough fresh meat and produce to provoke food riots in the Soviet Union.

Wanxian was another of those cities along the river that benefited from the British ability to get trading concessions in the confusion of the last days of the Manchu dynasty—or, in this case, in the early moments, equally chaotic, of the Chinese Republic, in the idealistic period before Sun Yat-sen's death opened the way for Chiang Kai-shek; there were still old buildings that didn't require plaques to tell the story. The central city had a few hundred thousand inhabitants at least, tightly packaged into a small space, as the contours of the river and mountains insisted. It was big enough and busy enough to suggest a need for traffic signals; the total absence of any such devices increased not only the congestion but also the sense of excitement, the realization that what you were seeing was the urban experience, Chinese style.

We were underway again at first light, and within an hour the river had started to boil and churn. But this was only another of the signposts along the route. When it finally began, Qutang, the shortest and swiftest of the gorges, came up suddenly and was over too soon but really was magnificent while it lasted. We had two more towns to pass before the ride could begin—Fengjie, not far from the head of the gorge, and the Baidicheng, or White King City, a place whose mythical associations were buried now in coal yards and boat yards. This whole part of the valley was particularly rich in archaeological sites, including some dating to the Stone Age, for that was how long the river had been sustaining people here. We made our way into the canyon, which was only eight kilometres long, playing tag with other boats. The experience was a bit like being on a roller coaster that never left the ground, but with high stone walls racing past on both sides.

The second gorge, called the Wuxia, was more dramatic and more than twice as long. The mountains reminded you of photographs of the Andes perhaps, with the tops in cloud cover. Right in the middle of the gorge was a town called Badong, where it had to be difficult landing under certain conditions. The vegetation along that section was markedly different from what I had seen the previous day, with more conifers, and I began to notice a difference in the rocks as well: high white shale cliffs rose along one section, with a wavy fern-like pattern to them.

Thereafter the river widened for quite a spell and grew calmer. We saw butterflies in profusion for a few moments and could hear birds chirping, could in fact eavesdrop on the conversation of men in sampans and small motor launches a considerable distance away. This went on for some while until, mid-afternoon, we entered Xiling Gorge, the last and longest. It ran for 80 kilometres, not roaring or bubbling but sending the boat along at a fast steady pace, past rock formations riddled, high and low, with caves, some of them quite large and some, it was said, used throughout ancient times by successive cultures. Such matters were of little interest to most Chinese. It was perhaps significant that although the gorges generated attention abroad, the real excitement for most of the passengers came only later, when the boat passed the huge power station connected to the Gezhouba Dam, a famous Chinese mega-project of which everyone remained most proud. It was begun on December 26, 1970, Mao's 77th birthday, and opened to the public in 1981. The boats there had to pass through a lock, which they did four at a time. Crowds of people atop the lock stared down excitedly as the passengers stared up in turn at the man-made wonder. The people on one boat called out to those on the others. Cameras appeared and everyone was happy, awestruck by the majesty of—progress!

After the dam, the river quickly returned to its broad, muddy, moderately paced old self, and the mundane nature of Chinese country life enveloped people once again. Paul Theroux took the inaugural run of one of the first-class tourist boats in the early 1980s, producing a small gem of a book, *Sailing Through China*, one of his most satisfying efforts. He hit upon a striking truth when, in watching this part of the river float by, he observed:

> Our future is this mildly poisoned earth and its smoky air. We are in for hunger and hard work, the highest stage of poverty—no starvation, but crudeness everywhere, clumsy art, simple language, bad books, brutal laws, plain vegetables, and clothes of one colour. It will be damp and dull, like this. It will be monochrome and crowded—how could it be any different? There will be no star wars or galactic empires and no more money to waste

on the loony nationalism in space programmes. Our grandchildren will probably live in a version of China. On the dark brown banks of the Yangtze the future has already arrived.

Travellers had the option of continuing for three more days, to Wuhan, where they could take another boat all the way to Shanghai. I was eager to get to Shanghai more quickly, because it was another of my must-sees and because I had begun to sense that the authorities didn't want me to get there at all, for they had been hinting, suggesting, and inveigling me to change my itinerary in favour of Guangzhou (Canton). I could only guess that they feared I would ferret out some radical democrats in the former place. But I remained determined to get there if only to see the old foreign concessions and other surviving evidence of past clashes between Chinese and Western cultures. A compromise was reached. I would go to Shanghai, but quickly, and not stay for long, and they would continue to argue in favour of Guangzhou (which, I told them, I could visit anytime on a day tripper's visa from Hong Kong).

I talked with various people on the boat. There was an electronics student, 22, in whose eyes I could see vital questions she wanted to ask about politics in the West but was too frightened to say out loud. And there was a chemical salesman, in his mid-forties, who was still shaking his head in disbelief at what the post-Tiananmen crackdown had done to his state-controlled company. "We were still making the transition to the market economy and I was building up our overseas business," he said. "Then suddenly all that we had built was torn down and we were back to central planning." His expression and the motion of his shoulders said: "It's crazy! Nobody can work like this."

We got off at Yichang, a place that was said to be the throat between the head of Hubei and the stomach of Sichuan. The phrase had a smooth tourist-board sound to it, but there were complicated emotions beneath the surface. The locals spoke with something very close to the Sichuan dialect. They deeply resented, however, not being thought of as citizens of Hubei. Yichang was another old treaty port that once had a large British community, then almost totally lost touch with the West, and the West with it. "Before 1970," I was told, "many people here had never actually seen big-noses." That was the year when almost everything in Yichang started to change. Work on the dam and the lock had begun. Then, the next year, a long railway-and-highway bridge across the Yangtze was opened, based apparently on the one completed at Wuhan a dozen years earlier. The Wuhan bridge was the first Chinese-built span to cross the river, for although Chinese bridge engineering had once been quite advanced (Peter the Great summoned Chinese experts to St. Petersburg), it atrophied after foreigners came in great number. The pre-Gezhouba population of Yichang (which got a modern port in the bargain) was 170,000; by 1990 the city had 400,000, though like all Chinese cities it looked smaller than it was.

Wen and I barely had enough time to catch our CAAC flight to Wuhan, assuming that the flight still existed and that it hadn't been unreasonably delayed. This entailed a wild ride from the riverfront to the airport over a temporarily unpaved road filled with holes the size of small bomb craters. Prosperous commercial Yichang was only a few streets deep. The rest was like rural China plunked down in the middle of an urban area. Housing ranged from mud buildings at the low end to modern blocks of flats at the high, with the mean being quite adequate. I didn't see as much evidence of economic freedom for small entrepreneurs as I had in other cities. People grew rice and cotton, and I saw others flailing grain—with wooden flails, I mean—and using round baskets to separate out the chaff. There were water buffalo—morose creatures they were—being coached through the paddies, a sure sign that although I was still on the north side of the river I had crossed some invisible boundary into southern China. By passing convoys of soldiers and honking at deaf animals and endangering people on bicycles, hazy figures encased in clouds of dust, we managed to get within sight of the airport. A field nearby was littered with the hulks of DC-3s and other vintage aircraft. We made it to the terminal with moments to spare before we began a long wait for the plane. On previous CAAC flights we had been given perfectly adequate box lunches. I was ready for another. This time they gave us fans made of sandalwood.

The Canadian embassy in Beijing had told me there were reports of anti-Canadian sentiment in Wuhan; I didn't catch details, but *immigration* and *Vancouver* seemed to be the key words. To people in Canada who reached their majority during the Lester B. Pearson era, the whole notion has an absurd ring. One might as well speak of demonstrations against the Swiss, or of anti-Belgian riots. But times change, which is to say they deteriorate, and I kept my ears and eyes open over the next couple of days, but heard or saw nothing to report. If my presence wasn't enough to provoke back-lash, I reasoned, there was likely no merit to the story. Yes, I felt myself starting to become just the slightest bit paranoiac by this stage. Nothing clinical, you understand, merely defensive; I almost thought it might be expected of me, and I had no wish to appear rude.

At Wuhan the Yangtze was much wider and slower than it was at Chongqing, and the bridge did add a note of dignity. Wuhan was also broader and more up to date than Chongqing, though its contemporari-ness was not the source of whatever charm and interest it possessed. It had quite a bustling indoor-outdoor market along Thousand Families Street, full of the customary snake sellers, dog-meat merchants, curbstone physi-cians, key-cutters, and people with medical scales offering to tell you your weight for only a few fen. All this in addition to the packaged goods ranging from wart-remover to Fancy Smell Biscuits. This was the only market at which I saw people with bamboo beds slung from wires above their stalls so they could sleep there as well as do business. This might—or might not, I couldn't determine—be related to the fact that Wuhan was not so com-mercially free as it was before Tiananmen; new confiscatory taxes were all but wiping out the entrepreneurs' profit. Yet there was still prosperity to be had for the shopkeeper there, a fact most obvious in, for example, the many electronics dealers' and clothing stores in Dr. Sun Yat-sen Street, which looked and felt remarkably like Charing Cross Road in London.

A lot of history showed through in Wuhan, though it was little enough considering the past the place had had. Wuhan was actually three cities joined under a single municipal government for administrative reasons, though the components stubbornly retained their distinct identities. Their functions overlapped a bit, but the pattern was for Wuchang, once a walled city, to be the political and cultural centre, while Hankou, where the for-eign concessions had been, was mostly for shopping, and Hanyang for the most part industrial—famously so. The first of these was on the east side of the river, the others on the west.

Wuhan had often been at the centre of important events. You could see that by the presence of more foreign buildings than in either Chongqing or Yichang, though not so many that its character was defined by them, the way part of Shanghai's was. It was here that the revolution of 1911, ending 267 years of the Qing dynasty, had its beginning. This was also the first piece of China to see massive industrialization on the Western model and also therefore the first Western-style labour violence. The nationalists took it over, the Japanese seized and destroyed much of it, and Mao, for some reason, had a special affection for it. It was to Wuhan that he would come annually, until well into his sunset years, to show his strength by swimming in the Yangtze. He was also, it was said, particularly fond of one local restaurant, the Laotongcheng.

It would be inaccurate to say that Wuhan staggered under all the historical baggage. The main sites to which visitors were dragged were a Russian-built hotel in imitation of the Temple of Heaven and a huge five-storey ersatz Buddhist temple completed in the mid-1980s on a high promontory overlooking the bridge approaches and the river. In the morning when I went out, a platoon of soldiers with automatic weapons was doing close-order drill in front of the hotel; they were still at it when I returned in the evening. And if the temple was full of only sham Buddhism, there was genuine peace to be found elsewhere. Wuhan University in Hankou is one of China's oldest and most important and has an ivy-league sort of campus, belying the violence that erupted there during the Cultural Revolution. I strained to hear indications that today's students were under special suspicion, the way those in Shanghai and particularly Beijing were, but I picked up no such vibrations. It was a well-behaved place, Wuhan. The newspaper had a brand-new office building and printing plant. "That shows how powerful they are," I was told.

Another peaceful spot in the city was East Lake, a large lakeside park with nature paths and some surprisingly quaint amusements, such as shooting galleries, a small private-sector zoo under canvas, and the Chinese equivalent of a Punch and Judy show. On a slow weekday, people could walk there with thoughts disturbed by nothing more jarring than the discontinuous tinkling of bicycle bells, one of the pervasive and characteristic sounds of China.

4

The Buzz on the Shanghai Bund

When I arrived, bedraggled and fatigued, there were two signs, one on either side of the lift, in the lobby of the Peace Hotel in Shanghai, the lovely old Peace Hotel of so many people's warm recollection. One informed patrons that the staff were renowned for their clean linen and attention to personal hygiene. The other said: DUE TO NECESSARY RENOVATIONS, THE JAZZ BAND WHICH NORMALLY IS TO BE FOUND IN OUR LOBBY MAY NOW BE HEARD ON THE EIGHTH FLOOR TEMPORARILY. OUR APOLOGIES FOR ANY INCONVENIENCE. YOU ARE THANKED.

I wanted to stay there because the Peace is of some importance to the history of Shanghai's involvement with the West (and Shanghai was and in one sense remains the most Westernized city in China). The story is so fiercely complex that readers new to the subject might not be annoyed by a thumbnail sketch.

Everywhere I went on this journey I am describing I was plagued by anniversaries of this or that war or founding father, all of them dates put on the calendar for immediate political purposes. During my time in China, schoolchildren in Tianjin, Shanghai, and Nanjing were being prepared for celebrations marking the sesquicentennial of the start of the Opium Wars. The conflict had its origin in the late 18th century, when factors of the East India Company began paying for Chinese tea and silk with opium rather than with silver. The opium, most of it from India, was so cheap that the British could afford to dump it on the Chinese market, causing widespread addiction and thus increasing demand. In all, 4,000 chests of opium were imported in 1800, the year the emperor tried banning the stuff (the edict had no effect—even his court was hooked). By 1821 the annual figure was 21,000 chests. In time the administrator of Canton took it upon himself to close down the opium dens in the city, burn stockpiles of the drug, and behead Chinese traffickers. In 1840 the British fought the first skirmishes to protect the trade. By 1842 they had defeated the Chinese government and forced China to empty the treasury, cede Hong Kong, and grant concessions in other cities. These cities became free ports of a kind, in which the British built their own institutions and conducted trade immune from Chinese law. Their success sparked other opium wars on the part of the French, the Americans, the Japanese, the Russians, and others, all of whom also exercised their extraterritoriality, as is was called. Shanghai, as China's biggest port, was at the centre of such activity.

The fourth and final opium war was concluded in 1860, which was a crucial year also because it marked the date when the West finally made up its mind about whom to support in the Taiping Rebellion, a massive peasant uprising led by one Hong Xiuquan, who believed himself to be not the resurrected Christ but rather his younger brother. Preaching a kind of Christianity and promising land redistribution and other social reforms, including a ban on opium, he put together an army of well over a million and took control of the Yangtze valley and, in fact, all of southern China. If *war* seems too grand a word for the opium wars, then *rebellion* is too mean a one for the Taiping Rebellion, which claimed millions of lives. The already demoralized Qing government was on the defensive, and the West hesitated whether to support the regime or wait until the fighting stopped to endorse the Taipings. Finally they came down on the side of the Qings and helped to defeat the rebels; Hong killed himself when cornered, and the threat collapsed. It was in this action that General Charles "Chinese" Gordon acquired his sobriquet—though his greatest fame lay a generation in the future, when he let himself be martyred in Khartoum by the Madhi, another such messianic leader, who claimed to be the Prophet Mohammed returned to Earth and who preached his own kind of anti-foreign message.

With the Taipings vanquished, the Westerners now tightened their control even more, perhaps making inevitable the Boxer uprising at the close of the century when another peasant movement based on xenophobia formed an unlikely alliance with the empress dowager to drive the foreigners out. The most dramatic incident in the Boxer conflict, one much beloved by Hollywood and by patriotic illustrators of the Frederic Remington type, was the siege of the foreign legations in Beijing, with a multinational relief force of British, Americans, Japanese, and Europeans coming to the rescue. After that, a few warlords and pirates notwithstanding, the British and others enjoyed clear commercial sailing until the Japanese and then finally the communists expelled them.

In the 1920s and 1930s Shanghai was fully deserving of its reputation for wickedness and intrigue, but these qualities were not limited to Westerners except in the sense that the city was divvied up geographically between Chinese and foreigners. Because it was the place where Chinese sovereignty was most laughable, it was where Chinese dissent was loudest, a city full of revolutionaries and political philosophers. André Malraux is too out of favour even to qualify as a writer who is neglected, but I have always thought that his novel *La Condition humaine* must be pretty authentic in the way it describes this underground milieu. It was in Shanghai, in 1921, that the Chinese Communist Party was founded. And it was in Shanghai, in 1927, that Chiang finally turned on the communists, in the celebrated coup and massacre that Malraux describes. The spark was the discovery in the French Concession of a large arms cache that had been confiscated from one of the warlords. The Green Gang, or Green Circle, the organized crime ring that ran most everything in Shanghai that wasn't already run by foreigners, wanted the guns for its own purposes. The communists, who by that date controlled the labour unions, had plans for them as well. One source says that to even enter Shanghai, Chiang had had to pay tribute to one of the Green leaders, who was driven through the streets in a bulletproof limousine with gun-toting outriders hanging on the running boards. But Chiang made an alliance with him over guns. They were two of a kind.

In 1990 the city had six or seven million people, the district twice that number. It is a simple matter to divide it into three parts, one might say into three levels of consciousness.

First is the foreigners' Shanghai of old, consisting of the former International Settlement and the Bund with its famous skyline, which represents early modernism at its most self-caricaturing, like Buffalo's before urban renewal ruined it or like that of Gotham City in the original *Batman* film. The skyscrapers still stand shoulder-to-shoulder alongside the bend in the Huangpu (Whangpoo) River. But the Hongkong and Shanghai Bank at No. 18 was turned into government offices, and the British consulate at No. 33 became the Friendship Store, and the Shanghai Club, which claimed to have the longest bar in the world and stood in snooty opposition to the Cercle Sportif Français, was transformed into, of all things, a hostel for Chinese seamen.

Bund is the old Anglo-Indian term for an earthen dike or levee. Its use is fitting in that this was the stronghold of the British imperial presence, though any discussion of the foreigners' quarter must also include the quite separate French Concession, or Frenchtown, and some of the other foreign enclaves. While it lasted, the foreigners' Shanghai was a community of a few hundred thousand set inside the world's sixth-largest city, a kind of multicultural canton (no pun intended) where the various language groups mixed with one another as well as with the natives but operated pretty much as they pleased. To quote a 1934 guidebook: "The entertainment is variegated, a Hawaiian hula, Russian mazurka, Parisian apache, negro musicians, Siberian acrobats, London ballroom exhibitionists, American jazz, the Carioca, the tango, the 'dancing hostesses.' Ah!" Originally most of the dancing hostesses were White Russians, an ethnic group conspicuous even in Shanghai with its 20,000 European Jews, 25,000 Japanese, uncountable British, Americans, French, Belgians, Brazilians, Danes, Swedes, Spaniards, Italian, Dutch—and who knows how many of those curious and wonderful people (I'm always attracted to them) who appear to be all nationalities and none in particular, who seem to speak every living language and accept every currency at par, without fuss or ostentation. Of all the foreigners, only the Russians, Germans, Austrians, and Hungarians were subject to Chinese law.

The guidebook to which I refer has a few ads for doctors who specialized in venereal diseases and many for nightclubs. Sometimes the copy is quite revealing. When you read that the Canidrome Ballroom ("The Rendezvous of Shanghai's Elite") was featuring music by Buck Clayton and his Harlem Gentlemen, you get a pretty clear picture of what passed for sophistication in that time and place—and what didn't register as racism. By comparison, the Ambassador Ballroom in the avenue Edouard 7e in Frenchtown, where "Shanghai's boasted Night Life is at its gayest," promised "100 of the prettiest dancing hostesses for your entertainment." Not to be confused with the Majestic Café, which trumpeted "100 charming dancing hostesses." In any case, 100 was clearly the magic number, as it also was for the Shanghai Secondhand Store, whose proprietors could "command the resources of over 100 of the leading pawnshops in Shanghai" and so offer "bargains in rare jewellery, curios which have been the proud possessions for many generations of aristocratic families...."

The whole concept of foreignness, of being a foreigner in a place one has been taught to consider inferior, runs through the book like a red line. Readers are given a quick lesson in pidgin ("Catchee one piece rickshaw" means "Get me a rickshaw") but are warned not to insult well-spoken Chinese with such talk. The Palais Café, "Shanghai's premiere Cabaret [which] with its host of dancing partners and Peppy dance music is THE place for an EVENING of fun," unwittingly summed up what must have been the prevailing attitude when it announced the three foundations on which its business was based: "High Class Drinks. Good Service. Foreign Management." Seldom can such a hopeless place have been so hopeful, and it is in connection with such contradictions that the Peace Hotel fits so snugly. It occupies both sides of the Nanjing Road, formerly the main street of the British settlement, at right angles to the Bund. Actually it is two hotels now merged into one. The Palace, a four-storey red-brick building, was built in 1903. It is still somehow splendid but now rather cheap. Almost 60 percent of the rooms are retained permanently by foreign companies, for what made the location so desirable in the old days—its proximity to the British banks and trading houses—still applies insofar as Chinese banks and trading houses are concerned; the attraction could only grow when Shanghai succeeded in having foreign financial institutions and insurance companies readmitted to the Bund. Opposite is the younger, taller, grander former Cathay Hotel, opened in 1929. When it was still brand-new, and still the last word, Noël Coward put up there and wrote *Private Lives* in a suite with a sweeping view of the Bund. I prevailed on the good-natured manager to let me into the room with his passkey; the space had been remodelled almost out of existence, but the panorama remained, with a limitless crush of humanity immediately below the windows. The only hostility I felt directed at me anywhere in China was from young men who stared with genuine hatred as I strolled along the Bund— ironically the spot in all China with the greatest claim on cosmopolitanism and hence, or so one would hope, on tolerance as well.

Several young Chinese I spoke with said that they knew next to nothing about pre-liberation Shanghai, only that it was wild and famously sinful. "We were not even taught that much but have learned it from outside school," one explained. They were curious for more, and so I found myself in the unlikely position of telling them about their city. I tried to explain what the European buildings were supposed to represent in European terms—what Threadneedle Street and Lombard Street meant, for example— of how, for all its wide-open atmosphere, there was a countervailing if not very important element of community pride and boosterism. There were protests and demonstrations in 1932, for instance, over the opening of Josef von Sternberg's film *Shanghai Express*, in which Marlene Dietrich utters the imperishable line, "It took more than one man to change my name to Shanghai Lily."

Such was the commercial past. The commercial present, while less romantic, was considerably more pleasant. The communists had a formidable job making Shanghai work again after Liberation. When they took over, they found 30,000 prostitutes and probably the most extensive drug-addict population in the world at that time. Another legacy was balkanization. The foreigners' Shanghai was so divided that each nationality operated its own dairy, not trusting the other people's milk in a place where lack of pasteurization posed a health hazard, though hardly on the scale of cholera and typhoid. Even 40 years later the city was a maze of 24 different standards for sewer systems and electricity grids. Of course, this was also another example of how the Chinese both embraced and rejected change. A further instance would be how Shanghai's night soil was still collected in the traditional manner, even though it was no longer used by nearby farmers, who unfortunately had switched to chemical fertilizers.

If it is true to say, as I believe it is, that not even the Cultural Revolution, reign of terror though it was, was able to extinguish the spark of life in Shanghai, it is equally true to say that Shanghai returned the favour by showing communism at its most workable and livable. This second level of Shanghai consciousness is best seen along the stretch of Nanjing Road from the Bund to Nanjing Xilu, the former Bubbling Well Road, a stretch once associated with nightclubs and coffin-makers' premises but now the main shopping and business street. Nowhere else in China were people so stylishly dressed, nowhere else was such a variety of consumer goods available (a high percentage of them Shanghai-made, with electronics gear being particularly conspicuous). Only Canton had more to offer in this regard, but so much of what it bought and sold originated in Hong Kong.

In the old days there were four famous department stores in Shanghai. They were still there when I visited, with new names. They could be recommended for the sceptical (but certainly not for the claustrophobic): everything was available all the time but everybody was grabbing for it all the time as well. From certain angles, this chic and brightly lit part of downtown Shanghai resembled a vast and infinitely more complex version of Montreal—except the signs were in English.

Shanghai has always been the place to honour the past while experimenting with the future. Pedicabs were introduced in 1926 and within a generation they had doomed the rickshaw. Similarly, today you see only a few junks, unlike two decades ago and unlike present-day Hong Kong. You do, however, spot former junks, with their high sterns cut down; the last ones probably won't disappear for a decade or more. That is the normal pace of Chinese progress, but in Shanghai time generally passes a little more quickly. It was now one of several cities with a stock exchange (a misnomer; so far, trading was mostly in government bonds) and had more automobiles than anyplace else in China and, what was perhaps more telling, more telephone pagers for businessmen. To ride down the river the 25 kilometres or so to where the brown Huangpu meets the yellow Yangtze is to get a sense of what commerce is all about. For more than an hour you pass a solid row of deep-water shipping, some naval, such as the destroyer escorts and even a few old submarines, but mostly merchant vessels of every description, not only Chinese but incoming ones of many flags. People are quick to say that the citizens of Shanghai are less outward-looking now than the Cantonese, who can stay in touch with the West through Hong Kong, but the difference between the new commercial Shanghai and the pre-Liberation one—aside from a great increase in moral restraint, that is—is that the former was copied from other cultures and the latter is sui generis.

The Chinese leadership wanted slow, steady economic change but with political sameness. Sometimes the two policies came together. After Tiananmen Square, the government began punishing urban residents by making them take a portion of their salary in five-year bearer bonds—in effect, imposing a pay cut while raising money for various modernization schemes. Comparisons with the Soviets and with Eastern Europe were inevitable but maybe also without much value. The two socialisms were always different enough to deny logical collation as well as to preclude cooperation between them. Shanghai seemed poised to take advantage of whatever repercussions might follow a renewal of the pro-democracy agitation. One couldn't know what might happen following the death of the aged Deng Xiaoping. One had no way of knowing which rumours might be true. Did the government really execute a number of generals following the generals' massacre of the students? Or was the People's Liberation Army the real secret power now, with the party little more than a shell? Whatever happened, life in Shanghai didn't actually seem too bad, not as contrasted to its previous recorded high and not as compared with the rest of urban China.

The third Shanghai is the residential one that lies behind the glitter, far from the banks of the Huangpu. There was much that remained to give the feel of an old Chinese city, even if some of it included Western buildings. Life in the lanes and back streets was earthy but not squalid. Apartments were small, even smaller than in Beijing, and one of the common sights was families drying their laundry by putting bamboo poles through the sleeves and leg holes of their clothes and then shoving the poles out the window until the streets seemed to be bizarrely decorated for some holiday.

Daily life for most people was given shape by two bureaucracies, the cradle-to-grave paternalism of the factory (odd how much Chinese socialism resembles Japanese capitalism in this respect) and the equally intense pressure of the neighbourhood committee, whose members, sometimes distinguished by the armbands they wore, kept business hours in small storefront offices that you could recognize without being able to read the signs. Much in people's lives depended on their personal relations with the committee members as well as on the luck of the draw, but I was told that the neighbourhood committees in Shanghai were generally liberal and understanding, if not as compared with those in Guangzhou then certainly alongside Beijing's or the rural equivalents. I was told of a woman who recently had gone before the committee to seek permission to conceive her one allotted child. She was told that her timing was poor, for the neighbourhood had already exceeded its quota; she would have to wait. She then confessed that she had fibbed a bit. She was already pregnant and had come forward on the assumption that it would be easier to secure permission than to obtain forgiveness (my own experience of bureaucracies suggests precisely the reverse). Normal practice would have been to order an abortion—though others denied this when I repeated the story later. Instead, the committee managed to barter some perk it had lying about for one of the unused pregnancy authorizations of a committee a few streets distant, and no one was any the wiser. At age one and a half the child was to be sent to a sort of day-care centre.

Abortion, as in the Soviet Union, was free and required no one else's permission but the woman's. But unlike the Soviet Union, China had other forms of effective birth control. Condoms were free in factories or could be purchased in chemists' shops; in Shanghai two local firms manufactured them. Compared with repressed Beijing, social life was easy there. The shoppers and office workers were gone from the Bund at night and replaced by strolling lovers. Not far away in Nanjing Road was a news kiosk that even the most unobservant passerby could see was the local meeting place for gays.

Everywhere I went in China I got some sense that the level of religious activity permitted locally was another small indication of the amount of freedom in people's lives. In this respect no place was freer than Shanghai. I couldn't help but compare the Jade Buddha Temple, completed in 1918 as the resting place for a large jewel-encrusted Buddha brought from Burma a century earlier, with temples in Wuhan and elsewhere. It was closed in 1949 and narrowly survived the Cultural Revolution only to be reopened in 1980 and the monks allowed to serve the community once more. Guidebooks sometimes depict it as a tourist come-on, and to some extent that may be true; that photography has recently been permitted inside is one sign of this. But clearly this is also a genuine place of worship.

I saw young people, local people, lighting joss sticks and reciting their prayers. Christianity is the religion practised with the least interference— none that I actually witnessed. Mass is once again celebrated at St. Ignatius Cathedral, whose spires were truncated during the Cultural Revolution, and there is an American Protestant church, which I was informed had a few parishioners from beyond the small U.S. business community. There were familiar signs of a loosened grip in the Soviet Union. Certainly the Soviets had come a long way from the days when Stalin tore down the Church of Christ the Saviour to put up a building that was to be crowned with a statue of Stalin 30 metres high (the structure proved too heavy for the spongy land and a swimming pool was built on the site instead). The difference is that in the Soviet Union I still would have needed permission from the state religious affairs office to venture very far inside a working church or synagogue, especially if I wanted to talk to a priest or rabbi. In China I refrained from talking to a Christian cleric for the simple reason that I didn't actually see one, and I didn't want to intrude on any of the Buddhist priests, as the ones I saw always seemed to be at prayer.

Near one religious shrine in Shanghai I saw something that eroded my friend Tian's assertion that in China the size of the fine or penalty for a misdemeanour must always be ominous but nonspecific to make the people cower. The sign I saw clearly stated the fine for public expectoration was one yuan. Of course, this was a prohibition that no one seemed to obey, so maybe he was right after all.

The buzz in Shanghai when I was there was all about politics. The party bosses in Beijing had three concerns. That President George H. W. Bush, kowtowing to pressure from Congress, might not renew most-favoured-nation status with China. Indeed, this fear extended to the possibility that Bush might damage the economy more not only by cutting down on imports from China but perhaps by causing a big pullout in the foreign investment that China had been courting with such success right up until the time of Tiananmen. As it was, the Italian partners in one major joint venture in Shanghai had announced their intention to withdraw because business had been so poor since the massacre, only to be told that China couldn't afford to buy them out—a different situation from the one in the Soviet Union, where foreign partners were frustrated by lack of sophistication in the government and the market and the nonconvertibility of the money.

The second Chinese worry was that the pirate radio ship *Goddess of Democracy*, conceived by exiled pro-democracy students and their sympathizers, would begin its propaganda operations. In any event, America extended China's trading privileges and the radio-ship project had to be abandoned after the United States, Japan, and Taiwan closed ranks to prevent it from getting the equipment it needed. At a certain level governments always stick together, sometimes even when they are at war with one another, for war can be a kind of military collaboration against civilians. This trip was not having the slightest effect on my view of socialism one way or another, but I confess that it was adding another layer of cynicism about government.

Beijing's third fear was of course another outbreak of protest on the June 4 anniversary, and about that one they were more nervous than one might have reasonably expected them to be. With the day in question a week or so away, Jiang Zemin, the party leader, went so far as to say that security forces were being ordered to stop the hunt for students who took part in the movement. I wondered what people like Fang Lizhi and his wife Li Shuxian, who were still in hiding inside the U.S. embassy a year after fleeing there to avoid arrest, thought of that. Soldiers were out in force in Nanjing Road doing public relations duty—shining people's shoes, giving them free haircuts, testing their blood pressure, and performing other small public-health tasks.

So the place was jittery and reacted excitedly to the news, smuggled in from Hong Kong via Guangzhou, that the senior Beijing official in the Crown colony—Xu Jiatun, head of the New China News Agency there and so a kind of consul-general in waiting—had defected to California. Defection had never been an important part of the Cold War in the Pacific the way it was in relations between the Western allies and the Eastern Bloc, and indeed it wasn't entirely clear whether Xu had truly defected or had taken it on the lam; the story had a sharp effect nonetheless. Suddenly the usual Western newspapers were not on display in the hotel patronized by foreigners, and the satellite feed of CNN reverted to snow and static for a minute or two during the world news roundup. Now I found myself in a tight situation, for the stupidest of reasons.

When I had finally got my journalist's visa from the Chinese consulate in Toronto, I had given the staff there a copy of the itinerary I had already been through with the embassy people in Ottawa, and explained that I would be crossing the border by train at a certain point on such-and-such a day. They professed to understand me, and I foolishly did not bother to check their arithmetic once they returned my passport with the visa stamped inside. A chance look at it now while changing some money showed that I had been travelling for days on a visa that had expired. The consulate still thought I would be flying from Moscow to Beijing and had allowed only one day for the trip. After having so much trouble getting into China, here I was in the ridiculous position of perhaps not being able to get out.

Summoning all his reserves of calm, Wen Dong told me not to worry. These little errors in addition did happen from time to time, he said. But I could see his anxiety growing, and he would disappear at unusual times to return to his hotel room to telephone his superiors in the building on Tiananmen Square. Could they fine me for visa offences? Would they actually detain someone they were clearly hoping to be rid of? At the least I was no doubt prejudicing my future relations with the Chinese, such as the prospects were (though I was hoping most earnestly for a warming in the future—and still am). There was another problem as well. I had to be on a certain Hong Kong flight in order to make a connection to Bangkok, and now the reservation had disappeared from the computer—vanished totally—with what seemed, for a day and a night, to be slight hope of rein-statement. There were no other flights available.

We needed a plan. If some airline didn't come through with a flight out of Shanghai in time, then Wen would throw me on the train to Guangzhou (they were determined to get me to Canton one way or the other!), whence I could take another train to the frontier before it closed at 8:30 or 9:00 at night and then catch the hovercraft to Hong Kong. That still left the prob-lem of the visa. The answer was to get the Foreign Ministry to spew out some additional documents, an extension and a safe passage, and fax them to Shanghai. I gathered from Wen's expression that this was by no means so easy as it sounded, but on the third try the fax arrived. It remained only to be seen, he said, whether the notoriously officious passport officers at Shanghai airport (for by then a seat had opened up) would accept a mere facsimile as being the same as a piece of good paper with red seals and real signatures. To be safe, he called in a government specialist in VIP-handling, who had a security pass for the whole airport and seemed to know all its employees and guards and the latest triumphs and tragedies in their respective families. While I tried to look as innocent as my meagre acting talent would permit, she joked and cajoled us through customs and into the departure lounge for immigration control. Two guards stamped my passport without even looking at it. I thought I was home free.

INDOCHINA 1990

When I arrived in Bangkok, I discovered that the hotel at which I had a reservation did not exist, at least under that name and at that address. Coming as it did at midnight, after a long day of flight delays and customs queues, this was particularly discouraging. Using gestures and what he believed were a few English words, a taxi driver recommended another place, and we took off down back streets and over flimsy bridges, only to pull up at a brightly lit massage parlour several storeys high. I ventured far enough inside to see the teenage masseuses sitting in a Plexiglas room, wearing porcelain number badges on their cocktail dresses. The place was presided over by a formidable, taciturn woman who sat at the till, under twin portraits of the Thai royal family. Seeing my suitcase, she finally stirred herself enough to convey that the hotel I wanted was across the road. I left with the impression that the two businesses enjoyed an interlocking directorate.

The hotel did indeed have a room, and I dragged and pushed myself up to the top floor. There was no lock on the door. I resolved to get some sleep but to find someplace else for my second night in town before departing for Vietnam. When I awoke in the morning, there was a gecko on the wall opposite the bed. When these lizards are in a disposition to mate, they puff themselves up like Dizzy Gillespie. But this fellow was perfectly still, trying to act as though I hadn't seen him.

To my intense, almost heartbreaking disappointment I didn't make it inside Vietnam, though I did succeed in getting some fresh information about conditions there. I fear the reader may be losing patience with my tales of bureaucracy, yet I feel I should explain my failure. I shall try to be brief.

I knew of course that Vietnam was something of a shambles economically. That much had been assured by the United States, which since the end of the war in 1975 had continued to pursue its embargo against the country under the Trading with the Enemy Act of 1917 and other legislation. Only the ubiquitous and oleaginous Ted Turner had somehow managed to carry on business with them. Other nations that might have invested heavily there, such as Japan, had put in some capital but had also joined with Washington in blocking funds for Vietnam from the World Bank and the International Monetary Fund. The United States still clung to the pathetically sad notion that there continued to be American POWs held in the remote jungles. It had also gone on hating Vietnam for following its own example and invading Cambodia, which the Vietnamese did in 1978, putting an end to the four-year bloodbath of the Khmer Rouge but setting off in turn a complex four-way insurgency that only recently was showing signs of winding down.

The Vietnamese, nothing if not patient and resilient, tried to pull themselves up. For example, they revived their fishing industry, which had nearly collapsed in the late 1970s and early 1980s because so many of the fisherman had used their boats to flee the country. They climbed into the number-three ranking in world rice sales, though this was mainly a reflection of the fact that Vietnamese rice is far cheaper than, say, Thai or Chinese rice; it must be so, because it is irregularly shaped, has a nutty taste, and none of the fragrance of the competition's. Each month Vietnam sent two shiploads of rusty metal picked up from the battlefields and got two shiploads of Indonesian cement in return. Officially the economy was growing, slightly, but this was statistical distortion. Unemployment, once unheard of under socialism, was high, some said 30 percent; income was low, about US$120 per year on average. Everything except some staple foods was scarce; petrol was sold by the bottle. The foreign debt was more than US$13 billion, and one estimate put the foreign exchange reserves at only US$50 million. In 1986 the government announced its own version of *perestroika*, called *doi moi*. What choice did it have? Yet it feared the political agitation that seemed inseparable from such restructuring, judging by the very different examples of Eastern Europe, the Soviet Union, and China. Like Cuba, Vietnam saw itself standing alone and had nightmares about a U.S.-backed Contra-style insurgency that would topple the regime and exact revenge for 1975 when the tanks finally came rolling into Saigon from the north. It had gone so far as to accuse its neighbours and near neighbours, from Laos and Cambodia to democratic Thailand, of harbouring CIA-backed guerrilla training bases. Who knows?

Clearly two forces were competing for the vital energies of Vietnam's leaders: anxiety that the government might start to unravel through a combination of external pressures and domestic discontent, and a desperate need to get more foreign cash. I could tell by following the Hong Kong papers that the two were approaching a quiet collision. Officially this was "Visit Vietnam Year." Tourists were being enticed and even implored to come. But there were few facilities or guides and interpreters for them, and few approved places where they could eat. At the time of my visit there were only 1,150 hotel rooms in Ho Chi Minh City, compared with 12,000 in Bangkok, 27,000 in Hong Kong, or 27,900 in Toronto, three tourist destinations of the same population class. France and Australia, each with very different interests in the region, put some money into building up the tourist infrastructure, but most investors were reluctant because the economy was so weak. It was a vicious circle. Also, Hanoi had cracked down on individual travellers for political reasons; the issue was apparently another of the many that still divided the northern and southern parts of the country, to say nothing of the various factions within the government itself. Visit Vietnam Year was further marred, to say the least, when the police began arresting people.

In February, when I was still in Toronto wrestling with the Chinese visa problem, Hanoi started to pick up persons whom it claimed were involved in activities such as distributing subversive literature. Intellectuals and writers and Roman Catholics, both lay and clergy, were the most frequent victims. There were often assertions that the suspects had links to the United States, Britain, or France. In March a Politburo member was removed from his post for saying publicly that political liberalism could not come too soon if dissent on the Eastern European scale were to be avoided. The government was especially nervous in April, fearing that the 15th anniversary of the fall of Saigon on April 30 would be the excuse for a Tiananmen Square type of demonstration (it wasn't). May saw a similar threat in the 100th anniversary of Ho Chi Minh's birth (which turned out, by all reports, to be a rather pleasant political event—the Vietnamese don't seem to blame Ho for what has taken place since his death, the way the Russians had begun to blame Lenin and the Chinese, Mao). Yet it was also true that one of the reasons the celebration went smoothly was that so many of the potential troublemakers were locked away. Hanoi admitted arresting 14 persons in February and March. An exile group based in Paris, the Vietnam Committee on Human Rights, put the number at 6,000 for May alone, bringing the total to 14,600 for a six-month period. Yet if the Vietnam War taught the world nothing else, it taught us never to put much credence in body counts. No matter what the source. As for such dissent as remained, it took the form of agreement in principle but disagreement about methods, rather like Yeltsin in relation to Gorbachev. The Committee of Resistance, a group of heroes from the war against the Americans, believed that reform should be swifter and more sure; two of the movement's leaders were removed and placed under house arrest, the favoured method of dealing with dangerous people, real or suspected. The Committee of Resistance was linked to the north-south tension whose full extent it was difficult for an outsider to comprehend except to know that it was great. Official sources admitted that the Vietnamese army, once the world's third largest but now reduced to fewer than one million men, had a serious desertion problem. In one unit 20 percent of conscripts had gone over the hill, 34 percent in another, 50 percent in still others.

This was the atmosphere in which, while still in Shanghai, I received the alarming news about Michael Morrow, an American journalist during the war who now published *Petroleum News*, a trade magazine, in Hong Kong. By coincidence I had been reading about him only a short while earlier, about how in 1971 he broke the story revealing how Laos was permitting Yao tribespeople trained by the CIA to penetrate as much as 320 kilometres inside China on espionage missions. I knew little else about him, except that in addition to his publishing activities he did a lot of business consulting in Vietnam and that now, on his 20th visit there since the war ended, he had been picked up for spying (he was held three weeks). Technically the charge against him, according to both the *Standard* and the

South China Morning Post in Hong Kong, was that he was found in Danang, a city not named on his visa as one he was cleared to visit. The Vietnamese, I was then forced to presume, must follow the Soviet practice of listing all one's destinations on the visa and checking it at every spot. This prompted me to look at my own, which had been procured by a Vancouver travel agency that was a joint venture with the Vietnamese government. It specified no cities whatever and indeed did not seem to me, on close inspection, to be very official-looking; it was a small form that had been filled in by hand, the mistakes being covered over with correction fluid. I thought I had better make certain that I had the document I needed.

If I had begun the whole trip a few months later, I probably could have flown directly from Hong Kong to Ho Chi Minh City on Cathay Pacific. But for the moment, except for a few departures from Indonesia, Malaysia, and the Philippines, the only way into Vietnam was through Bangkok on the twice-weekly flights run by Vietnam Air, the domestic agency in partnership with Thai Airways International. The Vietnamese liked to keep control of who was coming in and when.

There was no Vietnamese consular representation in Hong Kong, only a one-person trade mission, and the person in question did not answer the phone. So when I continued on to Bangkok I called Thai Airways International, reasoning that, although it had not assisted with my own visa, it must assist with other people's, when dealing with package tours and the like. Besides, as the business partners of Vietnam Air, Thai Airways might have current information. It is often only Thais in the upper-middle class or higher who can communicate effectively in English, and of course they tend not to be people found in the service industries. That plus the Thai reluctance to conduct business over the telephone made me hire a tuk-tuk and go to the office. Mainly what I learned there was that they were pretty sure all visitors to Vietnam must arrive and depart via the same airport. This was a blow, as my ticket called for me to enter at Ho Chi Minh City and leave from Hanoi (only later did I learn from a report by the Canadian journalist Murray Hiebert in the *Far Eastern Economic Review* that Hanoi had been off-limits to foreign journalists and businesspeople for the past month). My ticket was for the following day. I tried to change it, but there seemed nothing I could do. Flights were fully booked for another two weeks and I couldn't count on travelling even then. There was virtually

no chance that a wait-listed passenger would get on. In fact, doubly recon-
firmed executives and tourists who turned up at an early hour to make
certain their names were on the handwritten departure lists were routinely
bumped off the flights anyway, after waiting half a day with their tickets in
hand; there were accounts of this mess in the newspapers. Visit Vietnam
Year indeed.

I tried to call on the Vietnamese embassy in Bangkok, hoping for I
don't know what, a kind of low-level miracle, I suppose. The legation was
right in Wireless Road, in the heart of embassy row. Less than a block away,
guarded by Gurkhas, was the sprawling and impressive British embassy,
with its famous statue of Queen Victoria—famous because some Thai
women considered it a statue of a fertility goddess and made floral offerings
to it. The Vietnamese had the most modest mission of the lot, a nondescript pale green building located, in an irony lost on no one, within sight
of the rather formidable U.S. one. The Vietnamese did, however, have the
higher flagpole. The old Vietcong ensign fluttered above the tops of the
bottle palms, slapping the face of Uncle Sam every time the wind blew.
The phone was not working, and when I did get through I exhausted five
staff members in turn, trying to explain my problem, first in English and
then in the Diefenbakerish French that is the strongest cultural bond
between the Vietnamese and the people of English Canada. All I knew at
the conclusion was that I needed a Mr. Dhan or perhaps Dhang and that
he wasn't in. Owing to the unrelieved traffic congestion, movement in
Bangkok is slow to difficult. A German entrepreneur had told me at breakfast that he could do only two or at most two and a half brief appointments
per day, owing to the tie-ups. When I got to the embassy, it was siesta time.
When I returned later, Mr. Dhan had not reappeared and was expected
only vaguely at some point in the future. The flight left without me.

But failure releases its own type of adrenaline, and I was determined to
make the best of the situation. I was in Bangkok after all, which even during
the war years was the primary listening post for Vietnam, not least because
it has a fairly large Vietnamese community going back to the days of the
French-Indochina war in the mid-1940s. Now that it was the only real
means of access and egress, it was even more full of Vietnam-watchers than
it had been for years, including the hustlers and promoters sniffing about
for something to buy or sell and the staffs at the 50 embassies in the city.

What's more, a colleague had kindly provided me with a letter of introduction to surviving cronies from his days at the *Bangkok Post*. I would set up a hectic schedule of buying drinks for people and see what I could learn, using the nights, when it was somewhat cooler, to write up these notes of the trip to date.

What I found out is what I have set down so far, but with an abundance of other detail and a bit more context. The whole region was changing quite as much as Europe was, with some developments almost as abrupt. While I was in Bangkok, for example, Burma, which has been more or less forbidden territory to foreigners since the end of the Second World War, locked in its own complex internal struggle, held its first election in 30 years. The losers (the military, who clamped down on a democracy movement in 1988) appeared determined not to vacate the palace without a fight. And the possibility of peace in Cambodia held out promise, not least because it would help end Vietnam's diplomatic isolation, particularly from China. That would affect Vietnam's potential for foreign investment; without China, and given the Americans' continued refusal to make up to the people whose country they devastated, the Taiwanese and the South Koreans would likely be the big players. Such news was another sign, as though another were needed, that a new Asia had emerged without the sort of reference to the West that had existed in the era whose artifacts I had been seeking out with an antiquary's interest: an Asia as cautious as it was monolithic.

Not that the West isn't persistent in Asia. For example, the British bank Standard Chartered, which began doing business in Saigon in the 1870s, then opened its own branch in 1904 and managed to hang on until 1977, through three wars and two years of communist rule, was moving back. In fact, for various reasons, most of them global rather than regional, English was replacing French as the second language of Vietnam. This was at least one of the pieces of news that had rankled the French, who saw their cultural stake in Vietnam, Laos, and Cambodia as inseparable from any revival, on a small scale, of their commercial interests there. "When you get to Vietnam," someone told me, "you will find French businessmen in your hotel. Most of them *are* French businessmen." The suggestion was that the others would be from the Direction Générale de la Sécurité Extérieure or some similar agency. Two diplomats told me that Canada was in an enviable position to invest in Vietnam should relations between the two countries be re-established anytime soon, in view of the special trust that attached to Canada's being French as well as English. But they felt that Canada would probably miss its chance out of deference to Washington.

No doubt I had failed to get into Vietnam by being too prudent (that will teach me), but it certainly seemed as though the Vietnamese didn't want me and that had I got in I would have had trouble getting out if for no other reason than that the authorities there, in their uncertainty, kept changing the rules every day. The Soviets didn't want me, the Chinese didn't want me, the Vietnamese didn't want me either. A less insensitive person than myself might have begun to notice a pattern. But me, I was merely glum with immediate disappointment, and in that condition I found Bangkok a demanding place to be. I went there hoping, for instance, to see a performance of the ancient *lakhon ling*, or ceremonial monkey theatre. What I saw instead, in a smart shopping street in Bangkok, was a woman with a poor dog she had dyed bright yellow.

The Thais have done a fine public-relations job on the rest of the world. Their advertising slogan is "Land of Smiles," and the visitor is bombarded with the image of happy people performing the *sawasdee* in greeting or farewell as they bring their palms together in a prayer-like gesture and give a little bow. I learned nothing of the countryside; I had planned one day to travel to Chiang Mai in the north but stopped in disgust when I read in *The Nation* that morning that the American FBI was there that week, running one of its National Academy in Asia programmes, designed to bring Thai police up to date on interrogation techniques. So I speak only of Bangkok.

Tourists are somehow led to believe that the city is as ancient as the authentic Thai culture, which began to form when the Khmer civilization was driven out some 800 years ago. In fact, Bangkok was decreed into being in the late 18th century because its defensive position on the Chao Phraya River made it a difficult target for the Burmese (who had already invaded twice, on battle elephants, and had been expelled) or the Vietnamese or the Lao. The place was meant to recapture the glories of

Ayuthaya, which had been destroyed after serving as the administrative centre for four centuries. Ayuthaya had been quite a town: it had 400 wats, and as early as the 17th century there were 47 kilometres of paved streets there. Bangkok (*bang kok*, village of the plum-olive trees) was a poor substitute, despite a system of canals, which are mostly now either filled in or stagnant.

I had the poor luck to be there when the weather was both too hot and too rainy. You had only to step outside early in the morning to be bent down by the heat, which had the force and effect of gravity. Then the rain would descend. It was a punctual, work-to-rule kind of rain. Once a year the river spills its banks and inundates the city to a depth of a metre or more. The floods are a little worse each time because Bangkok, like Shanghai, is built on ooze and is steadily sinking—in Bangkok's case by 12.5 centimetres per annum.

Thailand managed to escape colonization by the British, Dutch, or French, but sided with the Japanese in the Second World War and so briefly became a colonial power itself when it was given parts of Laos and Cambodia as an immediate reward (but was forced to return them in 1945). Then it came into the American orbit. After a series of coups and counter-coups, the most recent in 1981, it remains what it has been for so long, a constitutional monarchy that is more or less run by the military. Still, the country is far less authoritarian than Singapore, and quite stable as well, despite having had 11 constitutions since 1932. Thais are also the world's most vocal monarchists. They are serious about their Buddhism as well, though devotion varies according to generation and locality. Most people practise Hinayana Buddhism, except for the Vietnamese and the residents of Chinatown, who are Mahayana Buddhists; there are also more than two million Sunni Muslims, mostly in the south, and a couple of hundred thousand Shi'ites. Bangkok, where monks often have their photographs taken blessing new places of business, has a lot of wats for the tourists. While I was there I was struck by a press report from Phuket province of a monk addicted to heroin who beat a brother monk to death inside their temple with a wooden pole; the motive was robbery. Section 206, subsections 2 and 7 of the Criminal Code make it an offence "To use the lower part of the body to point to a statue of Buddha, pagoda, stupa, mosque, or cross" and "To put a statue of Buddha, or the head of such a statue, in a wardrobe together with men's or women's clothing."

Of all the world's peoples, perhaps only Americans are more patriotic than the Thais. Like many others before me, I have often observed that this emotion is sometimes found in conditions that are favourable to the cultivation of hypocrisy, and I couldn't help but notice that movies shown on cable television are censored, clumsily and heavily, to remove the slightest reference to sex. I speak not of what Americans call X- or even PG-rated movies but of routine inoffensive Hollywood films. "The censors," I was told, "apparently have an interest in the video stores, all of which have uncensored films for hire in the back rooms. Everyone here is on the fiddle, you see." Notwithstanding that perfectly logical if inaccurate explanation, I found such censorship, and Thai prudery in general, somewhat curious in a place where sleazy sex is one of the biggest industries, employing, if that is the right word, up to one million Thai women, or one in every 55 citizens, and bringing in uncounted wealth in foreign exchange.

Everybody knows about Patpong, the sex district—actually Patpongs I and II, a couple of parallel streets, now augmented by such others as Soi Cowboy off Sukhumvit near Soi 21. Defenders like to suggest that this represents the continuation of a tradition with roots in ancient Thai culture. In fact, Thailand's first massage parlour opened only in 1956, offering the sort of legitimate "traditional" or "Thai" massage once administered by masseuses outside wats. The place had a mainly Japanese clientele and was soon driven out of business by "massage" parlours. Bangkok was the closest and least expensive of the R and R destinations for American servicemen in Vietnam, and it is widely supposed that it was they who remade the face of Patpong, as they did Kings Cross in Sydney. "But in the days before the Vietnam buildup," writes Alan Dawson, a Canadian journalist who was given U.S. citizenship for fighting on the American side, "Patpong was without doubt a respectable street, although a drink was available." Girlie bars didn't begin concentrating there until the 1970s. But it is easy to see how the misconception began, given that the dominant type of performing was and remains what was called (I write this for the benefit of Young People) go-go dancing. Sex-for-hire as an economic staple came slightly later. Live sex acts on stage as a form of theatre arrived only in the mid-1980s; the first establishment to make a speciality of them was owned by a former police officer. Yet if it is not literally correct to say that the Vietnam War made Patpong what it is today, it is surely true to say that the Vietnam

War aesthetic still flourishes there—after a rough couple of months killing Buddhist rice farmers, what better relaxation than enslaving young Thai girls from the countryside (the legal age is 13 and the slavery is disguised by contract)? The sex shows are nothing that a grown man hasn't seen before without any benefit whatsoever and that women would wish to see even less—prostitutes shooting darts at a balloon using only their vaginal muscles, for example. As for actual sex, all other considerations aside, a person would have to be suicidal to buy any in Bangkok. AIDS is a touchy subject, related as it is to the balance of payments, but various estimates put the rate of HIV infection among massage personnel at between 50 and 80 percent, rising as one goes farther down the price scale, which tracks the educational curve. The newspapers accept advertisements for heterosexual sex only, but to judge from the abundant promotional matter of other types, perhaps half of the sex-for-sale is gay sex, and this no doubt has some influence on the AIDS problem.

The area is not without its crime problem as well. I copied the following from a handbook of advice for visitors. It was written by a local solicitor whose knowledge of English is less advanced than his practical counsel:

> I have known some message from a newspaper that there are evil person gangs act in a manner likely giving well-intentioned advice by volunteer to keep a credit card of tourist by using any means of fraud until a tourist approves. And then the evil persons gangs will take the credit card to change money wonderfully that the tourists has not known about this. The tourist has known that not money in his credit card when he has come back to his house. Then it is too late. So you should keep your credit card with yourself all the time.

Under a government and a military so conservative that a core of powerful people persisted in prepping mentally for a Vietnamese invasion, Thailand longed to practise slash-and-burn capitalism. With commodity prices up, manufacturing coming abreast of agriculture, and exports bounding, there was money in the air. In 1989 the U.S. economy grew by 2.9 percent, the Japanese by 4.8 percent, and the Thai by 11 percent. But the price of profit was high. The country's attitude towards the environment had always been casual, and now air, water, and land pollution were becoming alarming; I saw a few people in Bangkok wearing face masks, in the Japanese manner. Urban planning and even zoning were primitive and the construction boom was rapidly depriving Bangkok of its old charm. There were over 30 million people in the country's labour force (70 percent of them still in agriculture), but that figure took into account ones as young as 11. Many workers first had to buy their jobs from employers for cash. But every month 4,000 Thai technicians, some of them the best-trained individuals in the labour pool, left for contract positions in Saudi Arabia—or did, until the Iraqi occupation of Kuwait. This outflow was halted at one point after three Saudi diplomats were assaulted in Bangkok and in retaliation the Saudis stopped giving out work visas; at the time of the Kuwait invasion, which changed the whole picture in the Middle East, there were believed to be 150,000 Thais working for the Saudis.

Like the Soviet Union, like China, like Vietnam, Thailand was undergoing a kind of revolution or counter-revolution or whatever you wished to call it. Like the Soviet one in particular, it had less to do with ideology than with necessity, but the aim was similar in all these cases: to create a middle class where there was none before. Hong Kong was different. It had a middle class but was having difficulty holding on to it.

In 1990, 500 resident Canadians in Thailand were registered with the Canadian embassy in Bangkok, which was one of the Fort Zinderneufs of the external affairs department; there were probably as many again who had not checked in. But fully 100,000 Canadian tourists travelled to Thailand every year, a threefold increase since 1985. By comparison there were only 200,000 U.S. visitors in Thailand annually, an indication that a decade and a half after the late unpleasantness in Vietnam, the Americans were still skittish about Southeast Asia. Hong Kong, though, had 30,000 Canadian expatriates, and the Canadian commission there was by far the busiest post in our diplomatic system insofar as visa applications were concerned. The reason of course was that so many Hongkongese were attempting to get into Canada.

At the time about 600 per week were boarding what people there called the Maple Leaf Express, and the number was climbing quickly. Some upper-middle- and upper-class Hong Kong people had begun to send their friends emigration cards. These were similar to change-of-address cards and often concluded with the sentiment, "We look forward to seeing you in Canada." One Hong Kong newspaper columnist observed that when a person idly asked an expectant mother where she intended to have her baby, the woman answered not by specifying a hospital but a country— Hong Kong or Canada. This atmosphere was reflected in ways both subtle and obvious. Suddenly the *Globe and Mail* was easy to find in Hong Kong. And whereas Canadian furs were all but banned from the marketplace in Europe, they were very popular in stiflingly hot Hong Kong, as long as the shop had *Canada* in its name and the goods were expensive.

Education was another field where Canadianism was a fashionable necessity. "School here is a business," Margaret Greer, 28, told me. "Only 30 percent of students attend the fully funded government schools." The rest went to privately funded ones like Delia School of Canada, where both she and her husband, Garry, 38, taught for almost two years before returning to their home in Kingston. The oldest, most exclusive private schools in the colony, such as King George V School, locally known as KG5, were still the most desirable, but lately there had been a boomlet in schools that had accreditation from one or more Canadian provinces and thus promised the graduate easy passage to some Canadian universities. The Delia School had about 525 primary and secondary students learning the Ontario and the Nova Scotia curricula respectively. The Canadian Overseas School, across the harbour on the Kowloon side, offered the Ontario curriculum exclusively; a school opened in autumn 1990 offered the Manitoba programme. Not since Expo and the Centennial had Canadian culture been so popular anywhere outside Canada, but this time the reasons were different. Not admiration but panic, not respect but curiosity and fear of the future.

Hong Kong became a British Crown colony of immense sophistication and enormous wealth as a result of the biggest drug deal in history, and now the deal was turning sour, almost a century after it went down. In the Convention of Chuen Pee at the conclusion of the opium war of 1841, China was compelled to cede Hong Kong Island to the British in perpetuity. In 1860 the tip of the Kowloon Peninsula and a dollop of land called Stonecutters Island were also signed away forever. But in 1898, in the Second Treaty of Peking, the British didn't press so hard to get freehold;

the 588 square-kilometre area called the New Territories was leased for only 99 years, like a London townhouse. As the last few precious years drained away, people grew uneasy, then worse than uneasy. The negotiation that began in 1982 and concluded in 1984 about how the People's Republic would take over and manage the colony was little comfort. After the slaughter in Tiananmen Square and the ongoing repression that followed, whatever hope there was turned to dread, even terror.

The deliberate shows of confidence in Hong Kong that were underway before the massacre were carried forward (though when I was there, Hong Kong came to realize that Donald Trump, given his financial reverses in New York, would not build a Trump Tower in the colony, as he had planned). Certainly many locals, as well as the British, continued to invest and breed, attracted, to no one can say what extent, by gambler's daring and the smell of a bargain. Yet such activity seemed to be so much whistling past the graveyard. On closer examination the rats, such as Rupert Murdoch, who sold his half-interest in the *South China Morning Post*, were deserting, or at least making contingency plans, and the most conspicuous new building in Hong Kong, and perhaps its most conspicuous man-made landmark, was the tower of the state bank of the People's Republic of China. Beijing also announced its intention of helping to build the new airport that would stabilize confidence and be a symbol of the continuity of capital.

What all this meant for Hong Kong citizens was that those who could secure a foreign passport were doing so. One New Canadian in six was from Hong Kong. To stem the flow into Britain, the government, after a lengthy debate, reluctantly announced that it would grant U.K. passports to 50,000 administrators and officials in the colony—about 250,000 people in all, when family members were included. The plan was that, by dispensing such peace of mind, London would be permitting the colony to run smoothly for the next several years, because the key personnel would know that they had a place to go after the changeover; but Beijing saw this merely as a way to ensure British influence into the new century. Meanwhile, at the level of individual souls, the desperation became more apparent. People whose whole lives were rooted in the concept of the family shut up aged parents in nursing homes and disowned children with handicaps so that nothing would impede their desirability as immigrants to Canada or some other place. Dead relatives were less of a problem: cremation, which took place in only 50 percent of cases a decade earlier, climbed to 90 percent, as Chinese emigrants took their ancestors with them. The love and enjoyment of wealth, with which Hong Kong had been associated for so long, seemed now to be giving way to a deeper greed, as people attempted to make as much money as they could as quickly as they could, in preparation for a rainy day—the skies were darkening already.

I found three sets of public-service ads running on television one evening. The first urged citizens to turn in members of the triads who might try to extort money or do violence against them. The second pleaded with gang members to turn themselves in (which they were all the more reluctant to do because it had been understood that organized crime infiltrated the Royal Hong Kong Police). The third advertisement was for more police recruits.

There was in-migration to counterbalance but by no means cancel out the out-migration: the Vietnamese boat people who started coming in 1978. The pace of reform in Vietnam remained such that Hong Kong, for all its problems, looked pretty attractive. The thought of Hong Kong under Chinese rule was of course less terrifying to the Vietnamese than it was to even the smallest of Hong Kong capitalists, not only the silk-suited young men with their cell phones who made deals on street corners but even those sampan-dwellers with their pocket scales for weighing small quantities of fish and rice.

Hong Kong had been inundated with refugees before, after the collapse of the Qing dynasty in 1911, after Shanghai fell first to the Japanese in 1937 and then to the communists in 1950. However dislocating those movements were, they also benefited Hong Kong by remaking it, reinvigorating it. The colony's history as a textile centre, for example, might be attributed to Mao Zedong. But this time the situation was different. The arrivals were locked up until they could be sent back home.

The profile of the boat people was changing, and various authorities professed to find good news in the shifting statistics. When the Western media began repeating the horror stories about Thai pirates preying on boat people, the government in Bangkok responded by setting up a commission for the suppression of piracy, which then claimed to show that its efforts cleaned up the sea lanes. In fact, the number of reported incidents—

of the small percentage actually reported—declined because most of the refugees were, in fact, ethnic Chinese from southern Vietnam who could smuggle themselves across the border into the People's Republic and only then use a boat to descend the Pearl River to Hong Kong, where some 90 percent of them were turned away on the grounds that they were merely economic migrants, not refugees. The others were sent to detention camps to await enforced repatriation. The month I was there 800 boat people still made it to Hong Kong, compared with 9,000 in the same month one year earlier. At the same time the police made a sweep of one camp, Whitehead, acting in response to stories of gang violence inside, and took away 180 people, some of them minors, and then made the rounds of the other camps scattered in secluded spots round the territory while a special facility was set aside for troublemakers. The camps were overseen by the United Nations High Commission for Refugees, but the agency was quickly running out of money.

My last day before returning to Canada I talked my way into one of the camps—Bowring, in the Tuen Mun District. It was only one-fifth the size of Whitehead but housed about 1,000 men and women (average age 35) and an equal number of children. They were crowded into Nissen huts formerly used for British troops and now fitted out as crude dormitories, the tiers of bunks separated by blankets. The air was heavy with the smell of cooking fish and the odour of too many bodies in too small a space. The light was poor, and people's laundry hung everywhere. There was a school and a small library within the compound. Atop a tiny hill, isolated from the other buildings, was L Block, a brick building divided into 10 airless cells, each about 1.5 by 2.5 metres. This was where the problem cases were kept. Problem cases were defined as those caught stealing or fighting or abusing women. A week earlier Hong Kong police made one of their surprise inspections at seven in the morning and confiscated a quantity of homemade weapons, yet the owners of them weren't put in the cells. The people at Bowring were Vietnamese rather than ethnic Chinese, and they were all from the north. Those from the south and those from the north had to be kept in separate camps lest they killed one another; perhaps this was the most telling of all indications of what Vietnam was like 15 years after Reunification.

"This is an open centre," William Lau, the head of Bowring, explained to me as we tramped around the compound, with small children darting round us but the adults keeping their distance, pretending to be busy and otherwise avoiding eye contact with us. "This means that under the reforms that came into effect last month, the people here are free to find jobs on the outside and return at night." They left their identification with the guards when they went out and retrieved it when they came back in the evening. These were all legitimate refugees fleeing persecution, the others having been screened out and made to wait to be returned. They were to stay here "a year or two" before they moved on to a third country, assuming they had relatives to sponsor them in Canada, the United States, Australia, or elsewhere. It was expected that by 1997 there would be a buildup of as many as 30,000 people who could not return but were rejected for life elsewhere.

Lau told me, "We have many voluntary agencies involved here, and Hong Kong people run a job placement bureau." The most common jobs were as labourers. "Sanitation is a big worry. Health care is generally better. We have an English nurse." A sort of prisoners' committee met every Wednesday morning to work out complaints and resolve difficulties with Lau and his staff, who spent some of their time arranging for donations of food. Someone gave one tonne of candy, which just before I arrived had been made up into individual bags.

After the tour, we repaired to Lau's office, where I saw the results of the morning's roll call written on a chalkboard: "In camp, 2050. Missing, 157. Detained by police, 1." He asked me where I was from, and when I told him, he replied, "Ah, yes, Kingston in Canada, a beautiful spot. I have taken a boat tour of the Thousand Islands."

I expressed surprise that he had been there. He answered that he knew Ontario well, because his brother now worked for IBM in Toronto, their parents had moved to Don Mills, and he was hopeful—though he hadn't heard the decision yet—that his daughter might be accepted at the University of Toronto.

As I was leaving, he said to me, "Perhaps you and I shall meet again one day when my work here is done." He was not being sly or ironic.

"Maybe so," I replied. "That would be pleasant." We shook hands, and he walked me to the checkpoint where there was a gate in the barbed-wire fence. Two English guards were cracking jokes on the other side.

TAIWAN

Prologue

I stood on the spot where the Third World War almost broke out—twice. I was on the island of Kinmen, then known as Quemoy. Kinmen is one of two tiny subsidiary islands (the other, Matsu, retains its old name) that were the subject of ongoing disputes between the Chinese nationalists of the Republic of China on Formosa (now Taiwan) and the Chinese communists of the People's Republic of China. I was on my second sojourn in Taiwan, completing a self-assigned mission to make a complete circuit of the island. The visit to Kinmen was a side-trip but, to me, a vitally important one.

Kinmen, about 1,200 kilometres from the Taiwanese capital of Taipei, is only three kilometres wide at its narrowest and approximately 20 kilometres long; it is a low, desolate sort of place, a brown-and-green land of sand dunes and caves, of razor wire and camouflaged bunkers, and it is surrounded on three sides by fingers of the communist Mainland. At high tide the two ideologies are separated by only 2.2 kilometres of water; at low tide, 1.7. I clambered up onto one of Kinmen's uncountable defensive works to squint across the water at members of the People's Liberation Army who, I had no doubt, were squinting back at me. Such situations imparted an eerie feeling.

In a sense, my generation had grown up with the events that happened, or threatened to happen, there. In 1949 the Chinese civil war finally ended when Generalissimo Chiang Kai-shek abandoned Mainland China to his old adversary Mao Zedong and retreated. Chiang took the entire infrastructure of the Kuomintang (or Nationalist Party) with him, and reassembled it on the offshore province of Formosa, only recently returned to China after a half-century occupation by the Japanese. Assured of continued U.S. support simply because he opposed communism, Chiang dug in and awaited developments (while misappropriating billions of U.S. dollars—1940s and 1950s U.S. dollars—for the benefit of the Chiang family).

Chiang didn't have to wait long. In October 1949 Quemoy was attacked by 10,000 communist troops, who were repelled by the nationalists. There was always the fear, the danger, the presumption, that the United States would come to the nationalists' aid militarily, not just economically, as it would continue to do for another 30 years. The touchiest moment was August 23, 1958, when Mao's troops tried again. On the ground the two sides engaged in an artillery duel that lasted 44 days; in the skies the nationalist air force, showing what was called the *chien-chia* spirit of the Second World War, shot down 32 Soviet-made MiG-17s. One day three nationalist generals were killed by an exploding shell; Chiang's life was spared only because he had gone back for his hat.

The crisis atmosphere waxed and waned but never seemed to vanish. Today the 1960 presidential debates between John F. Kennedy and Richard Nixon are remembered as a test of the candidates' telegenic attributes. We've forgotten that one of their major arguments was over the crisis on Quemoy and Matsu. As recently as the late 1970s, the two Chinas were still firing artillery shells at each other (although only on alternating days, so as to conserve ammunition).

The Taiwanese still had 30,000 very lonely troops on tiny Kinmen and another 100,000 in reserve, ready to be moved there on short notice. But the tension between the rivals, each claiming to be the legitimate heir to Sun Yat-sen's overthrow of the last imperial dynasty in 1911, had changed focus. It had changed focus geographically (recently the potential flashpoint in the war of words between the two contenders had moved to the Spratly Islands in the South China Sea). But it had changed focus politically as well. There was current talk in Taiwan of turning Kinmen into a tourist area (an idea I couldn't imagine working unless the planners visualized a Cold War theme park).

Some thought Prime Minister Pierre Trudeau's official recognition of the People's Republic of China in 1970 was the beginning of the end for

Taiwan's claim to importance, especially when President Richard Nixon, for his own reasons, followed suit, recognizing the government at Beijing and cutting off the one at Taipei. There the standoff remained until the sound of a ticking clock grew louder. Everyone knew that in 1898 the British had taken a lease on most of Hong Kong for only 99 years. As 1997 drew nigh, the whole complexion of Asian politics began to change. Beijing's massacre of thousands of pro-democracy demonstrators at Tiananmen Square in 1989 only increased fears of what sort of repressive measures might be brought to bear on a Hong Kong grown used to British-style democracy.

In Beijing, Deng Xiaoping had been experimenting with vast economic reforms (such as ending communal farming, and encouraging limited capitalism, including stock markets). But these changes brought no significant improvement in human rights. To be sure, life was better in Mainland China than during the terror of the Cultural Revolution in the 1960s, but no better than it had to be to keep the peace. Beijing had promised that Hong Kong would have special status within the People's Republic, for it was, and is, a valuable magnet for hard currency: controlling Hong Kong is like owning a giant casino. But to people living in the colony, the prospect of being run by the People's Liberation Army was not a happy one. The result was a great new Chinese diaspora that changed the faces of such cities as Vancouver and Sydney, making them wealthier than they had ever been.

Another of the urban centres to benefit, although somewhat differently, was Taipei, which hoped (and hopes) to gain if Hong Kong turns sour under the communists, by becoming a safe harbour for free enterprise and state-of-the-art communications. Even if Hong Kong were grafted back onto the body of China successfully, the Taiwanese, or some of them, still stood to benefit. If Hong Kong could be smoothly reintegrated into the life of Mainland China after only 100 years, then why not Taiwan after only 50?

These questions described the schematic lines around Taiwanese politics. One faction of the ruling Kuomintang (much improved from the KMT of Chiang Kai-shek) was still in power at the time under discussion, despite the end of martial law and the beginning of democracy in the late 1980s. It continued to maintain, officially at least, that Taipei was the capital of all

China. Younger people, most of them born after their parents' or grandparents' relocation to the island, rejected even the faintest trace of this polite fiction. They sought to declare a new and second Chinese republic that would scheme and beg for admittance to the United Nations, the World Bank, and other international bodies.

Any move in such a direction, however, provoked a near-violent response from the People's Republic. The most recent manifestation had started in the spring of 1995 and had sunk Sino-American relations to their lowest level since the Tiananmen shootings. For 16 years Taiwanese officials had been refused entry to the United States for fear of irritating the People's Republic. But with the Republicans resurgent in Congress, a decision was made to allow Taiwanese President Lee Teng-hui to appear in Ithaca, New York, as a private citizen to make a non-partisan convocation address at Cornell University, his alma mater. Beijing was furious. In the West the slick and patient Taiwan lobby was delirious. Both sides saw Lee's visit as the thin edge of the wedge. Which was why standing on Kinmen was charged with such symbolism. Metaphorically the gap of 1.7 kilometres was either about to widen considerably, or to close up entirely.

Early in 1996 Taiwan held its first-ever free election for national president. This was an election that Canadians should have paid attention to for several reasons. It was going to affect the face of what was virtually the only country in East Asia where human rights and democracy, while far from perfect, were rapidly improving. More parochially, the vote promised to affect one of the trading partners with whom Canada's relationship was growing. By 2020 total economic activity in East Asia will exceed the combined total for Europe and North America. Taiwan is one of our best opportunities to wring some advantage from a transition we can do little to influence.

But I was also drawn to write about Taiwan for its own sake. This nation or province (the term you choose reveals your sympathies) has had a turbulent and schizophrenic past but is now at some sort of crossroads, for the ambitious capitalist state that has become one of Asia's great economic powerhouses is also a self-conscious semi-nation struggling for respect in the shadow of its nearest neighbour. Something about Taiwan will strike Canadians as familiar.

1

Taiwan 1991

My timing was impeccable, as usual. People kept apologizing, saying, "This is the last typhoon of the season," as though I had arrived just a few days earlier than I should have to discover their dirty little secret. The long flight from Los Angeles took no cognizance of Typhoon Ruth, as this one had been named by its proud parents at the Central Weather Bureau. By the time we arrived at Taipei, however, the storm was moving northwest from the top of the Philippines, across the Bashi Channel. Such was the usual avenue.

There was probably never any fear that Ruth would trigger one of the official CWB Emergency Alerts ("Move furniture away from windows...roll up rugs and place them on your furniture"). But a Condition 24 was certainly likely ("Fill your vehicle with gasoline"), perhaps a Condition 12 ("Store extra drinking water"), maybe even an old-fashioned Condition 6 ("Do not travel unless necessary"). Like the evil spirits of Chinese mythology that move in straight lines, the storm lost much of its power by making a sharp change in direction, until it travelled at 60 metres a second over a 300-kilometre front. Its main effects seemed to be this extraordinary rain, which gave every pedestrian a perfectly horizontal shower bath, and the fact that 700 tourists were stuck on the Pescadores, in the Taiwan Strait, and on Lanyü and the other islands on the Pacific side. Alas, those were my destinations.

The little 28-seat aircraft that made the one-hour trip to those places were grounded. When the storm passed, they stayed in their hangars one more day, for prudence's sake. Then yet another day, just in case, while I twiddled my thumbs in the capital, window-shopping, reading the newspapers, staying out of trouble. Then no amount of coaching could bring the planes out, at least for as long as I remained in Taiwan. "You would require a guide and the guides don't go at this time of year," the Government Information Office told me. I came just at the moment when summer became winter. So I sat down to enjoy some winter days in Taipei, where at least the politics were interesting, where in recent years fistfights and brawls had become common in the legislature.

In 1949 the communists drove Chiang Kai-shek and his Kuomintang political apparatus, his army and supporters, from Mainland China to the offshore province of Formosa, about 160 kilometres away. From then until 1989 the two countries were officially at war. On occasion there would be threats of violence to back up the mere theory. The tension level was not directly related to the fevers and bouts of hypothermia that made up the Cold War in Europe. But the cycle was similar, because at base the antagonists were the same.

On the one hand, there were the Americans who had been pouring money into Chiang's army and government since the 1920s in an effort to maintain China as a right-wing totalitarian country, and on the other, America's supposed nemesis, the worldwide communist conspiracy (Chinese branch). In more recent times, as other concerns came to occupy Washington's attention in Asia and elsewhere, the standoff in China cooled, but in cooling it solidified even harder, like lava turning into obsidian. Even after Chiang's death in exile in 1975 (an exile he made into a kind of rival reality), the Taiwanese nationalists and the Mainland communists would still cling to their respective policy-fictions.

The People's Republic of China claims to consist of 22 provinces— 21 on the Mainland and the rebellious Taiwan a short distance across the water. Taiwan, for its part, claimed with equal conviction for more than a half century to be the real China, the Republic of China, from which the other 21 provinces had broken away, with their illegitimate and bogus government in Beijing (which Taiwan calls Peking, refusing to adopt the Mainland romanization reforms). In the official view of Taiwan and the

Kuomintang (or in the Mainland spelling, Guomintang), which still ruled it, this island was not the home of a government-in-exile but of the legitimate Republic of China established by Sun Yat-sen in 1912 following the overthrow of the last imperial dynasty, the Qing. The fact that Taiwan is less than 400 kilometres long and had 20 percent fewer people than Canada, while the People's Republic is 9.6 million square kilometres and had 1.2 billion, a quarter of the world's population, did not influence the mutual make-believe, the suspension of belief that was American policy from the start and continued until Richard Nixon recognized the People's Republic, and Taiwan's diplomatic integrity started to bleed away.

America long maintained its own double standard with a two-China policy (first postulated by Canada in 1966). This was useful during the Vietnam War when Taiwan was needed as an ally in a hostile region (and as yet another R and R site). In 1978, with the Vietnam War over, Jimmy Carter called a halt to America's part in the charade by ending U.S. diplomatic relations with Taiwan in order to placate the People's Republic. Taiwan then withdrew from the United Nations, refusing to take part as long as the People's Republic was a member. Today Taiwan enjoys normal official relations with few other countries but vigorous trade with many, making do with a tangle of trade missions, foreign chambers of commerce, and other sub-diplomatic structures to facilitate communication and consular necessity.

So the Asian Cold War lingered on. It was coming to a conclusion only now, owing not to the economic collapse of one side as in Europe but rather thanks to an economic boom on the other. By 1991 Taiwan had a per capita income of about US$20,000 (as against about $24,000 in the United States itself), and was the world's 12th largest economy (Canada ranked seventh). Of all the economies of Asian countries, including those of Singapore, South Korea, and Thailand, only Japan's had had faster growth. Taiwanese were still forbidden to trade with the Mainland directly, but through intermediaries in Hong Kong they now owned 3,000 factories and other businesses in the People's Republic. Like Americans relocating below the Mexican border, they were going where labour was cheap and environmental laws lax. And there was the added dimension of racial, national, and familial loyalty as well.

A number of Asian countries are referred to in the media as "economic miracles." In Taiwan's case the miracle has certain appealing aspects not so easily associated with other places where there's a Rolex on every wrist and a Rolodex on every desk. When Chiang set about digging in at his former fortress of an island, Taipei was a poky, dusty place of low stucco buildings with red tile roofs. (You can see a few of them yet, hiding in the shadows of the office blocks and hotels that line its straight, wide boulevards.) Its population was only 600,000 and people got around by bicycle or three-wheeled pedicab. Today, with slightly fewer people than Toronto, Taipei has more taxis than either London or Paris, and is materialistic to a fault but not to the point of pathology like Hong Kong or Tokyo. The crowds and the traffic were a nightmare made worse by the construction of an enormous elevated rapid transit system. But it's peaceful and clean next to Bangkok, say. And while the Kuomintang continued to reign, Taiwan as compared to Singapore was no longer a particularly authoritarian place, or at least it had become far less so recently. The instructional video shown on incoming China Air flights was out of date in suggesting that strict foreign exchange controls were still observed or that one couldn't bring in *Playboy* or decks of playing cards. Taiwan wallowed in foreign-exchange reserves, and at one point the government even tried operating casinos to encourage tourism in remote areas: an experiment that failed only because it wasn't making enough profit. Only murder and kidnapping still carried the death penalty, making Taiwan far more liberal in this respect than the United States.

Under Chiang Kai-shek and his family, there were opposition parties in Taiwan in name only. But now there was a real one, the Democratic Progressive Party. There was also freedom of expression. Although 80 percent of the press was still controlled by the KMT, the remaining 20 percent was unmuzzled to a remarkable extent—certainly as compared with television, which was still licensed by the Ministry of Defense. There were movements towards a new kind of democracy—halting, uncertain, sometimes grudging steps, but the thrust was clear. In this instance they seemed inseparable from the rise in living standards, education, and general prosperity. In one long generation the Fujianese and Guangdongese who fled to Taiwan did amazingly well for themselves. Now in their twilight years, some of them were beginning to look back at the land of their youth, where many already had investments. This pragmatic nostalgia was becoming a powerful force in the politics of Taiwan and the region, but the island and the Mainland have had a longer, more intricate relationship than most of us with comparatively little past have realized.

Typhoon Ruth never rose to its full potential (nor did Seth, which followed immediately), but neither did it go away. The manager of the nondescript hotel where I stayed set up a visual aid in the lobby, a plywood map on which he plotted the storm's progress by moving a red ball higher up the display, like a local United Way chairperson showing how much money had been collected thus far and what the goal was. My hosts were probably right to be concerned. Conditions to the south remained unpredictable. On the third day a freighter bound from Hong Kong to Taichung was thought to have gone down in heavy seas near the Penghu archipelago, or the former Pescadores, with 18 crew members missing (in fact, it ran aground and all were rescued). For the time being we remained in the north and I looked elsewhere for what I was seeking, which was some place that showed in sedimentary strata some of the pre-Kuomintang history of Taiwan. A pretty consistent history it is, too. Hundreds of years before the communist revolution, the island seems always to have been someone's refuge and the refuge in turn a provocation to the conquerors from whom the people had fled.

Most Taiwanese live on the coastal plain facing the Mainland, which is industrial and agricultural by turns. The plain on the Pacific side is much narrower and less productive (cement and marble quarrying are its two big industries). It is therefore less populous as well. The middle of the island is taken up by the Central Mountain Range, which keeps cross-island communications rather basic, especially during landslide season. In the half-light of a misty morning these mountains, rising two, three, even four thousand metres in one case, look as if they've come to life from a scroll painting.

In the mountains and in some of the places around the edges, and on islands such as Lanyü, live a large but diverse group of aboriginal peoples, descendants of those who came originally from the Philippines and other spots to the south or from Polynesian islands far to the east. These peoples were driven into the mountains by the Hakka, a despised minority from northern China who had been pushed off the Mainland and across the strait. The descendants of the Hakka still constitute about five percent of Taiwan's population. Taiwan has been a nest used by successive generations of birds, each forced out by the next—until now. It was the same with the Europeans when they arrived. The Portuguese got there first (hence place names such as Formosa and the Pescadores), but they had the island to themselves as a staging area for the China trade for only a few years, until 1624, when the Dutch East India Company established itself on the south-west coast. In 1641 the Dutch forcibly put an end to a Spanish incursion in the north and became thereby masters of all the commercially desirable parts of the island for the next 20 years.

Taiwan has three national heroes of ultra-legendary status. In reverse chronological order they are Chiang Kai-shek, his mentor Dr. Sun Yat-sen, the founder and first president of the Chinese republic, and Cheng Chenhkung, a Ming general and sometime pirate who defeated the Dutch in 1661. Like Chiang 200 years later, Cheng, who is usually called Koxinga in English (on the Mainland, Coxinga), was blown across the strait by events he could no longer control. The arrival of the Manchus from the north having put an end to the Ming dynasty, Koxinga fled to Taiwan with 30,000 soldiers in 800 war junks. Six months later he had driven the Dutch from the island and began dreaming, like Chiang Kai-shek after him, of reconquering the Mainland. But instead the Mainland invaded Taiwan (as had been about to happen to Chiang when the Korean War intervened and the Americans interposed the Seventh Fleet between the two enemies). Now the Mainland itself was a kind of colonizing force and Taiwan, as usual, the unwilling host. Not until 1887, when it already had a population of 2.5 million, did Taiwan become a full province of imperial China, rather than a mere county of Fujian province.

With Typhoon Ruth now downgraded to mere tropical-storm status, but with the wind still kicking up, I set off northward out of Taipei along the Tanshui River to the town of the same name, a not very popular tourist destination where much of Taiwan's history converges in a cluster of build-ings called Fort San Domingo. I've always been attracted to structures that bear the cumulative traces of sequential occupation, particularly if the remnants are highly improbable or contradictory. There's a building on a side street in downtown Toronto, once a synagogue, which I've watched become a Korean Baptist church, a community crisis bureau, and a day-care centre, as the texture of the neighbourhood has changed. Not far away is the site of a tiny storefront, now razed, which I can remember being the headquarters of every conceivable political group over the years, not excluding the Trotskyites. Fort San Domingo is similar in a way.

As its name suggests, this mountain outpost overlooking the sea to Kuanyin Mountain is evidence of the brief Spanish interlude in Taiwan, practically the only such evidence left today. The Spanish rebuilt it following an attack by the aboriginals. It fell to the Dutch soon enough (which explains its Chinese name still in use today: Hung Mao Ch'eng, "the castle of the red-haired people"). Then the Chinese under Koxinga took over. Each time it was destroyed the town was rebuilt in a different style. This is what gives Fort San Domingo its charm—this and the fact that it occupies such a peaceful spot. A Spanish arch standing on a Dutch foundation that post-dates it is one of the anomalies that resulted. Actually it's an exaggeration to call it a fort at all, much less a castle. It's a kind of stout two-storey block-house. But, in truth, it's hard to tell what it must have looked like at any of its previous turning points because it was remade yet again in the 19th century, this time by the British, who leased it in perpetuity in 1867. A tablet that was once part of the complex but now stands apart, like an old tomb-stone detached from its proper place, bears the inscription "V.R. 1868."

This was the age of the treaty ports following China's humiliation in the Opium Wars and the Taiping Rebellion when the European colonial powers, and the Japanese, too, won extraordinary concessions from the Qing rulers. Tanshui, though it was then the largest port on Taiwan, still remained pretty much off the beaten path of British hegemony. But the Americans, by this time the great rivals of the British in the China trade, had been sniffing about and indeed would probably have simply snatched Taiwan outright if it hadn't been for their Civil War at home. So both the British and the Americans kept consular missions in Tanshui. In 1891 the British went so far as to add a quite splendid official residence on the grounds, a two-storey affair with Romanesque touches, similar to some at the old fort, part of which was now a jail for British subjects (who, under the principle of extraterritoriality, were immune from Chinese law).

Although it does not lie in the same county as the capital, Tanshui has long since lost its identity as a distinct city. It still relies heavily on its fishing fleet for sustenance, and a long row of seafood restaurants lines the highway. The community is also a bedroom development for Taipei, and the one road that links the two places no longer offers much countryside to look at, just urban sprawl. Given the waning of British power in the Pacific, and Tanshui's decline into civic irrelevance, it is surprising that the Foreign Office in Whitehall kept the consulate open until 1972, after which they gave it over to the Australians, who passed it on to the Americans, before, finally, in 1984, it became a museum.

It is an anomaly whichever way you look at it. Fort San Domingo, with its hints of ancient diplomatic intrigue (two wall safes, one very old indeed, and a primitive stove for incinerating documents), is a babble of different periods and architectural styles, a kind of folly almost, such as an eccentric lord might have built from scratch, imitating the caprice of history to make a centrepiece for the gardens of his vast estate. And then there is the consular residence, with its reception- and morning-rooms and separate quarters for staff and servants. By the look of it, the British must have left much of the furniture when they finally decamped.

Curiously Taiwan, with its violent past, is as poor in old fortifications as peaceful Bermuda, say, is rich. San Domingo is very far from the most complete, and is not really what it claims to be at all. Its importance is simply that it occupies a spot—a lovely spot, high above Shalun Beach, where surfers cavort during certain seasons—where so many of the currents of early Taiwanese history happen to come together: the Spanish and the Dutch traders, the aboriginals, the first definite influx of Chinese under Koxinga, but not, curiously, the British themselves. In stark distinction to the Chinese Mainland and the forces that shaped it, Taiwan is a place in whose development the British played almost no role (and the French even less). The Americans were always the rulers and the cultural models here— the Americans and the still-hated Japanese, who took the island in 1895 and ran it ambitiously but with a certain cruelty until forced to cede it back to China at the end of the Second World War.

This is another reason that the old consulate is so interesting: one is hard-pressed to find the slightest sign of British civilization in Taiwan, while signs of the American equivalent are so abundant that they seem almost natural. The floor above the ground floor is called the second, not the first. Yet there is no triskaidekaphobia as in North America: the tall buildings all have 13th floors. Many of them, however, do lack fourth floors, and houses with fourth floors are difficult to sell, owing to bad feng shui. Advertisements calling for applicants with American accents reflect more than simply the ubiquity of CNN. How unusual it is for Americans to find themselves not the most disliked of foreigners in a place. Yet that's not to say they're perforce the most admired, at least not distinctly so.

There was a time, 250 years ago, when Formosa was all the rage among the British intelligentsia, in whose midst had appeared a charismatic foreigner named George Psalmanazar, a friend of Samuel Johnson's. Psalmanazar, who claimed to be a citizen of Formosa, had written a very popular and completely counterfeit history of the place and was soon teaching a language he called Formosan to Oxford divinity students training as missionaries. In 1747 he confessed publicly to having made it all up, and he became known, in the words of his biographer, as "one of the most successful liars of all time."

Today English is taught in Taiwanese schools from the earliest levels as a matter of pragmatism, though with wildly varying success, of course, and a degree from an American or at least Canadian university is almost de rigueur in certain professions and for those aspiring to public life in the generation that lies ahead. Some of the preferred schools might sound odd; the University of Missouri, for example, is an enclave of ambitious Taiwanese. Citizens now 75 or older are likely to speak Japanese as well, as a result of the long occupation. When a young reporter from *Asahi Shimbun* or *Yomiuri Shimbun* or some other Japanese newspaper came to interview Premier Hua Pei-tsun in his office in the Presidential Building (built by the Japanese before the war, like the Foreign Ministry and other public structures in Taipei), he found that they could communicate quite effectively without the presence of a translator. This eliminated the premier's young Taiwan-born aides, who sat in on the meeting but had no idea what was taking place.

This strikes me as a telling anecdote. While being thoroughly Chinese, the people of Taiwan are struggling to make something quite new from the mixture of qualities they admire in America and Japan, both economically and now, more slowly, politically as well. So far the resulting social concoction is much more pleasant than either of the ingredients on their own might lead one to expect, though it has not been without its problems, not by any means.

The rain was still coming down like a waterfall and the wind looked ready to start tearing the leaves off the palmettos. I told my Taiwanese companion, a young communications student who had agreed to serve as translator and explainer, that I had never been in a typhoon before, not even what they called a baby typhoon. A hurricane alert in Florida once was the nearest sensation I had experienced. He told me about the most recent typhoon and also entertained me with his favourite earthquake memories.

"Do they have such things in your country?" he asked.

"Our disasters are usually man-made," I replied.

"Ah, politics," he said. "We have those here as well."

Before the end of the year there was to be an election in Taiwan; the odds-makers, seeing the Kuomintang's almost uncanny ability to embrace just enough change to stay in power, were predicting a victory for the admittedly somewhat volatile status quo. The issues were democracy, nationalism, and the generation gap. The last of these, in a curious way, actually provided the key to the other two.

In 1948 President Chiang Kai-shek announced a "period of communist rebellion." This was a state-of-siege declaration, giving extraordinary powers to him and the Kuomintang. The next year he and the government, faced with defeat by the communists, retreated to Taiwan and settled in for a long rule. Chiang was genuine in his hatred of the communists. To the Americans, this was more important than his affection for fascism or something very close to it, and he used this fact to squeeze all the money from them that he could. As Harry Truman is supposed to have said, "He may be a son of a bitch, but he's our son of a bitch." In fairness Chiang could have expressed precisely the same sentiment about Truman—or Eisenhower or Kennedy or Johnson or Nixon...but there the chain stopped. Nixon recognized the People's Republic as the real China. Then in 1978, a few years after Chiang died and was succeeded by family and friends, Taipei broke diplomatic relations with Washington. Only in 1987, when the

Emergency Decree, as martial law was called, was lifted, did life begin to grow freer, particularly under Lee Teng-hui as president. The situation was hardly without its tensions, however, as the government tried to maintain change at the present pace and its antagonists tried to speed it up.

Lee was mayor of Taipei and governor of Taiwan province before achieving the presidency. But the most significant line on his CV was the fact that, although 68 years old, he was—in the sense of having been born in Taiwan and not on the Mainland—a member of the younger genera- tion. For it is on this point of birthplace that the generation gap comes into play and informs, even defines, the future of the constitution.

As part of the hypothesis that Taiwan was the real China and the People's Republic an imposter, the National Assembly in Taipei had always been run by persons born on the Mainland. Nominally they represented not just Taiwan but the other 21 provinces as well. Such Mainland-born people, together with their Taiwanese-born offspring, made up only about 15 percent of the population but held 80 percent of the seats in the assembly— held them indefinitely, while controlling the mechanisms for amending the constitution. The same situation also prevailed in the other, less powerful chamber, the Legislative Yuan. There had always been a few small parties, such as the Labour Party, whose most famous member gathered a crowd on the hustings by performing a striptease act. But the first real one wasn't founded until 1986, and didn't begin to gain great strength (30 percent of the popular vote in one election) until after suspension of martial law.

The Democratic Progressive Party is unusually named in that it is actually democratic and progressive. It favours direct election of a simplified gov- ernment instead of the system in which the president appoints the premier who then appoints the ministers. The Democratic Progressives are also dominated by native-born Taiwanese who are usually far younger than Lee and without his commitment to business as usual. The most controversial plank in the DPP platform calls for an end to the hopes of reuniting the two Chinas and simply declaring Taiwan an independent republic, seeking readmittance to the United Nations, and otherwise getting on with the realities of life.

It's dangerous to generalize too much about either party. The Kuomintang, for example, included everyone from relative liberals to former brownshirts—as does the DPP itself, by way of being a coalition of sorts.

But on the fundamental question of "independence" not from old colonial power but from old romantic ideology, there is a clear polarity that need not be tinctured by too much qualification. All other questions—the necessity of direct representation and what kind of constitution is best— flow from that. The DPP adopted its position on the matter at some danger to its members, given that Lee still controlled the formidable anti-subversion machinery and hadn't hesitated to use it in the past.

The DPP was certainly driven in part by a grassroots pro-democracy sentiment similar to that which the communists crushed on the Mainland. But the way the KMT met the threat more closely resembled the situation in Poland or the former Soviet Union in recent memory: they permitted dissent, but only up to a point. And necessity kept changing what the point was. For example, one of the most important opposition leaders, Hsu Sin-liang, had been a political prisoner not all that long ago. Yet much of the agitation had to be done from bases overseas. People from those bases who returned to Taiwan did so at their peril, as when Kuo Pei-hung, leader of the U.S. branch of the exiled group called World United Formosans for Independence, slipped in and was promptly arrested. The case that made the biggest splash in Canada was that of Y. S. Leo, a Toronto bank analyst who returned to Taipei and was charged with false entry. Later, after Ottawa refused to listen to a plea on Leo's behalf from the United Nations, a charge of sedition was added. Leo was the first Canadian citizen ever designated a "prisoner of conscience" by Amnesty International.

The DPP's historic decision to make an independence plebiscite part of its policy was taken at a party convention on October 13. The next day the government began ferreting out still more oppositionists, as the local press called them. By the time I arrived almost three weeks later, the total of newly arrested leaders stood at 11 and was climbing. Meanwhile the cabinet ruled the DPP plan for a vote on independence illegal and ordered it changed or else. The "or else" was taken by some in the DPP to mean that their party would be disbanded. The tough talk was clearly designed in part to placate Beijing.

Until the massacre at Tiananmen Square and the world's reaction to it, the standard interpretation of Chinese-Taiwanese relations was this: hard-line communists on the Mainland relish the thought of reunification on their own terms as much as KMT hard-liners cherish the quixotic dream of reunification on theirs. Of course, acting on either is a very different matter. But as the pro-independence movement grew more vociferous, so did the People's Republic make a display of becoming restive. At length Beijing went so far as to make at least a thinly veiled threat to invade Taiwan if the island ever did declare independence. To sensitive individuals the whole notion sounded quite far-fetched. The same folks who could get back Hong Kong merely by waiting for a century, or get back Macao by waiting for five centuries, weren't likely to fly off the handle—especially given that they were still smarting from the world's criticism of the one instance when they did indeed overact so terribly in putting down their own student protesters. The KMT, however, used this ominous statement to justify its crackdown on the DPP policy, while extending the deadline for its repeal.

Yet even as these deadlines were being ignored, the Mainland took the unusual step of commissioning a public poll on the subject of Taiwan— and the still more unusual step of releasing results. The survey showed that 58 percent of those asked felt that the People's Republic should not interfere in the course of Taiwan's political future. Finally, but well before its last deadline, the DPP rejected the demand that it rescind its policy. And nothing happened, except that more people were arrested and some of those arrested were deported back to exile.

The Asian equivalent of *perestroika* would continue on its own timetable, slowly but steadily, without any of the unexpected and violent turns seen elsewhere, both sending a signal to, and taking a signal from, the concurrent example of the two Koreas, which sometimes seem to be moving towards their own kind of reconciliation. That was where the matter rested when I was there, when local turf accountants were giving odds that despite the probability of large DPP gains in the December election, matters would still unfold slowly, with the country, having already moved away from sham elections, progressing towards elections in the Chicago manner and from there maybe real democracy.

Having put into motion its own eventual obsolescence, the KMT also set loose an elaborate plan to postpone the day of reckoning as long as possible. Just weeks after declaring an end to the 40-year "war" with the Mainland (and delicately sidestepping the issue of who won), President Lee and his more conservative premier, Hua Pei-tsun, announced implementation of the Six-Year Plan. This was a public-works scheme of unprecedented size and scope, designed to plough a lot of Taiwan's new commercial wealth back into the country—and make the KMT all the more difficult to remove from power. New highways, railway systems, and airports were being built along with new shopping centres and parks, to a total of about US$300 billion. The opposition would be hard-pressed to whip up dissatisfaction with go-getting on such a grand scale.

But the KMT knew that it had to do something else as well: address the insecurity of so many Taiwanese, young ones especially, who had grown up in an atmosphere of isolation from the West and a sense of betrayal by the United States and others. They were the people who provided grassroots support for the DPP's vision of a new kind of nationalism, totally different from that of Chiang in his day, based on pride in material achievement despite what were for so long such overwhelming odds. The change began in the late 1980s when Taiwanese were permitted to travel freely to the People's Republic to see relatives (a particularly shrewd move since it led to so much Taiwanese investment in their ancestral homeland). It continued with an elaborate and effective diplomatic offensive against what once had been, when Taiwan was comparatively poor, an indifferent world. Canada, along with Australia and New Zealand, had already (while ignoring mutterings from the People's Republic) opened direct air links with Taiwan and taken other such steps the Taiwanese found promising. Italy, France, and most important of all, the new united Germany, actually came round to full diplomatic relations. Much more activity of both kinds was expected to follow soon from other members of the European Community. Meanwhile the Taiwanese were quick off the mark (much quicker than Canadians, for example) to elbow their way into the new markets opening up in Eastern Europe.

What did the KMT have in mind for the long term in order to keep all factions happy and to rejuvenate itself? Clearly some kind of sovereignty association with the Mainland in which, unlike Hong Kong, Taiwan would run its own political institutions and have a separate presence in the world while enjoying some type of relationship with the People's Republic that would go well beyond free trade but fall far short of surrender. For anything of this type to happen of course, Taiwan must continue to make lots of money. Fortunately it has the knack.

The false news in November 1991 that the Taiwanese were paying US$2 billion for a 40 percent stake in McDonnell Douglas created quite a sensation in the business world. It was taken as a signal that yet another important American industry—aerospace—would have to compete against Asians. This was a sign that Taiwanese in particular had suddenly (to Western eyes) come up in the world, to the point of posing a threat. Taiwanese dynamism should have been obvious long before. It was certainly obvious from within Taiwan, looking outward. In many societies architectural landmarks and institutions recall past glories. In the Republic of China, which Taiwan has been for only two generations, they instead tend to reflect present realities and future probabilities.

The finest place to visit in Taipei is the National Palace Museum, which houses the world's most important collection of Chinese art and antiquities, including the former contents of the Forbidden City in Beijing. The collection has its origins in the Southern Song dynasty (960–1279), but the present building, in the Shihlin district on the north side of Taipei, dates only from 1965. Boyle Huang was the architect; he later became a Chinese-art consultant in Toronto.

The museum was long thought to house an extraordinary 700,000 items, but the official total keeps growing, thanks not only to purchases and donations but to a new inventory system; at present the figure stands at 760,000. The most extensive holdings are in the areas of porcelain, ceramics, ritual bronzes, and painting and calligraphy, but the mandate extends to books and manuscripts, which are all far more than simply representative.

Collecting began through the efforts of the Song emperor Taizu and was carried on by his successors down through the centuries until artistic treasure filled display rooms and storerooms of the capital. For most of this period this was Beijing's Forbidden City, where none but members of the court and royal household ever saw the collection. That it was maintained throughout various wars and upheavals is little short of miraculous. With the collapse of the Qing dynasty in 1911, gathering came to an end, but the new Chinese republic opened the hoard to the public. After 1925, when Puyi, the last emperor, had been banished, authorities began cataloguing the treasures and designated the spot where they were to be kept as the National Palace Museum. But that was only the beginning of the incredible story of the collection's survival.

When the Japanese invaded Manchuria in 1931, the collection was moved south to Shanghai for safekeeping. Then it had to be moved again—this time to Nanjing. When the Japanese occupation became an actual Sino-Japanese war in 1937, most of the objects were hidden in three widely scattered locations as far away as Sichuan, more than 1,600 kilometres up the Yangtze River. One lot of 7,000 crates was removed from a building in Hunan Province only one day before the site was destroyed. The last survivor of this heroic preservation effort was Na Chi-liang, who was now 85. He lived rent free at the rear of the museum grounds, a national hero.

The treasure had to remain hidden for years, as the Sino-Japanese conflict blended into the Second World War. After the peace in 1945, the government of Chiang Kai-shek reassembled all the old imperial collections in one place: Nanjing, the nationalist capital. When, in a few years, it became clear that the communists under Mao Zedong might overrun Nanjing, most of the pieces, including all the choicest ones, were removed from the Mainland and taken to Taiwan.

The pieces were kept in Taichung before facilities were ready in Taipei. For its part the People's Republic opened its own National Palace Museum in the now sparsely endowed Forbidden City (as well as establishing other new institutions, particularly the formidable Shanghai Museum of Art, which opened in 1952). Thus there came to be two National Palace Museums, unwitting symbols of the two governments, each of which claimed to be the legitimate government of China.

The Taipei museum is immense, with display areas and offices totalling 8,300 ping (27,870 square metres) and employing 600 people. Of course, only a small portion of the vast collections, between 7,000 and 9,000 items, can be shown at any one time. So there is a large permanent exhibit, "The Relationship Between Chinese and World Culture," on the ground floor, to give visitors an overview and provide a necessary foundation for the various other displays, such as paintings (changed every three months) or ceramics (changed every one to three years). There are naturally many famous works by individual artists and craftspeople: virtually all the greatest names in the history of Chinese calligraphy are represented, for instance. But I found, as

I imagine many visitors do, that I came away with the most vivid memories of some of the smallest and least-touted objects.

Perhaps the site that people in the city most enjoy showing guests is the mammoth complex that comprises both the National Cultural Center and the Chiang Kai-shek Memorial Hall. It is imposing. It is meant to be. The Cultural Center is an elaborate concert hall and an equally grand theatre famous as a venue for Taiwanese opera, which is more colourful, more gestural than the Mainland kind, with firecrackers at times and certainly a freer interpretation of the classic texts. Because not everyone speaks both Mandarin and the Taiwanese dialect (called Hokkien), written characters are often projected down to the stage from the fourth balcony to help the audience along. Like all such subsidized palaces of art, this one reflects a kind of official charade. The real world of Taiwanese culture is business, and as in all other Taiwanese businesses, the atmosphere is cutthroat. Even in the shadow of Hong Kong's famous film industry, Taiwan made scores of feature films a year; it now was only making six or eight—and the big studio was more a tourist attraction than a place of creative enterprise. The Taiwanese can't compete against the Americans when it comes to visual trash. Conversely the Mainland Chinese can't compete against the Taiwanese for the aural kind: Taiwanese rockers and pop singers (the most famous one was named Su Rui) are the stars of the People's Republic, thanks to radio signals that penetrate far beyond the coastal areas, to as far west as Sichuan.

The Memorial Hall, which opened in 1980 to mark the fifth anniversary of Chiang's passing, is covered in local marble and approached by means of a long avenue, flights of mammoth steps, and a 16-metre-high bronze door weighing 75 tonnes, behind which is the message: NO ENTRY FOR THOSE WEARING SLIPPERS OR SLOVENLY DRESS. It is a monument to Chiang's personality rather than, strictly speaking, to his life. The exhibits relaying the biographical facts make no mention of, for example, the Green Circle, the criminal syndicate that ran Shanghai in the 1920s and 1930s and sheltered him when he needed help. This curatorial approach allows Chiang to be seen to be more flexible in death than he was in life, more like Abraham Lincoln in that respect than Mao, say. Two of his limousines are on exhibit, one of them a 1955 Cadillac with special bulletproofing. A third limo is seen in Kaohsiung in the south. One begins to suspect his automobiles are as numerous as Lenin's overcoats, or places where George Washington slept, or pieces of the True Cross.

The real monument to the Chiang legacy is the Grand Hotel, despite its age one of the fanciest and most famous in Asia (what the Taiwanese call a five-blossom hotel). It was built to resemble an enormous Chinese palace and sits atop a mountain called Round Hill, commanding a view of the city to the south. It was constructed by a group of investors led by Madame Chiang (who died in 2003, age 105, after living in seclusion in New York State). But unlike, say, the Acropolis in Athens, the Grand can't usually be seen from the city below: the buildings are so densely packed down there, and the smog so bad, that being in the Grand is like looking through a one-way mirror—you can see them, but they can't see you. The Grand, which boasts of having the largest classical Chinese roof in the world, is in two sections, an Old and a New, the former built back into the lush side of the mountains. That the whole place is huge—enormous imperial buildings linked with gardens and pathways—and yet has a combined total of only 575 guest rooms, gives some indication of how generous the suites are.

The Grand is a shrine to prosperity rather than to memory, and in modern Taiwan, that seems altogether appropriate. It overlooks all the other recent landmarks where money is made and managed. This is somehow symbolically correct. Off in the distance, for example, I saw the tallest building in Taipei, the five-year-old World Trade Center, or rather the 34-storey tower of the China External Trade Development Council which, along with a hotel and an enormous convention centre, make up the complex. The convention centre is booked with trade fairs from now until doomsday. When I passed through on my way to interview the head of CETDC, carpenters and gaffers were descending on the scene like insects, striking the Taipei International Medical Equipment and Pharmaceuticals Show, replacing it with booths and displays for the Taipei Aerospace Technology Exhibit. Even more telling is the adjoining exhibition hall: six floors of small cubicles where thousands of Taiwanese manufacturers display their wares, from computers to gadgets and gimcracks. It's as though an invisible motto hangs over the place for the benefit of the 3,000 or so business people who come through every day: "Whatever you want, we'll make it cheaper." This is how Taiwan had come out of the blue to have the world's largest container fleet and, now that Japan was dumping dollars to prop up the yen, the world's largest foreign-exchange surplus. Increasingly, though, manufacturing itself was being exported, a trend that must continue for a number of reasons.

One reason is concern for the environment. This is a matter Taiwanese politicians cannot afford to ignore, given the smog and the general ecological deterioration—and the ease with which they can score points abroad, as when the government agreed to ban drift-net fishing. Another is the abiding search for ever-cheaper labour. The People's Republic might seem a limitless resource in that respect, but the need to seek out the willing poor must to some extent be as much behind diplomatic overtures to places such as Vietnam as the need to create more markets by investing in them. These trends dovetail with Taiwan's inevitable wish that, as its economy grows, it will become more complex and sophisticated as well: that Taipei will become less a manufacturing centre and increasingly a financial one. There was reason to believe that this would happen. One study had put the shortage of capital in financial markets at about US$140 billion, of which Japan, the dominant force in Asia, could offer only about half. There was plenty of room for subsidiary centres in the region. That was why I hurried off to take a look at the Taipei Stock Exchange.

Such concrete institutions as the Taipei Stock Exchange, as distinct from abstract ones, such as the constitution, were already fully formed, which made the West's astonishment about the Taiwanese economy itself all the more surprising. But the Exchange, though opened for business as long ago as 1962 as a sort of in-house curb market, was only in the 1990s beginning to take off. All the signs were present, including infantile volatility and a sense of go-goism that even the old Vancouver Stock Exchange might have envied.

When I was there, recession had taken some of the shine off the figures, but the atmosphere was still quite extraordinary. Part of the cause of the excitement, and some if its effect, was a tenfold increase in the number of brokers at the very end of the 1980s and the start of the 1990s, to the point where there were two reps for each listed company. The Taiwanese are *avid* for golf, but they're *obsessed* with the stock market. In the period when the board was flashing like a flight deck of a spaceship (the exchange uses the computer-assisted trading system developed by the Toronto Stock Exchange, with Japanese modifications), it was common for ordinary citizens to quit their well-paying jobs and spend all day at their brokers', transfixed by the spectacle. Towards the end of 1987 the Taipei index stood at 1,000. It had climbed to 12,000 by March 1989 when it promptly fell to 2,000, only to reach 12,000 again in February 1990. During my stay in Taipei, the index stood at about 4,300. One day it jumped 127 points following news that a political demonstration on the independence issue did not end in violence as had been feared.

The exchange itself, as a physical place, is not what's interesting. Electronics have imposed a postmodern distance in such situations anyway, and nowhere else more than in Taipei. The growth in trading has caused the exchange to be spread across the city in several different buildings, only one of which, the data-processing centre, was purpose-built. The administrative offices, where I went for a briefing, are on six floors of a nondescript structure near City Hall and directly opposite police headquarters (a tall and somewhat scary edifice with an American-style eagle on the front and a heliport on top). The whole system had several revealing peculiarities. A board lot was not 100 shares but 1,000, as would be true in Canada only of junior resource stocks and other penny dreadfuls. And the market traded only from 9:00 a.m. to noon (as well as from 9:00 a.m. to 11:00 a.m. on Saturdays). But the level of regulation this suggests is not apparent otherwise. Consider the fact that dealers, brokers, underwriters, bankers, and insurers can all be one and the same. Yet *deregulation* is not quite the correct term either, since there's little heritage of claustrophobic supervision to react against, except in terms of allowing foreign investment—and that was coming soon, as soon as it could be achieved with a degree of orderliness. Which is to say, as soon as it was politically safe to cut through the tangle of regulations prohibiting it. In the meantime the finance minister wanted to see new flotations by the larger state-run companies—China Steel, China Shipbuilding, China Airlines, and the three largest commercial banks—to pump up volume and make manipulation more difficult. To that end a new private bank was being established, and its shares, too, would be thrown into the pit. This was all according to the famous Six-Year Plan for national reconstruction.

None of the change was fast enough or dangerous enough to contain the citizens of Taiwan. Each business day stocks traded on the exchange had a total worth of somewhere between 40 billion and 90 billion New Taiwan Dollars (NTs). But on some days almost as much was traded on the official and highly illegal underground exchange, and one Chinese-language business paper, the *Commercial Times,* estimated that on occasion the underground action reached NT$200 billion a day. Actually the underground exchange isn't an exchange at all, as no shares change hands. It's more of a cross between a futures market and the numbers racket. People phone their bookie, er, broker, and lay bets on which way individual stocks, or the entire index, will move. Some of the biggest financial names on the island were involved in this activity. Some went to jail. The underground market led to the creation of complete underground banks. One of them was discovered to have illegally accepted nearly NT$85 million in deposits. In all, 58 of the bank's officials were convicted. Wonderful stuff.

Some on Taiwan contend that the people there are growing lazy, smug, and non-productive. One hears a great deal of anxious chatter about yuppies. Those local councils controlled by the DPP and other opposition parties cut back the civil-service workweek to five days. Then came talk that the central government might permit its people to take off the final Saturday of each month. And in a few months there might be another national holiday for everyone: Children's Day, April 4. This would be tantamount to a spring break, since Tomb Sweeping Day falls on April 5. As it stands, the Taiwanese celebrate 17 national holidays, as compared with a mere 11 for Canadians. There is a fear in some circles that the whole society is growing soft and flabby. The average Taiwanese works 45.5 hours a week. That's three and a half more than the average Japanese, but far behind the average South Korean who works an incredible 54 hours. How can we hold up our heads, people say, when we're losing ground to South Koreans? How indeed.

When Taiwan really began to boom economically about 1975, it expanded to the south and east. This was a matter of geography, but it was not without symbolic logic as well. As the northern part of Taiwan is better developed than the southern, so is the western more important than the eastern. Railways run up both sides of the island, for example, but the one on the west coast is electrified and that on the east coast, diesel. There are powerful historical reasons for this. The west coast after all faces the Chinese Mainland. It is also protected by the Central Mountain Range, which runs down the length of the island but slightly off-centre, giving the strait side a much wider coastal bench than the Pacific side enjoys. In the other typhoon season, from April through August, the mountains help to deflect the winds sweeping up from the southeast.

International air travel to and from Taipei, a matter of sub-diplomatic manoeuvring, was growing rapidly in response to bullish economic conditions, but flights within Taiwan were less of a priority: the weather was too unpredictable to permit strict schedules to be maintained. The main means of getting around is the Sun Yat-sen Freeway, a four-lane toll road, which on a map looks like the femoral artery on the island's anatomy. It begins at the top of the island, near Keelung, the second-largest port for container shipping, and runs 80 percent of the way down, to Kaohsiung, the biggest such port, and fourth largest in the world. I was finally breaking free of Taipei and striking out through some of the countryside between the two termini. My slow, discontinuous circumnavigation of Taiwan was finally about to get underway in earnest.

The government had kindly laid on a car and a driver. The former had two small ROC flags on the front, giving us the appearance of a one-unit diplomatic convoy; the latter spoke Taiwanese, very common in the south, which he used rather then Mandarin when conversing with the countrymen there. I wore a security badge identifying me as a representative of the Kingston *Whig-Standard*. The people in the Government Information Office in Taipei had some difficulty translating the name of the newspaper into written Chinese; after consulting various English-language dictionaries and asking the advice of fluent anglophones, they came up with something like "flag of the independent anti-slavery democrats." Not a bad description, I said to myself.

The boom made the middle class rich and created a new middle class from much of the rest, but poverty of course remained. I could see it as soon as I left the city—people living in dark slum buildings with old discarded tires atop the roof to hold the tar paper or the rusty iron sheeting in place. But this is by no means Latin America or even the poorest parts of the People's Republic. In sizable cities along the way your eye is naturally drawn to shop signs with pictures that tell you what sorts of businesses they are. I was struck by the number of commercial kennels advertising popular Western breeds of dog, such as Dalmatians or terriers. Some people still may eat dog, especially as a winter delicacy, as in the People's Republic, but a vast, newly prosperous middle class has taken to owning pets in the Western manner. One also sees a lot of restaurants with reversed swastikas painted on the front; this of course has nothing to do with Nazis but is an indication that the restaurant is run by Buddhists and is vegetarian. One also sees many large reproductions of the Statue of Liberty, including a particularly huge one towering over yet another restaurant. These aren't signs of solidarity with the pro-democracy movement in the People's Republic, where the students erected such a statue in Tiananmen Square shortly before many were massacred; they are indications of the Taiwanese love of most things American. Personally I found my first brush with a Statue of Liberty in Taiwan about as distasteful as my initial encounter with dog meat in a food stall in Beijing.

To mistake mere drabness for poverty was easily done, especially in Chinese culture, where colours sometimes served different functions than they did in the West. In Taipei, and in the small cities we kept passing through as we progressed down the coast, government buildings were decorated with what looked like festive abandon: bright red, yellow, and blue banners were draped permanently across the tops, and the signage had an almost carnival connotation to foreigners who couldn't read the characters. By comparison, places of business, even the mammoth department stores found everywhere in coastal Asia, seemed severely understated from the outside. And death too was every bit as colourful as government. Tooling down the highway we heard honking and loud Chinese music that gained on us from the other lane. The outside of the hearse was covered—sides, roof, hood, windows, wheels—with the brightest of flowers—not merely white for death but yellows, reds, greens. Following behind at a high rate of speed was a series of Japanese four-by-fours similarly adorned; each contained a cluster of musicians in the open back, blowing on horns and woodwinds, loudly and with independence of spirit, pointing their instruments skyward, like soloists executing a difficult passage. Given all this, I found it hard to know how to interpret the squarish concrete low-rises and high-rises seen all over Southeast Asia—grey, unpainted, with never enough windows and even those preternaturally small—buildings that always looked old and used-up even when they were new. Whether residential or commercial, the style was the same, down to the corrugated steel rain barrels on the roof. In fact, it was frequently hard to tell at a short distance to what use such buildings were being put. This was the other traditional architecture in China, the one behind the red-tiled temples and the like. Could it really be as ubiquitous as it seemed? Was it really as depressing as it looked?

Setting foot out of the capital is enough to tell you where all the merchandise displayed in the World Trade Center actually comes from: there are small factories everywhere, for every conceivable type of goods. It may not be quite true to say that the Republic practises manufacturing the way the People's Republic does agriculture: intensively, with every level square metre put to good use. But they each do what they do as though their lives depend on it (as indeed they do), and along the major transportation routes the results are obvious: factory after factory. But as you move down the island, farming is apparent as well, particularly the big cash crops such as sugar cane and corn and betel nuts. The last of these the rural Taiwanese chew addictively, despite government warnings that the habit may cause cancer. At lunchtime we stopped to get some ears of corn, boiled on the spot in a vessel made from a metal drum. The kernels were ivory in colour and twice as large as the variety we're most familiar with at home. They were delicious.

The high mountains appeared unbroken in the distance. Very Chinese mountains they seemed too, in the way the summits dipped down and swung back up at the ends, like the roofs of palaces all in a row. But near Changhua on the Tatu River we left the big dual carriageway and swung inland, heading for Sun Moon Lake, a famous scenic wonder high up in the Central Range, just about dead centre on a map of the island. As we climbed higher and higher, the mountains began to take on a different character: not jagged, sloping peaks in choreographed sequence but huge obstinate loaves, 1,000 metres tall perhaps, densely forested, and standing closely together, each blocking the view of the next.

Sun Moon Lake, 760 metres up along a switchbacking road, is a place of considerable loveliness and even more tranquility. The water is delicate blue, with jade-like streaks of green along the margins. At its bluest it looks like the glaze used in Qing porcelain. Its elevation, its calmness, its apparent remoteness from the world all call to mind Windermere in the Lake District, but Sun Moon Lake is far larger. There's an island sitting in it where Chiang Kai-shek had a holiday home (as cottages are called in Taiwan). I walked round the shore for a bit and found a spring percolating madly in a little inlet. This is the source of supply for the entire lake. Tall bamboo and giant ferns flourish near the shore. Other less delicate flora dominate the farther up you climb.

On the crest of the lake is a large temple, not as intrinsically interesting, I think, as one I saw earlier at Tanshui, where a golden Buddha with 21 hands is approached by tunnels bored through a mountain. The lakeside shrine is called the Hsuanchuang Temple—the Temple of Literature and Power, a reference to the scholars of the ancient court who wielded administrative authority only by working harmoniously with the military. The real man-made attraction of Sun Moon Lake is the nine-storey Tzuen Pagoda, built in the 1960s at the very top of one of the encircling mountains.

I could see that the morning fog was going to obstruct what people told me was the magnificent 360-degree view, but we trudged up nonetheless, simply to get a look at the pagoda itself. The long, tough climb exhausts many visitors, I was told. Among the dense foliage along the way were occasional papaya trees; the fruit was ripe that time of year, and Filipino tourists, seeing its yellow, were reminded of the pun involving a "red joke"—a blue joke, we would say. Poinsettias, which Taiwanese Christians regard the same way Western Christians do, as a Christmas plant, grow wild along the path. The pagoda is indeed a restful spot—and a rest is what's needed once you've gone round nine circular flights of stairs. The fog, which seemed to touch the shore at certain points and then pull back, like a blind person navigating among unfamiliar obstacles, made the scene all the more relaxing. We lingered a while.

An enormous bronze bell hung from a stout beam at the top of the pagoda. On close inspection we found that it carried the Taiwanese flag, not religious symbols, as its motif. Back down below, near the car park, there were shops selling large fungi, native crafts, and butane cigarette lighters with pictures of naked women on them. This was an unsubtle reminder of a more important fact: that Taiwan was not only far more Westernized than the People's Republic but far more traditional too, in some ways. After all, it hadn't had a Cultural Revolution and years of indoctrination camps to erase folkways and old beliefs. In any case, the incongruity of the selection struck me because it seemed to say a lot about how Taiwan looked at itself and its place in the world. As if to prosecute the point, a short distance away was the Formosan Aboriginal Culture Village.

There are 10 aboriginal tribes in Taiwan: the Ami, Atayal, Bunum, Paiwan, Puyuma, Rukai, Shao, Saisiat, Tsou, and Yami. All are quite different, and they are spread out across the island and offshore. One of the tribes is found on Lanyü in the Pacific, but most lived originally on the strait, where for years one tribe preyed on Chinese and European shipwreck victims. Still another practised a religion that involved use of their enemies' severed heads—a fact alluded to in the preservation of the ceremonial stone shelving where the heads were once kept, row on row. All had complex cultures long before the Chinese arrived in force. Their continued existence, both in their natural habitat in the mountains and here, as a tourist draw, speaks well for their resilience; the pressure to come down into the cities and marry Chinese is stronger every year. The village, however, does not give much hint of their political importance. Aboriginals have no special status, like Natives in Canada, but they have taken an important part in the movement for direct democracy and all that it entails.

The tragedy of the Formosan Aboriginal Culture Village is its entertainment value. There is a stage where members of the tribes put on a joint musical and theatrical performance, a kind of slick pastiche of the 10 traditions. For domestic rather than Western tourists there is also an enormous restaurant made to look like an 18th-century French stately home, complete with vast formal gardens in the European manner. Soon, so went the rumour in business circles, some Disney or at least Disneyesque theme park would be built adjacent to this. Conversely the value of the village is the way in which it brings together in one place some indication of the 10 tribes. Learning here is much easier than learning by tracking down separate sites in all 13 counties. The village consists of examples of the various types of dwelling used by the aboriginals. They are as different as a thatched hut and a stout house of flat stones piled up without mortar, resembling a structure you would expect to see in the Orkneys. Much of what's on display in the village no longer exists in the wild but is preserved or reconstructed from the field research done as long ago as the 1930s.

There is also an adequate museum, and examples of aboriginal carving everywhere, including much that is phallic in nature. An interesting difference this: in the People's Republic the aboriginals would have been at least

forcibly assimilated by the communists and probably persecuted quite rig-
orously, with the government all the while eulogizing them as special. In
Taiwan they are genuinely protected, even nurtured, but the nurturing
takes such a commercial form as to be destructive in its own way. On the
one side of the strait, all action regardless of the motive tends towards
struggle and opposition; on the other, all action tends towards business.
This is not a cultural stereotype ("Irrepressible entrepreneurs, those
Taiwanese"). It's a national trait incorporated into Taiwanese society as
necessary for survival. As the aboriginals have learned to sing and dance for
the tourists in order to earn the privilege of being left alone the rest of the
time, so the Taiwanese have learned to make money in the most competitive markets in the world in order to go on enjoying being Taiwanese.

We had to put up for the night at Taichung, as almost everyone who's
been in the mountains must do. Although it is Taiwan's third-biggest city,
after Taipei and Kaohsiung, it's a very distant third indeed. No cosmopolitanism here, just a sense of being in some inland provincial place that has
grown faster than its ability to metabolize change: a sense the traveller
experiences more often on the Mainland. We stayed in a nondescript
tourist hotel, and when we went for dinner we found we were practically
the only people in the ballroom-size restaurant, which nonetheless must
have had 12 to 15 waiters on duty. We packed up at first light, as the old
people were starting to gather in the park for their tai chi. Also, the first
few students were making a reluctant appearance: young girls in burgundy
blazers, carrying their school books in leather straps slung over their shoulders.

If the northern one-third of the island is conspicuous for light industry,
the middle third, from Taichung down to Tainan, is much more agricultural. There are rice paddies stretching on forever and fish farms in neat
artificial lakes making mosaic patterns on the landscape. Poultry is important as well. From a certain distance the masses of ducks waddling across
the scenery looked like white flowers waving in the wind. In this area the
mountains are no longer visible from the highway.

In less than a couple of hours you come to Tainan, the old capital of
Taiwan (until 1885) and the city with the most spiritual significance: the
Kyoto to Taipei's Tokyo, as it were. Mind you, this part of its character is
not always apparent at first look. But in the alleys off the main streets and
the lanes off the alleys, scores and scores of temples, Confucian and Taoist,

sit hidden—churches too, for Tainan is the most Christianized place in the Republic of China, with the baptized population exceeding 10 percent of the whole, according to one guidebook. At least two of the more important temples date to the 17th century. They hint at the wave of religious and cultural reclamation following Koxinga's defeat of the Dutch East India Company traders—of whom, by contrast, almost no reminders survive.

When Koxinga captured Casteel Zeelandia, he built his own stronghold atop it and named the result Fort Anping. (Six months later he was dead at the age of 37 or 38.) Nearly all of Fort Anping was destroyed in the 19th century in what must have been a formidable typhoon indeed. By that time the site, once right on the water, was rapidly becoming an inland one, as the harbour silted up. It is now not only dry but in the middle of a very urban area.

The reconstructed buildings that mark the spot today don't ask much of one's imagination, though on climbing to the top of a little blockhouse to look down on some old Chinese cannons with long carriages, I was delighted to see the semi-circular foundation of one of the Dutch towers still visible below. Its origins are unmistakable, being made of the thin yellowish bricks called *klompje baksteen*. In this instance the bricks had been brought from Batavia.

A short distance away is Yitszi Chin Cheng, a small moated fort built by French engineers in the 1870s when the Qing dynasty was worried, prematurely as it happened, about Japanese designs on Taiwan (a name, incidentally, first applied only to the Tainan area, before the rest of Formosa was developed). Yitszi Chin Cheng is an earthen fort with a traditional Chinese gate, boasting enormous old shore batteries built by Armstrong. Like some others, supplied by Krupp, which have since disappeared, they were in their day the last word in prestigious European death technology. Schoolchildren play on the guns now. How often old forts turn out to be peaceful, contemplative places—more so sometimes than many of the temples.

Tainan seems a world away from the heavy industrial sector in the south, whose nerve centre is Kaohsiung, long familiar to anyone involved in Pacific shipping (or anyone who likes to read about it) but now growing beyond its origins without actually outgrowing them. You see the industrial landscape changing kilometre after kilometre as you move towards the city. Agriculture gets smaller and smaller in scale, factories bigger and closer together. On the afternoon we were driving past, I fancied that we could tell the exact spot where the two worlds came together. A man and a boy in a conical straw hat were fishing with wispy bamboo poles. Their stream was a concrete culvert running alongside a refinery. Behind them in the distance a big red sign flashed letters one at a time—T-O-Y-O-T-A—followed by the complete word, TOYOTA, in endless alternation.

So it was a surprise to get into central Kaohsiung and find it so pleasant-looking—much more handsome than Taipei and more orderly as well. Like a just-bought shirt still stiff with sizing and full of pins, the major buildings hadn't lost their newness yet. But neither had they completely usurped the old low wooden structures of the past, which could be found not only on side streets and alleys but sometimes, in twos or threes, on the leafy thoroughfares as well. The city is bisected by the Love River, and the traffic bounces over the bridges in a multicoloured parade. The city and harbour sit in a kind of broad basin, with mountains in the middle distance most of the way around. Some of the mountains are green, but others have bare terraces in stripes round the top, the work of the cement industry thereabouts.

Environmental concerns are worrisome throughout Taiwan, and with reason. After all, it's a small island—six hours by car from top to bottom if conditions are right—and in only a few years it had gone from near insignificance financially to being the world's twelfth-largest economy. Such transitions exact a big price, but the politicians are determined that their cities won't become like Bangkok. To judge by the press, television, and what I got from 50-odd conversations round the island, the environment is a more frequent topic of public discourse than it is in the United States, say. The lifting of martial law, under which all public demonstrations were banned, doubtless increased the concern by providing outlets for pent-up anxiety. Not that long ago persistent protests actually had forced China Petroleum to cancel, or at least postpone, construction of another refinery in the city.

The saddest fact about Kaohsiung is that it is home to what is probably the world's largest scrapyard for ocean-going vessels: a heartbreaking place for people who love ships. Seeing it is almost enough to make you swear off air travel if you could, as a visit to a slaughterhouse is the surest path to vegetarianism. At least the yard has been moved a few kilometres out of sight, and no longer destroys the mood of Kaohsiung Harbour, which is definitely upbeat. In Kaohsiung all the personal luxuries both commonplace and exotic come from the profits of exporting. To understand what makes the place tick, you must plunge into this very competitive world of contracts and cargoes.

Cities like this in Taiwan and South Korea have taken over from places like Hamilton, Pittsburgh, and Sheffield. Steel-making is not a protected industry in Taiwan. It's quite laissez-faire, though China Steel Corporation, the biggest of the 300 mills on the island, was also the only one owned by the state, which was taking back 98 percent of the extraordinarily high after-tax profit (between 25 and 30 percent on sales). The China Steel facility was also the country's only integrated works, meaning that it imported the coal, coke, iron ore, and limestone to feed its three blast furnaces rather than buying ingots ready-made. The company employed about 10,000 people.

To North American eyes some of the business practices seem rather Japanese. When I was there, China Steel Corporation had a gym, a library, tennis courts, a post office, et cetera, for the workers, even a contemplation pond, made from one of the slagheaps and stocked with goldfish (a second generation of them by then). A dormitory capable of housing 1,000 unmarried workers charged about US$20 a month. The steel-making process is much more up to date than you might expect, given that the mills look very much like our own. Escaping heat from the furnaces (1,040 degrees Fahrenheit) is captured and directed to other purposes; there's little smoke emitted from the stacks and what there is, having passed through an elaborate filtering system, is white, not black. The site took up 220 hectares. As late as 1971, the land was still a canebrake.

Next door, at one of the two yards of China Shipbuilding Corporation, the story was the same. In 1974 this was a fish pond. By 1991 it was 120 hectares of immense dry docks and plate shops and had repaired, refitted, or jumboized 1,600 ships and designed and built 262 others—tankers, bulk carriers, container ships, passenger ships, and small naval vessels, such as patrol boats like the one I saw but was forbidden to photograph. The yard also turned out offshore oil rigs and was licensed to make nuclear-power-plant components. The competition is keen, the clientele worldwide. This is where most of Taiwan's own fleet has originated—the result of competitiveness more so than patronage.

"See that?" asked the official who showed me round, pointing to a nearly completed container ship of the local Yang Ming Line. "Two hundred and seventy metres long. Cost $60 million. Very cheap." His tone was that of a dealer in stereo equipment.

At the time China Steel had a fleet of four ore carriers, bringing in raw material from Australia, Malaysia, and Canada. The hull plates were made in their own continuous-rolling mills and the vessels designed and constructed by China Shipbuilding just over the fence.

"Everything was done according to tender," a China Steel rep told me. "Very, very above-board all the way." By an eerie coincidence the rep of China Shipbuilding used almost identical language.

On a small peninsula across the harbour from these two giants was the Kaohsiung Export Processing Zone, one of three special industrial parks in Taiwan where manufacturers could bring in raw materials and components without duty if they processed them on the spot and sent the results directly overseas. The other two were at Keelung, on the northern tip of the island, and near Taichung. The Taichung site was given over completely to computers, semi-conductors, and the like, of which Taiwan had become a significant supplier. At 25 the eldest of the three, I was informed, the Kaohsiung zone was also the one with the greatest diversity of tenants. Some small electronics companies were there, but other firms in the complex made appliances, toys, clothing, or sporting goods. A duty-free store for foreigners looked like one of those shops in the former Soviet Union where overseas visitors with hard currency could purchase luxury goods. The quality and range were depressingly about the same; there was simply not the breadth of design and cleverness here that you saw displayed so well at the World Trade Center in Taipei. As an instrument of economic policy, however, the zone had certainly done its job in contributing to Taiwan's almost embarrassingly favourable balance of payments.

Some of the companies in the zone leased their factories from the government, while others chose to buy the land and erect their own buildings. The whole place covered 86 hectares and employed an astounding 22,000 workers. Significantly, though, 80 percent of them were girls of junior-high-school age. This wasn't the place to create high-paying jobs for the populace; it was a place to make money for the entrepreneurs wishing to take advantage of what was still, by Western if not by Asian standards, very cheap labour. At the shipyard across the way, boys as young as 15 worked nine hours a day for three years while going to class at night as they finished high school. The Taiwanese miracle was not being achieved without a price. As I returned to Taipei to depart for Canada, I fancied that I could foresee the social unrest that this system must inevitably create.

2

Taiwan 1995

Those who follow these questions say that the two international airlines with the most stylish and punctilious in-flight service are Singapore Airlines and one of its rivals, Mandarin, which is owned by the government of the Republic of China. As I intended to avoid going to Singapore, an authoritarian state so strict that some believe people are hanged there for not rewinding videotapes before returning them, I had not flown with the former. But rumours about Mandarin turned out to be true. The food is superior, the level of comfort makes you feel guilty, and the flight attendants go so far as to memorize the names of all of the passengers. Such attention to detail is all to the good as I was on a 12-hour nonstop flight from Vancouver. There were *three* full-length movies—two from Hollywood and one from China. There were also Japanese and Taiwanese videos. The Japanese ones were expensively produced and tried, without success, to achieve a hint of MTV nihilism; one group actually called American Boyz turned out to be four Japanese youths who recalled the innocent shenanigans of the Monkees. By contrast the Taiwanese videos all seemed dreamily romantic, full of young women with bedroom eyes and yet full of anguish too. Perhaps they were performing ballads. It was difficult for me to know as I had a headset tuned to classical music. I was delighted at how well the music seemed to suit the action up on the screen, no matter what it was. After the triple feature, for instance, came some documentaries, including one about Antarctica. I marvelled at how perfectly Brahms's dramatic flourishes synchronized with the crumbling of the ice shelf, how his lighter moments mocked the silly strut of the penguins.

I knew I was flying straight into a bureaucratic bramble in a few more hours' time. I was eager to return to Taiwan to finish the circuit tour of the island that I had begun in 1991, and to see if the accelerated pace of development and investment had brought Taiwan any closer to its goal, so seemingly quixotic, of getting the world to recognize theirs as *the* government of China. Members of the Taiwanese foreign service are rotated to new postings every three years, so I had already been dealing with two successive representatives of the so-called Taipei Economic and Cultural Office in Toronto—part of a vast lobby and propaganda infrastructure poised to turn itself into a chain of diplomatic missions at a moment's notice. With the present one, C. I. Lai, a good-humoured former teacher turned PR type, about my own age, long conversations and longer lunches had taken place in which I made my case for visiting the parts of the country I hadn't seen. They were countered by the suggestion that I submit to formal interviews with minor government officials. Such stuff might fill the papers in Taiwan. But I would be hard put to find a Canadian magazine or newspaper willing to publish an exclusive one-on-one with Prime Minister Lee Teng-hui, much less some third- or fourth-rank cog in, say, the Industrial Development Bureau in the Council for Economic Planning and Development. It was travel-writing—descriptive travel-writing, adding up to some kind of current snapshot of the island—that my editors wished to print. I thought I had finally got through to the GIO bureaucrats in Taipei. But as I was about to depart Vancouver I got a fax of my schedule and itinerary. It was heavy with interviews with civil servants and with trips to the tourist sites already too familiar to me from 1991—familiar to the world of travel-writing and travel-reading in general.

I arrived at Chiang Kai-shek Airport (or, as they now called it, Taipei Chiang Kai-shek Airport, to add just a little more distance between themselves and the wily old bandit) on April 4. This was the 20th anniversary of Chiang's death, which that year coincided with Tomb Sweeping Day, when families pay tribute to the departed by placing fruit and other goods at their graves and burning paper tributes. Observance of both these holidays is down dramatically in recent years, particularly among the young, but there was a holiday feel in the air nonetheless: the big spring vacation had just come to an end and people were returning to school or work after one of the few sustained absences permitted by the calendar.

At Arrivals a young man in a plaid sportcoat stepped out of the crowd like a tentative assassin and called my name. He gave me his card: WEI-KWANG HAO, PROTOCOL OFFICER. "But you may call me Comrade," he said. This struck me as an unusual request, especially in Taiwan of all places, but I was prepared to go along with it. Comrade Hao whisked me out of the long customs queue and sent me through the hard-to-find wicket where diplomats are allowed to bypass the usual formalities. Feeling as though there was no time like the present, I told him about my Vancouver fax and made polite suggestions about how my itinerary would have to be revised if what was after all the stated purpose of the journey was to be achieved. He slipped back into the seat of the Mercedes that was to take us in and out of thick traffic, past factories, factories everywhere. Our destination was the Grand Hotel, the ersatz temple—a temple of luxury, certainly—that still sits atop Yuan Shan (Round Hill) overlooking the Keelung River down below and the entire city beyond. I had evidently been bumped up to the Taiwanese A-list.

I sensed that my comrade had had problems with itineraries before. He said he would see what he could do. We were to meet in the morning before 8:30 a.m. It was—well, I wasn't even sure what day it was, as the International Date Line has always confused me. But I was happy to be at the Grand, which was once highly recommended to me by someone whose name was worth dropping but which I've forgotten. (Next day: I believe it might have been Margaret Drabble.) Anyway, the Grand, which was built more than 50 years ago, never seemed to make it into the rankings of the world's best hotels as compiled annually, with Academy Award–like ballyhoo, by the New York business magazine *Institutional Investor*. But clearly it belonged, and no doubt the Taiwanese took this as yet another slur on their claim to true nationhood. There is nothing of the chain or group aesthetic here. No Hilton, no Four Seasons. This is absolutely a one-off hotel, inspired architecturally by the Forbidden City in Beijing and suggesting some quality you might expect to find at the Raffles in dreaded Singapore but wouldn't have thought possible to have been built from scratch as recently as the 1950s. The Grand is renowned for the way it harmonizes Western and Chinese furniture and decorative works. I was given one enormous and somewhat sparse room—of how many ping I could not calculate. The floor was teak and showed the marks of the craftsman's adze. On the nightstand was a card stating that a blind masseuse was available by pushing five on the phone. Being in a hotel such as this, one so huge it never gives any hint of being packed to capacity no matter what the occupancy rate, is like being on an ocean liner that never goes anywhere. At 3:00 a.m. local time I was wide awake and dressed, sitting on the balcony, watching distant traffic twinkle in the darkness. In three hours a room-service waiter would arrive with congee, a breakfast porridge that, I'm sorry to say, I've never mastered the art of keeping down. The morning burned away the darkness and the smog for which Taipei is justly famous took over.

The Taiwanese like to claim they're the true preservers of traditional Chinese civilization. They like to remind you they had no Mao to pull down the monasteries and the temples and the old city walls (even Beijing's). They didn't have to live through a period in which the practice of traditional arts and crafts was persecuted as a matter of politics. But it's also true that neither did the People's Republic take to the market economy with anything resembling the vigour of the Taiwanese (and then not until the 1970s and with increasing tempo only much more recently), whose concern is always with the present, or future, and interminable advancement—a factor you see reflected in the literature of the younger generation. In the People's Republic, particularly out in the countryside, travellers sometimes come across scenes that seem misplaced in time—a water buffalo pulling a plough in a field, for example. In Taiwan—certainly in urban Taiwan, which was mostly what I had seen so far—I got the eerie feeling that I was in the middle of some anachronism I could not recognize. Until it hit me: the Taiwanese are like U.S. Republicans of the sort now extinct in the United States itself. They couldn't be less like such extremists as Ronald Reagan or George W. Bush. But with their golf shirts and business suits and increasingly sophisticated near-constant deal-making—with, most important of all, their absolute commitment to orderly, moderate reform—they're like 1950s Republicans, Buick-driving, country-club Republicans, Nelson Rockefeller–moderate Republicans: a breed that has survived here in Galapagos-like offshore isolation while the American models, with their chrome tailfins and large dinosaur teeth, have disappeared from the Earth forever, recalled now only dimly as the butt of *New Yorker* cartoons.

Comrade Hao told me a little about himself. He was in his late twenties, married, commuted three hours a day between the GIO office downtown and his high-rise apartment in a northern suburb.

"Usually I escort the German-speaking guests," he explained, telling me that he had studied in Germany for three years. "But so many people at the office have the flu that's going around that the English protocol officers are sick and I've had to take over your file even though English is my third language." As he spoke, I realized that Comrade Hao's name was not Comrade. Most English-speaking Taiwanese take an English name for convenience when dealing with foreigners—Michael Wang or Helen Chung, say. My escort, being a German specialist, took a German one. His name of course was *Konrad*.

Which I commenced to call him, working his name into every sentence, like some annoying Dale Carnegie–trained used-car salesman, hoping to make up for the earlier misunderstanding.

I lost my first round with the GIO bureaucracy, as Konrad, after a series of long and complicated negotiations with his superiors, reported that we had to adhere to the schedule for the first three days, so that he would then have a trade-off to offer in rearranging the remainder of the trip. But as it happened I won on points, as the bureaucracy, which was normally so well lubricated, started to go awry.

Many Taiwanese are said to make a fetish of precision in arranging meetings. Konrad was to pick me up out front not at 8:15 or 8:30, but 8:20 exactly. Rain was coming down like a bed of nails, making a deafening racket on the upswept temple roof of the hotel. Visibility was very poor. The tropical foliage in the surrounding hills had blurred into a runny wash of dark green. The landscape seemed to be running a fever. Although CKS Airport wasn't far away and one could hear the jets arriving and departing, no trace of them could be seen. Taipei must be a pilot's nightmare.

Following strict custom (as agreed on by host and guest countries), our first meeting was with the director of the so-called Canadian Trade Office, which was really the embassy-in-waiting, pending the day, not expected any time soon, when the two countries resumed normal diplomatic relations, over the dead body of the People's Republic. The agency shared a floor with the Toronto-Dominion Bank and other Canadian companies in a building on Fu Suing Road, and it resembled every other small Canadian consular outpost on the Foreign Affairs map: the boring statistical publications strewn about the waiting room, the rather tacky Group of Seven print (though in this case of J. E. H. MacDonald's *Supply Boat*) in the adjoining boardroom. Typically the GIO and the CTO had not been interfacing properly (perhaps the weather caused atmospheric disturbances) and so none of the Canadians knew I was coming nor did anyone understand who I was when I got there. I escaped with a few questions addressed to an assistant, 29 or 30, I judged, wearing a nicely tailored suit of the boxy style and speaking in macros while sizing up his interlocutor. Foreign Affairs is still full of these people. As the Toronto police once recruited new cops by going into the Gorbals of Glasgow and holding up slabs of raw meat with which to incite entire street gangs into signing up, so someone at the Lester B. Pearson Building on Sussex Drive must continue to lurk in the ivy at McGill and Queen's Universities, tugging on the sleeves of upper-middle-class WASP kids, promising them lives of exotic adventure.

I was on a roll of good luck, for at my first scheduled chat, the victim, the director of the Sixth Division of the Industrial Development Bureau in the Ministry of Economic Affairs, was unavoidably detained, and the one after that—with the equally imposing title executive director of the Coordination and Service Office for Economic Policy and Development—had just left on his honeymoon (an embarrassed underling explained).

Being stood up saved a lot of precious time, as I knew, from my reading and my visit in 1991, what they would have said. After the usual ritual of slick pamphlets, and boiling water in paper cups, they would have explained how Taiwan has developed a systematic plan for becoming a more important "regional operations centre" once the People's Republic reclaimed most of Hong Kong from the British in 1997 and Macao from the Portuguese in 1999. They would have explained, with graphics and audio-visuals, how the island would spend billions to establish itself as a central place in East Asia for making and selling value-added products. Methods would include building up the port facilities at Kaohsiung and elsewhere and putting an entirely new airport around the present airfield in Taipei. There would be a dramatic upgrade in telecommunications, media, and financial markets. The government saw Taiwan emerging after the death of Deng

Xiaoping in Mainland China as a place where (for all its problems caused by wealth) democracy and human rights were to grow apace with innovation in the market. Virtually all of East Asia has shown that the two sets of concerns are not exactly inseparable; Beijing and Singapore actually find them to be mutually exclusive. The Taiwanese have no particular ideological stake in their position; it seems to them simply that the one makes more sense than the other. They are after all admirers of a more liberal kind of capitalism that in the United States has faded into history. The United States has become more like the intransigent-fortress Taiwan of Chiang Kai-shek's day, while Taiwan, for its part, looks forward with vigour to the America of the 1950s. Of the Taiwanese, this might truly be said: They Like Ike.

Freed early of my obligations, I put on stout walking shoes and set out to reacquaint myself with Taipei City (as the natives call it to avoid confusion with Taipei County). It seemed busier, more congested and dirtier than ever, more itself than ever before. Obviously the city makes some attempts at planning, but they seem pretty superficial. For example, in trying to preserve or reinstate the city's claim to continuity, many of the old traditional businesses, such as herbalists' shops and dealers in paper goods burned as offerings to the dead, had been brought together in a place called Chiu Street—Old Street. But many areas owe their distinctiveness to some other, more organic logic. There are two red-light districts, one American, the other Japanese. The former is called the Combat Zone, no doubt after the one in Boston (the Taiwanese love American names). With the same love of compartmentalizing, there is a distinct residential area for foreigners. Yet everything in Taipei—the financial district, the hotel row, the streets of department stores—seems to have taken shape without much overall forethought. Now that protest demonstrations were allowed, two of the most common varieties were those championing the quickly rising women's movement and those condemning poor, substandard, or overpriced construction. Taipei has wide boulevards and narrow pavements like most big Asian cities, but the former have been ruined and the latter made impassable by overhead freeways beneath which, in a wonderful use of space, outdoor markets take shape, particularly on weekends and holidays—one for books, another for jade, a third for flowers, and so on. Similarly there is a beautiful utilitarian symmetry, but it is not obvious to the person merely passing through. In Taipei the dawn is often a burnt orange—smog of a kind that stings the eyes and shakes the lungs—while the nightlife tends towards karaoke bars and their newer video equivalents, KTVs. (Hell, I believe, must be very much like Heaven, but with a Karaoke Nite.) In Taiwan there is no regulation of real-estate agents. All one needs to begin buying and selling is a business card. This seems to me indicative of a larger attitude.

All of which is to say that in the four years since my first visit, Taipei had become even more like it was. Yet I was never without the sense—no one could possibly be without the sense—that life there was getting better fast. A difficult realization to fully digest when you come from one of the cultures where things are only getting steadily worse.

Before liberalization in the late 1980s, in the days of martial law, Taiwan had 30 newspapers. With the end of government strictures, the number climbed to 300. Clearly there had to be a shake-out. But even in 1995 there were over 200 newspapers, including two with daily circulation of one million each and 10 with more than 100,000 apiece—followed by a ragtag cacophony of little newspapers espousing every possible viewpoint about everything. Similarly there were over 100 radio stations, one-tenth of them government-controlled, and twice as many illegal pirate stations. When I last visited, there were three TV channels, all with some degree of government participation (later rules limited government equity to 40 percent). But there was also something called the Fourth Channel, which was no channel at all in our sense of the word but a strange shouting match between cable operations from the United States, Hong Kong, and elsewhere. Rupert Murdoch has had his hand in, with a combination of cricket matches and American movies; so, even more inevitably, has Ted Turner. Or take health care. In an age when the United States is callously refusing to embrace universal health care, Britain is trying desperately to preserve some of its once admirable system, and Canada is losing ground every day, Taiwan simply started up one from scratch (though not without howls from the opposition DPP and others). The scheme covers the entire population and had been in effect only about a month at the time of my visit. Only an economy that is expanding with head-spinning speed could attempt such a feat in today's environment.

Let me make my prejudice clear. Taiwan's Americanism makes me edgy (I'm a BBC World Service and not a CNN International sort of person), and

I don't imbue democracy with great sentimental value in and of itself (who wouldn't prefer a benevolent monarch to an endless succession of elected despots?). Yet it was hard not to be heartened by what was going on there. The Kuomintang was still in power (and you could see how it held on to the reins by shifting left or right as necessary). But since my previous visit a new opposition party, called the New Party, composed of foreign-educated Young Turks, had come to prominence, provoking the old guard towards further liberalization, while the Democratic Progressives took the most important municipal and country seats of power. Early in 1996, Taiwan for the first time elected a president by popular vote. All this new freedom came because new riches brought new attitudes, especially among the young, which was just the opposite of the effects of economic liberalization in most of the rest of Asia, where prosperity had been purchased at the price of human rights—especially, and most noticeably, in the Republic of China's motherland and adversary across the strait.

When I began my journey around Taiwan in 1991, the Taiwanese were not permitted to invest in Mainland China directly, but through Taiwanese subsidiary companies in Hong Kong or Singapore they already owned over 3,000 factories and other businesses in the People's Republic (a name, by the way, that a ranking Kuomintang official used publicly for the first time the week of my return—a long-awaited and carefully planned slip of the tongue that made all the front pages). Most of these factories were in the nearest parts of the People's Republic, the provinces of Fujien and Guangdong, where many Taiwanese have family ties. Now, only four years later, the official Taiwanese count was 11,000 Taiwan-owned factories spread out in all but one or two of Mainland China's provinces and so-called autonomous zones, from Sichuan and even Tibet in the far west to Manchuria in the north. Radio broadcasts monitored from Mainland China put the figure much higher—20,000 factories as of 1994, worth an estimated US$20 billion. Seeking clarification, Taiwan's economic affairs ministry retained an academic think-tank to find out the true figure; the report came back endorsing Beijing's estimates as accurate.

Many of these factories dot the old lines of European colonialism. A

Taiwan company in one of the four big fields (electronics, shoes, plastics, metal processing) might decide to set up a branch of its Shanghai operation upriver in Wuhan, for instance. "In the future," an official at the Mainland Affairs Council told me, "these growth rates will decline, because Mainland China has brought in new labour laws and pollution controls." Also, competition among the Taiwanese themselves was hurting everyone. Mind you, the growth would still be fast by objective standards. Even then, wages in Taiwan were 10 to 15 times higher than on the Mainland. What's more, the family connection made the Taiwanese more successful than anyone else at penetrating the domestic Mainland market—not just on the coast but far up-country: a prize that has so far eluded envious Japanese, Europeans, and Americans. "It may be that in five years' time," my informant continued, "after Mr. Deng has died and also after we see how the Hong Kong problem is settled, that we will see another big boom" in Taiwanese investment. When I was there, it centred on small businesses, employing 500, 750, or even 2,000. But Taiwan's majors, such as the great petrochemical companies and motorcycle manufacturers, were ready to move in once they had some assurance that the market was safe, once they could devise some clear notion of what the future relationship between the two Chinas would be. That is why the next spring's presidential election would be followed so closely. The Kuomintang platform was for unification without two separate countries—that is, doing through economic means what Chiang had not the slightest chance of doing militarily: retaking the Mainland. Conversely the New Party promised simple "unification" and the Democratic Progressives of course wanted to declare a new republic, independent not only of Mainland China but of its old self, and the endless wrangling that had gone along with it. The attention of China-watchers was unusually rapt.

One day Konrad had to bring his son along because the boy's kindergarten had been cancelled due to epidemics of flu and viral pneumonia. The lad was five years old. Like so many Chinese kids, he was impossibly cute and wore what looked like the Beatles' original 1964 haircut. He also had a dreadful chest cold and was coughing incessantly in the air-conditioned car. "Young ones get sick very easily in Taipei because of the pollution," his father explained. Sure enough I caught the boy's ailment by the next morning, when I woke up voiceless and with a racking cough and a big lumpy immovable congestion sitting in my lungs like a ball of unbaked dough. I decided that my best course might be a sauna to dry out my innards.

Sauna and massage customs present much to interest the sociologist and anthropologist, as they still seem to vary from culture to culture, and from city to city, untouched by the homogenizing effects of mass communication. When I set off for the massage district, I certainly didn't know what to expect, except that I was not anticipating any hanky-panky (for that, the Taiwanese go to barbershops, which are therefore as ubiquitous as ATMs in Canada). I found myself surprised and delighted with a very small but perfect illustration of the workaholic business culture that had made this island such a success story both materially and culturally in such a short time. I have often observed how Taiwanese, like Americans, enjoy doing two things at once as they race through the day, trying to maximize every opportunity. In America's speaker-phone society one is expected to ingest vast quantities of information from the business section of the newspaper while getting one's shoes shined; otherwise, time is wasted. Similarly you often see Taiwanese picking their teeth with a toothpick while smoking a cigarette. The men's section of the sauna was located two floors below street level. I was the only customer. I checked my clothes in a locker, gave myself a hand-held shower, and then eased into one of the steaming-hot Roman marble tubs. One sat submerged on a tile ledge, gasping for breath in the hot dry air. The policy, obviously, was a combination of wet and dry steam, which were separate functions in the West. The spooky subterranean room was filled with vapour. One somehow expected a gondola to slide silently by. Or a dragon.

When I finished, I hosed myself off again, and a muscular young Chinese in skimpy jogging shorts motioned for me to lie down on a marble slab that looked like it came from the old Toronto morgue on Lombard Street. Then for the next half hour he used a series of loofah-like gloves to scrub away the dead skin cells. The mittens had the roughness of diamond-drill sandpaper, and he used the same one on every inch of me, face, back, torso, legs, genitals. Then I was whisked away by a middle-aged Chinese endomorph whose big round belly, like Buddha's, hung down beneath his shirt. He took me to a massage room where, in the most tender way possible, he beat my poor body senseless. He used some technique peculiarly unknown to me—not Shiatsu, not Swedish—but perhaps a spinoff from one of the martial arts. It required remarkable strength in the masseur and a great deal of agility as well. He became in fact a contortionist. At one point in his routine he was up on the table with both knees implanted in the small of my back, while with his left foot he stretched my right leg as wide as it would go (farther than I thought it ever would) and with his left hand performed the same function on my right arm. At that moment, as I stifled a cry of pain, he began talking in a loud state of animation, laughing and joking. I was able to crane my neck around just long enough to see that it wasn't me he was addressing: he was talking into a cell phone, which he held in his free hand. Just another business deal no doubt, routinely consummated in the course of a chiropractic torture session.

I was beginning to feel that the charms of Taipei were easily exhausted. Konrad too was betraying some eagerness to begin the journey down the rugged east coast. For him this would be a holiday. For me of course it would complete my discontinuous tour round the island and fulfill the purpose of my visit.

The railway that runs part of the way is largely a convenience for the east coast cement industry, its employees, and the denizens of the various little company towns. It weaves in and out of the narrow coastal shelf and the Central Mountains, so it wasn't ideally suited to what I wanted to do. Nor is it anything like a ring road in its completeness. Indeed, one section of railway recently had gone bankrupt in the wave of privatization that was attacking Taiwan, including the giant state shipyards and steel mills on the opposite coast that I toured during my previous visit. There is also an informal system of ferries round much if not all of Taiwan, but although their ports of call are more numerous on the remote eastern shore than on the western, the vessels don't cling to the shore—the reefs and currents make that proposition too treacherous. So the best means of going down (or up) the Pacific side of Taiwan is by car, along the provincial highway, without doubt the curviest road I've ever travelled. It is breathtaking and hair-raising by turns, paved all the way and for the most part two lanes. At some places it was being widened and at a few other points it funnelled down to one lane as a matter of habit, quite apart from the incessant rock slides and mud slides most of the year. Only constant vigilance, and lots of heavy equipment stationed at strategic points along the way, keep this extraordinary highway open.

Konrad and I slipped into the 24-hour stream of traffic and struck out for Keelung on the northeast coast, 16 kilometres distant. Keelung is to Taipei as Yokohama is to Tokyo and Long Beach is to Los Angeles: the indispensable port city. The two places have very nearly—but not quite—grown into a single conurbation. On our way out of town we passed the domestic airport, and I pointed out the two anti-aircraft guns on the roof of one of the main buildings. Konrad looked embarrassed. "Left over from past time," he said, "and very old-fashioned."

For kilometre after kilometre we saw buildings being torn down (or rather, being allowed to fall down) while new ones were hurriedly built. Construction cranes dotted the city; even as the countryside began to reassert itself feebly, we saw huge stockpiles of building materials—hectares of rebar, for example—stuck in the middle of nowhere.

Inside Taipei itself the Keelung River was domesticated: not straightened but given a concrete canal in which to flow. Now it reverted to its old clothes. There were sandbars at some of the elbows and patches of rough water that glittered in the morning sunshine. There were bridges that carried pipelines as well as bridges that carried vehicular traffic. Mountains loomed in the distance. *Loom*, I think, is the correct verb. The peaks were lined up in ranks, three and four deep, each one a little fainter than the last: a watercolourist's dream. Along the way were tacky hamlets 100 or so metres long—rough concrete buildings, sometimes with sandbags or old tires to hold the plastic sheets or corrugated metal roofs in place, running along both sides of the highway (but with no cross streets to form a plat). In many of these villages empty ship-rail containers were set down right by the side of the highway, presumably to rust, though I suspected that people were living in some of them. In one or two places we passed containers stacked three and four high and many more deep, at a distance giving the suggestion of multicoloured condos.

Almost every village had a business that sold what looked like elaborately decorated archery targets on tripods but were actually festival offerings meant to commemorate the opening of a new restaurant or some other small enterprise and bring it good fortune. Many places of business were hung with paper lanterns, including some in the shape of pineapples, the universal sign of welcome.

"Are these because of the recent holiday?" I asked.

Konrad laughed. "No, I think people hang them out to welcome visitors to their new shop when it opens, but many have been there for years. They have not removed them, maybe because they are lazy or perhaps because they don't want to remove the luck it has brought them." He laughed again. I guess it's like people who still have their outdoor Christmas lights hanging up in July.

As we neared the start of the coastal highway, the foliage became giant-size—huge ferns and palm leaves—and bamboo was more in evidence. Keelung didn't magically appear at the end of the road but materialized in a slow cross-fade of nature and anti-nature, announcing itself with a vast tank farm. As a city, Keelung seemed to offer little for the eye as we drove through it, turned right, and began our descent down the coast.

This stretch of the coast reminded me of Cornwall. Yes, that's it exactly, a kind of subtropical Cornwall. The surf bangs against the land, demanding admittance; the wind has cut some rocks off from the main mass and turned them into tall cones as though on a potter's wheel. Small wooden fishing boats, their hulls painted cerulean blue, rise and fall, rise and fall.

This may well be one of the most crooked highways on earth. Turns pile upon turns until you're no longer sure of the compass, or wouldn't be if it weren't for the Pacific (here, the colour of Windex) always on your left shoulder. The engineers who built the road weren't actually practising the engineering of least resistance. I began to keep track of the tunnels we went through—many of them long and slithery—but lost track after twenty-something.

But the remarkable fact about the coast—one could extend the statement to all of Taiwan in fact—is that it is so variegated and surprising within the overall context of its small size and relative homogeneity. At Fulung, for example, comes the first in a series of extraordinarily beautiful (and under-utilized) beaches: vast circles of fine pale sand, seemingly painted in great arching strokes of the brush. Another is at Toucheng, only 30 kilometres farther along, where on a reasonably clear day you can see the outlines of Kieisha, or Turtle Island, so named because its northern part does indeed look like a turtle's head. In between these two points, however, the road is all up and down and left and right, and the very geography appears to change several times. At certain places the limestone and the compound rock give way to little outcroppings of volcanic stone; fishermen sit on them, throwing out their nets time and again in a fine spray. The wind, rather than work on rock vertically, softening its edges, instead gives it a crenellated look, like the wall of a castle. At still other places the rocks are tall and deeply lined with furrows top to bottom. These formations with all their rugosity reminded me of a certain type of weathered, sagging face—the kind of which George Orwell and the later W. H. Auden are perfect illustrations.

The road makes travel slow, which adds to the impression that the island is bigger than it really is. It took us two hours to get from the Taipei suburbs to Toucheng, beyond which you start seeing rice paddies and even hay ricks when the road dips down to sea level. By then I knew that my attempt at heading off a chest infection by taking dry steam and trebling up on vitamins had not worked. In fact, I began to fear that I was about to be the latest victim of the viral pneumonia that was sweeping certain parts of the island. I couldn't stop coughing, a deep basso profundo cough accompanied each time by a strangely mechanical rattling that hung on, like a metallic echo, until the next round. I made an executive decision to use the antibiotics I always made a point of carrying on long foreign trips. What I had in my hypochondriac's bag, along with surgical gloves and emergency sutures, was a course of tetracycline, a drug to which many of the better educated pneumonia bacilli were now immune, but a broad-enough-spectrum medication with which, with luck, I might do myself some good over the next week. At the moment I was sweating like a sieve and my left hand was shaking uncontrollably.

There was not much traffic on the highway. A substantial portion of the coaches we passed were decorated to indicate that they contained groups of pilgrims, travelling to visit the towns associated with particular deities. But then a different kind of group outing started to become obvious: the package tour of Japanese mirth-makers. We were nearing the turnoff for Taroko National Park, which contained Taroko Gorge, perhaps Taiwan's best known scenic wonder. I too wanted to see it, and so we agreed to detour for a couple of hours.

The road into the park is itself quite an attraction. It was built in the 1950s by the one-million-strong nationalist army who were between communist invasions at the time. There is a bust honouring the military engineer in charge, as indeed there should be. At certain spots the road was less than two vehicles in width, with precipitous drops of, I don't know, hundreds of metres certainly. At one place there was a long single-lane tunnel, with stop lights at both ends, though part of the road was being improved. Welders were at work on a steel tube that would form the basis of a new tunnel; their torches pissed orange sparks in all directions.

The gorge is indeed a remarkable place, a long and incredibly deep and winding canyon whose blue-grey limestone sides are full of swallows' caves and mossy overhangs. Unlike the famous Three Gorges on the Yangtze (which the People's Republic was already destroying, by making way for its mammoth hydroelectric project), the Taroko is not navigable. But it's obvious that the water has raged out of control over the millennia, imparting a sort of black swirl to many of the rock faces. Knuckles whiten when you look up or down. I was struck by the presence of a two-tiered pool of jade-green water high up in one of the mountains, which drains off to make a spectacular cataract that falls straight down the gorge far below, as though through some invisible chute.

All the cross-island roads, this one in particular, are susceptible to rock slides and mud slides, but here, near the gorge, the problem is particularly acute, and that the road is kept open at all is only through permanent diligence by the government. Signs warning of the danger of falling rocks are themselves often damaged by falling rocks. So are vehicles. We passed one abandoned Japanese car that had been flattened by a direct hit on the hood by a boulder about the size of a refrigerator. Only two months earlier three visitors were killed when slag and muck buried their coach. Higher up on one of the mountains that make up the gorge is a temple built to remember 200 Taiwanese soldiers killed in a slide in 1958. The original temple was itself destroyed in a later slide, then rebuilt, then destroyed yet again— whereupon the government decided to re-erect the temple a little to the left of the site of the original tragedy. We threaded our way back to the coastal highway, pausing at the park entrance, where local aboriginals sold postcards and brightly dyed feathers from the backs of their motorbikes.

I was really starting to feel like hell, and asked if we might stop at a drugstore so that I might see what patent medicines I could find to supplement my own stash and at least mask my symptoms for a while.

Each time a stream struggles down out of the interior and mingles with the Pacific, a little village has taken shape, as though to celebrate the miracle of drainage. The majority are small and aren't even shown on most maps. They consist of the standard Taiwanese domestic architecture, which is unfortunately supplanting the traditional three-*jian* Chinese house with its interior kang, or brick platform, and its courtyard. The new vernacular tradition is a concrete structure, boxy, not very strong, and bare of every decorative art but kitsch, with a business, almost any kind of business, on the ground floor and family quarters above. Those people without the capital to set up a machine shop or a convenience store at street level often make do with hanging out a short rack of clothing, both new and secondhand: anything to bring in a few dollars to supplement the vegetable patch or the cornfield or the fruit orchard or the rice paddy. Sure enough one of these villages had a drugstore: not a herbalist's, but a miniature Western-style drug counter such as you might expect to find in the lobby of a lesser Ramada Inn. We stopped the car and as I stepped out I barely avoided treading on an enormous and recently deceased rat. It was lying on its back with its tail straight down and its legs neatly pointing in all four directions, its white belly exposed to the sun, as though intent on soaking up a few rays. My coroner's instinct put the case down to misadventure, probably by suicide, possibly an overdose.

The next sizable city is Hualien, approximately one-third of the way down the island. Historically its claim to fame is that this was the somewhat imaginative site chosen by the Japanese for their invasion in the 1890s, which gave them control of Taiwan until what the Taiwanese call "the retrocession" of 1945. Two days earlier Hualien had been struck by a 5.7-magnitude earthquake deep below the surface. Travelling through, I was surprised to see no damage—at least nothing I could establish with certitude as earthquake damage. The loss of a scale model of the Eiffel Tower atop one downtown building would have been a civic improvement.

We were now descending into the broad coastal plain, a place of lonely promontories and migraine surfs, of pineapples and mangoes and the occasional water buffalo. Further inland-turning roads led the way to Jade Mountain and other climbing spots. But we continued on towards Taitung, two-thirds of the way down. After we crossed the Tropic of Cancer, which bisects the island almost exactly in the middle, the air was even more tropical, though the elevation picked up again, so some of the difference I experienced might have been purely psychological. I was surprised to hear roosters crow—not because it was so late in the afternoon but because, being some sort of animal chauvinist, I associated the sound with more northerly latitudes. For a while the highway seemed to straighten. I was very feverish now but felt that there were some sights I shouldn't miss experiencing firsthand, such as Sanhsientai, a rocky island, and place of meditation, reached by an eight-hump bridge from the coast. There were also a number of mineral hot springs up in the mountains, renowned for their restorative powers, and Buddhist shrines in caves.

Two highways actually cross Taiwan east to west. The larger one, way up north, is habitually impassable due to rocks, mud, and cave-ins. The other, in the extreme south, at the place where the island begins to narrow to its pointy conclusion, is a mere arterial road, not a provincial highway. Stories of its hardships are legend, but it was usually passable this time of year, before the big rains. This, then, had been our plan until now: to cover the 200 kilometres from Haulien to Taitung and go to the small town of Tawu, where the cross-island mountain road began its torturous course southwesterly towards the Taiwan Strait. There we planned to pick up the much better four-lane highway on the well-developed west side of Taiwan and have an easy passage into Kaohsiung, the second city. All this would take another six or seven hours. I was increasingly uncertain just what sort of ailment I was suffering from; I knew only that it was centred in my lungs and I feared it might degenerate into pneumonia. If so, this would mean that I had suffered pneumonia on three continents— four, if you counted Australia, where I once had Waltzing Pneumonia. So another executive decision loomed. It was too far to turn back. And too far to proceed as planned.

Ahead at Chihpen, a short distance up in the mountains, was a hot spring with, it was reputed, a brand-new spa-hotel put up by and for the Japanese. Perhaps there might be room at the inn? I had to get under some warm covers and go to sleep. Yes, there was a vacancy, and it came with all the Japanese amenities, including one of those chest-deep bathtubs, which, in this case, was connected directly to the health-giving natural spring in the mountainside. I filled the bath. The water, though clean, was the thickness of mineral oil and smelled strongly of sulphur, as though the Devil had just entered the room unobserved. Bathed and kimonoed, I crawled into bed and shivered.

During the night, I awoke to what I first took to be my own chattering but turned out to be an earthquake—only four-something on the Richter scale. By morning the sheets were drenched and salt-stained with my night sweat, but I felt that the fever had broken—departed under cover of darkness, as it were. After some strong Colombian coffee (but after politely declining fish and gruel), I convinced myself that I was feeling quite a bit better, though my cough, brought back instantly by proximity to an air conditioner, continued to frighten young children and I still hadn't got my left hand to be still. Hell, yes, I was ready for anything now, I told Konrad, who looked concerned but made a display of telling me not to worry. He had seen guests much sicker than me, he said. And he told me the story of a German television producer who had to be choppered to hospital after being bitten by something poisonous—a snake or a rare insect, I couldn't be certain.

But I couldn't gainsay it: the morning had made me more hopeful. It was a bright day of exceptional visibility, and the coconut palms were motionless. To reach Kaohsiung, on the other side of the island at almost exactly the same latitude, would take us five or six hours if we drove down round the tip of the island, through Kenting National Park. There was hardly any traffic on the road when we started out. The Pacific was at its most peaceful. Every so often we saw fisherman (they worked in pairs), rocking gently on their small boats. On the other side of the highway were steep cliffs, sometimes with a red-copperish tint. We passed some lazy cattle and also the aroma of cherry blossoms. Small buildings with red flags denoted government checkpoints designed to prevent entry by illegal immigrants.

Kenting National Park, which was a Japanese scientific research facility before it was reclaimed by the Republic, expanded and opened to the public, covers 32,000 hectares, and is home to about 3,000 aboriginal people, members of the Paiwan nation. The attraction for Taiwanese and overseas Chinese is not anthropological but botanical and ecological. The park is partly underwater. Its reefs, including artificial ones formed by the hulks of old American and Japanese warships, attract scuba divers from round the world. Three hundred different corals are found there, and 1,000 species of tropical fish. For a couple of months each year, when the northern Taiwan coast is too cold, humpbacks and sperm whales migrate past the park, which draws about two million visitors a year of one sort or another.

It's a strangely beautiful place and more varied than I am making it sound. Within the park limits, for instance, there is an experimental cattle ranch. Yet this doesn't seem like ranching country. The air temperature at the park never falls below 68 degrees Fahrenheit and the vegetation, though thick, is not tall. Partridges, which the Taiwanese call bamboo chickens, run wild; orchids bloom and butterflies frolic year round. Abutting the park is the village of Kenting, a nondescript little touristy place on the site where the first ethnic Chinese came ashore in the 17th century. Most of the few thousand residents are either Paiwan or Mainland Chinese. One of the town's two landmarks is a lighthouse built by the British in 1882. The other, which you won't find on tourist maps, is a huge offshore rock that forms a perfect silhouette of Richard Nixon, the person who, the Taiwanese believe, stabbed them in the back when he recognized the People's Republic, thus condemning Taiwan to the crisis of self-esteem and diplomatic limbo from which it is still, ever so slowly, emerging. "We always seem to do much better with the Americans when the Republicans are in power," an official in Taipei once told me. All the more strange, therefore, to be looking into the gorgeous Bashi Channel at Richard Nixon Rock, as the rising tide crept up towards the old scoundrel's unmistakable ski-jump nose. "I am not a rock," the rock seemed to be saying, shaking its jowls ever so slightly. Or was I beginning to hallucinate?

I had to cover another 112 kilometres from Kenting and up the west coast as far as Kaoshiung, thus completing my stop-and-go circle round the island. Once you turn north, the road is well paved and flat and straight in parts. Approached from this direction, good old Kaoshiung doesn't look very attractive. But as we fought our way into the centre of the city at dusk I recovered the feeling that I had on my previous visit: this was a place that knows how to impress you with its closeness to life and the outside world—when it wants to. Soon it was dark and the skyline looked like a shorted-out control panel, blinking on and off unpredictably.

Epilogue

W hile still on the subject of Richard Nixon, my timing was, once again, unimpeachable. I returned from Taiwan just before the big storms broke. This time they were political storms. If they didn't exactly dominate world news, they certainly made an ongoing international story, one that carried the following message: the Taiwan problem (for such is how it came to be thought of once again) will not go away quietly.

I began with an expectant itinerary. So now I end with a brief chronology, to remind the reader of what happened next.

On June 1, 1995, the Taiwanese vice-premier, Hsu Li-teh, was in British Columbia to accept a doctorate *honoris causa* from the University of Victoria. This was a week before President Lee was scheduled to pick up his own honorary degree at Cornell in New York State. In the early 1970s Canada led the way towards change, with Trudeau recognizing the People's Republic long before Nixon did. But now Canada, in granting Hsu a visa, was playing catch-up with the Americans. The pendulum had swung the other way and the People's Republic was being dissed—or rather, Taiwan was finally being given a little overdue respect for all its achievements. Such acknowledgements of Taiwan irked the Beijing government. Indeed, if nations, like individuals, could suffer apoplexy, then the People's Republic would have done so at some point during the next few weeks.

By summer Taiwan had somehow become a subject in the accelerating run-up to the Americans' 1996 presidential election (shades of 1960). Relations between Beijing and Washington had broken down; the People's

Republic demanded that, as a condition of their repair, the United States publicly reiterate its policy that Taiwan is a mere Chinese province. At this point Madame Chiang Kai-shek, then 98 (or "thereabouts," according to the *New York Times*), tottered into the limelight one last time to speak to politicians on Capitol Hill, where Newt Gingrich, the House leader, called for U.S. recognition of a Taiwanese republic. Beijing responded by saying that his remark was a threat to world peace.

All this while the world wondered what would happen to Harry Wu, the Mainland Chinese who had become a U.S. citizen and had been arrested on one of his surreptitious re-entries to expose conditions in Chinese prisons. Also at this time the American First Lady, Hillary Rodham Clinton, was debating whether to make an appearance at the World Conference on Women's Rights scheduled to be held in Beijing at the end of the summer. At length the communists released Wu as a sign of good faith, and Mrs. Clinton, countering this improvement in the diplomatic situation, did attend the conference, where she made speeches condemning the Chinese for their human-rights record.

The best-selling book in Taiwan that summer was *August 1995*, a dystopian thriller, set in the present, about an invasion from the Mainland. The book sold almost half a million copies, largely because Mainland forces in July had begun "testing" missiles in the East China Sea only 100 kilometres from Taiwan proper, a mere 25 kilometres from one of the small outlying islands under Taiwanese control (causing the highly emotional Taipei Stock Exchange to strike its lowest point in 19 months). At almost the same hour, though, the brawlers and shouters in the Taiwanese national assembly finally passed enabling legislation for the election of a president by popular vote (though not necessarily a new president, as Lee announced that he would seek a second term—"throwing his hat into the powder keg," in the unusually sprightly phrase of the *New York Times*). The passage of the bill was a great measure of how far democratization had come since 1947, say, when Chiang Kai-shek's troops massacred more than 20,000 citizens, or indeed since 1979, when Human Rights Day in Kaoshiung ended, not in one of the playful miniature riots of contemporary Taiwanese affairs, but in a real and bloody one.

I would have enjoyed experiencing those times from back inside Taiwan, but I also found it instructive to observe them from my seat at home, monitoring the world press. Suddenly there was a 1950s feeling in the air once again. In a long leader the *New York Times* cleared its throat and made its position plain: "China has embarked on an escalating campaign of military manoeuvres meant to intimidate Taiwan and undermine its president, Lee Teng-hui. Washington, as much as it wants to calm troubled relations with Beijing, must firmly signal its opposition to this campaign." In Britain, *The Economist* went so far as to run an imitation communist poster on its cover with the tagline "Containing China." The inflection was unequivocal. Not "Containing *China*" or even "Containing China?" with a question mark, but rather a flat statement of what *The Economist* believes to be a bald necessity.

Suddenly I felt as though I was back on Quemoy where, for years, the young soldiers were ordered to wear earplugs at all times to blot out the sound of the communist propaganda broadcast from the Mainland and where I saw rusty tin cans still strung on barbed wire by the tide line—the first line of defence against an amphibious assault. Past and present, quaintness and danger, were mingled once again, causing a sensation that I now associate with my journeys to Taiwan.

AFTERWORD 2004

How could I have thought that Moscow and Beijing were not, relatively speaking, heavily polluted? I don't know. Maybe what I was suggesting when these notes were first published in different form was that the two capitals fell short of their potential as health hazards or at least didn't quite fulfill my apocalyptic expectations. Or perhaps I was being naive. Yes, I think that's it: I was being naive in this and in other areas.

I didn't know, for example, that the Chinese feared I was a spy, though the difficulty I had getting a visa should have tipped me off. I learned the truth one day back in Canada after I received a surprising call from Wen Dong, who announced he was defecting (to use the word usually only employed in connection with Cold War Europe and not Asia). When the time came for his annual holiday, he flew to North America, with no intention of ever returning. We once again found ourselves spending time together because I was helping him with his claim to refugee status. During one particular evening together, I asked what information about me he had been giving to his employers in Tiananmen Square. "Oh, I telephoned them every day and then had to write very long reports," he said. "It was quite a lot of work. You see, they thought you were a spy."

I laughed. "What tipped them off?"

He laughed back, to be polite. "Getting your foreign minister to help get you a visa was of course most unusual. Also, you came to China by land from Russia. No one does that." Then he paused, thinking he might have hurt my feelings. "Do not feel bad. They tend to believe that foreigners are usually spies."

Wen's refugee claim dragged on through the first couple of bureaucratic strata until, growing fearful that he might not be admitted, he disappeared, utterly and thoroughly. My guess is that he slipped across the border, carefully getting lost in the Chinese community in New York City. I've never heard from him again.

I was also giving both China and Russia too much credit for official religious tolerance (perhaps *indifference* would be a better word), but how much of this retrospective insight derives from more recent events is hard to say. In both countries, but China especially, appearances are customarily deceiving. On the surface, for example, Hong Kong seems fundamentally unchanged under Beijing's rule, but we know from sources there just how much control the central government maintains over every aspect of life in the former colony. All the more surprising, then, that in 2002 the PRC permitted the last 1,400 residents of the camps for Vietnamese boat people—a third of whom were behind the walls—to take up unfenced residence in the city.

In my defence I was correct about the population of Chongqing, which is thought to be 2.2 million not counting transient agricultural workers or 2.4 million with them. The *New York Times* recently put the figure at 15 million; such misstatements arise from confusion over the large administrative districts called *shi*, which means *municipality*, but in English is often misleadingly translated as *city*.

I have been back to a number of the places written about in the preceding pages, including Taiwan, where politics continue to change but not always grow and the standoffs with the Mainland have repeatedly taken on a dangerous cast. The one constant has been the West's hypocrisy in claiming to promote and cherish democracy while continuing to give in to the PRC's blackmail by subjecting Taiwan to even more isolation. The West's interest is the marketplace, not democracy.

One of my major regrets is that I was so rude about Bangkok, which since that time, as I've grown more familiar with it, has become one of my favourite cities, especially in that it's so like a thousand urban villages jumbled together. One of my satisfactions is that I did indeed later get to Vietnam (and saw the body of Ho Chi Minh, thus completing my collection of famous communist corpses). Other sites, however, I can never return to. The Three Gorges Dam is now operational; as a result, the gorges have ceased to exist along with the historic cities that lined them. The Chinese government has now moved on to what's believed will be the world's largest infrastructure project: diversion of part of the Yangtze to water the deserts of Mongolia thousands of kilometres away.

For its part Russia has been altered almost beyond recognition in economic, social, political, and cultural terms. Some of the changes, however, have been short-lived, making it even more difficult to know in which direction one is heading as one plots a course from Gorbachev to Yeltsin to Vladimir Putin.

Yeltsin's strange reign began when he clambered atop a tank in August 1991 to oppose the abortive coup against Gorbachev by Jurassic hard-liners, and it was full of contradictory signals. On the one hand, Yeltsin often appeared to be some type of populist democrat. On the other hand, he seemed like a nationalistic rightist. Sometimes the two hands were clasped together. Yeltsin both prevented the curbs on religious freedom and forced through the building of the giant Cathedral of Christ the Saviour, a replica of the one Stalin ordered blown up in 1931. But the first of these was an act of openness, the second a display of raw power of the sort that Stalin always admired in himself.

Pravda ceased publication—sort of—in 1996, its circulation having plummeted from 11 million to 200,000. By that time two opposing factions of the staff were putting out competing versions, one of which survived the closure, only to be ordered by the courts in 1998 to alter its design and change its name to *Slovo* (*World*). First under Yeltsin and then, with increased speed, under Putin, the Russian media, freed from state control, were taken over by conglomerates with (the phrase is euphemistic) close ties to whoever controls the Kremlin. The last independent newspaper voice was *Izvestia*. Having flourished for a few years following the end of the Soviet Union, it was acquired by Yeltsinite moneymen in 1997. The last independent TV channel in Russia went into liquidation in January 2002.

In the new Russia, book publishing has bloomed. Many observers, however, feel the disappearance of the old restraints has left a generation of Russian writers too confused and melancholy to articulate what they now have the means of expressing. Who can begrudge them a period of befuddlement when Moscow is now the world's most expensive city for business travel and the one with the most decadent nightlife, a place where everything is for sale to the public, even the services of Lenin's embalmers? As for the talk of burying Lenin with the rest of his family, as he himself wished, it lasted only briefly, despite the fact that Leningrad was permitted to revert to the name St. Petersburg and the remains of the last tsar were reinterred there.

St. Petersburg's architectural silhouette has lost its attractive integrity in a rush of high-rise construction (as has Shanghai, which now has the world's tallest building). Moscow, far from having a manageable number of private cars, has so many that 200 people a day are injured in street accidents (while in 1996, Beijing, for its part, began banning cars on alternating days). Since I rode on it, the Trans-Siberian Railway has filled with *chelnoki*—"suitcase traders"—and Lake Baikal, seen from the carriage window, is threatened by reckless overdevelopment as well as by pollutants. But even in a world where part of Beijing's Summer Palace has been razed for a hotel, entertainment centre, and parking lot, and where movies are sometimes shown in the Great Hall of the People, I occasionally find evidence that places have retained their old character even as they undergo elemental change. *Of course* Shanghai would become the site of the PRC's first stock exchange, with issues denominated in both Chinese currency and American dollars. And *of course* illegal traders would sometimes receive the death penalty, a development naturally seized on breathlessly by the *Xinmin Evening News*, the city's slangiest and largest newspaper, second in size only to the *People's Daily* in the country as a whole. But generally speaking little is the same as when I set out more than a decade ago. The era I described in my notebooks is now part of the past, though an interesting enough part, I hope, to justify the preceding pages.